Gospels for Sundays and Feasts
The Biblical Message — *Cycle A*

GOSPELS FOR SUNDAYS AND FEASTS

The Biblical Message
Cycle A

M. Miguens, O.F.M.

ST. PAUL EDITIONS

NIHIL OBSTAT:
　　Rev. Richard V. Lawlor, S.J.

IMPRIMATUR:
　　+ Humberto Cardinal Medeiros
　　Archbishop of Boston

ISBN　0-8198-3015-1 cloth
　　　0-8198-3016-X paper

Copyright ©1981 by the Daughters of St. Paul

Printed in the U.S.A. by the Daughters of St. Paul
50 St. Paul's Ave., Boston, MA 02130

The Daughters of St. Paul are an international congregation of religious women serving the Church with the communications media.

CONTENTS

Purpose	11
Advent Season	15
Christmas Season	29
Lenten Season	49
Easter Season	71
Ordinary Time	116
Solemnities	230
Index of Sundays and Sequential Feasts	259
Index of Solemnities	260
Alphabetical Index of Solemnities	260
Index of Gospel Passages	261

Purpose

The editor of a local paper requested me to write a column for a given period of time on the Sunday gospels. This gave me the idea and the stimulus for the present work. The short commentaries in the paper were, in fact, favorably received and even sought after. The experience taught me that this kind of work answers a real need in the religious public of this day. Thus a broader project was designed; a new direction was taken; and the few commentaries on some Sunday gospels were extended to the entire three cycles of the liturgical period. Not only the Sunday gospels, furthermore, were taken into account, but also the gospel readings of feasts of obligation and a few other major feasts.

The commentaries intend to disclose the theological meaning of the gospel passage assigned for a given day. It is the doctrinal message of the evangelist that these commentaries purpose to capture and to convey to the reader of the gospel today. The modern critical analysis of the gospels underlies every line of this work, but it is the message itself that is given top priority, because it is this that must come through with all its clarity and smoothness, without interruptions and obscuring complications. The advertent reader will perceive that the ongoing debates and discussions are reflected in the exposition. Still, no polemic is intended or conducted here; a constructive and positive approach seems to answer best the needs of the religious audience in today's world. It is not debate and doubt, but religious truth and firmness that can be meaningful today and bring home a message of faith, hope, and love.

The presentation itself is stripped of every unnecessary complication, technical terminology or academic intricacy. Simplicity and accessibility were actively and positively pursued, that the gospel message may gain that freshness, immediacy, power and persuasiveness that it certainly brought to the minds of those who listened to Peter, Paul, John and other early missionaries, with an open mind and a will to believe and be saved. In its concern for having Christ's message received, the original Christian mission cast the saving news into those unsophisticated and even artless stories that today make up our gospels. It was the word of God that came through those simple, unpretentious narratives, and with all its convincing power spread to the world and changed it—like the leaven that ferments the dough.

It is the word of God, again, that these commentaries intend to let flow through, and reach man's mind as smoothly and directly as this can be possible. If the word of God was cast in unsophisticated, plain forms, a channel devised to make the gospel narratives accessible to God's people serves its purpose best when it comes as close as possible to the naturalness of the original forms.

The concern of these commentaries is, in point of fact, pastoral and, in that sense, popular. Their purpose is to lend a helping hand to pastors, priests in general, religious, and lay people, to all those who in one way or another are involved in pastoral work, missionary activity and teaching apostolate, or are in any way interested in knowing better the gospel message in view of their own Christian life, spiritual meditation, or religious instruction. To all those who in whatever form or for whatever reasons want or need to know the real teaching of the gospel, these commentaries bring the essential and genuine message of the good news of salvation as they were recorded by the evangelists and as they were used by the early Christian apostles/missionaries, inspired preachers, pastors, teachers, catechists, and saintly persons.

It is the gospel message, and nothing but the gospel message, that is presented here. No application or adaptation to present day situations is attempted. And deliberately so. Pastoral or ministerial needs and situations change from place to place, from time to time. Any application of the gospel message must be suggested by the local prevailing condition at a given time. This is why any sort of moralizing tendency is absent from this work.

Our conviction is that, just as in olden time, today also, "being inspired, all Scripture is useful for teaching: for reproof, correction, and training in holiness" (2 Timothy 3:16), and that, as in early times, we should today also keep our attention closely fixed on the message of the gospel "as we would on a lamp shining in a dark place until the first streaks of dawn appear and the morning star rises in our hearts" (2 Peter 1:19). After all, no less than at any time in the past, in its perennial vitality "God's word is living and full of energy, sharper than any two-edged sword; it penetrates and divides soul and spirit, joints and marrow; it judges the reflections and thoughts of the heart" (Hebrews 4:12). The Lord himself is even more trenchant: "the words I have spoken to you are spirit and are life" (John 6:63). It is the words of the Lord that the gospels are all about. They certainly have enough energy, power and life to be meaningful and inspiring in whatever situation may prevail in a Christian community.

The three-year liturgical period itself suggests a natural structure and division of this work. Three different parts correspond to the three cycles/years A, B, C. Within each cycle the liturgical year indicates the mandatory sections: time of Advent; Christmas Season; Lenten Season; Easter Season; Ordinary Time. The "feast days" that have a *fixed* place within the sequence of the liturgical cycle are kept in that sequence, e.g.: Christmas, after the fourth Sunday of Advent; Epiphany, after the second Sunday after Christmas; Ascension, Pentecost, Holy Trinity, Corpus Christi, Sacred Heart —they are all kept within the liturgical year.

Those feast days, however, that are attached to a given day of the *civil* calendar, with no fixed place within the sequence of the liturgical cycle, are treated in a separate section devoted to "solemnities." Thus the Solemnity of Mary, Mother of God, appears in this section on January 1; the Solemnity of St. Joseph appears on March 19 and the Annunciation on March 25; and so forth.

The feasts of the Baptism of the Lord and of Christ the King are attached respectively to the first and last Sundays in ordinary time. This is why they are included in the section of Ordinary Time.

At any rate, an index of "Sundays" and "feast days," as well as an index of "gospel sections" treated, will render this work totally functional and of easy use for everyone. It is assumed, of course, that the reader will have his Bible at hand, and read the section assigned for a given day before he goes into the present commentaries.

Advent Season

First Sunday of Advent

Matthew 24:37-44

It is well known that Matthew articulated his gospel on five main discourses of the Lord; and that, as a matter of fact, these discourses are as many small treatises, each one devoted to a particular subject. This also is true of chapters 24-25 where the evangelist puts together the Christian teaching concerning eschatological/apocalyptic matters. The long discourse is presented as Jesus' answer to a question of his disciples. Christ had just told them that all the beautiful structures in the temple area would be utterly destroyed: "not one stone will be left on another" (24:2). It is in reaction to this that the disciples ask: "when will this be and what is the sign of your coming 'parousia' and the consummation of the world?" The question clearly contains two parts: 1) When will this be, namely, when will the destruction of the temple occur; 2) What sign or indication will forewarn man that the Lord is coming in his "parousia" and that the world will come to an end.

This is why the discourse has two parts. The first (vvs. 4-35) is devoted to the destruction of the temple together with Jerusalem and the Jewish state, which is described in apocalyptic cliches derived from the Old Testament. For this event there are forewarning signs of every kind (wars, persecution, preaching of the gospel, abomination, false Messiahs, etc.); just as from the fig tree it can be learned that the summer is near, so also, "when you see all these things happening, you will know that it is near, at the door," even more: "I assure you, the present generation will not pass away until all this takes place" (24:32f.).

But in v. 36 the Lord says that "concerning 'that day' and hour no one has any knowledge—neither the angels, nor the Son, except the Father only." Obviously, this sentence cannot apply to the foregoing section where "the Son" pointed out so many forewarning signs in the life span of the present generation. With this general ignorance of the day and hour of "that day" the second section of the discourse begins, in which the Lord answers the second part of the question mentioned above. The concept "that day" is a stereotyped expression that in early Christianity became the technical term for "that fateful day" (such is the force of the Greek term) of general reckoning. The evidence for this comes precisely from Matthew 7:22, among other passages, where, without any reference to any previous day or time or event the Lord says that "on that (fateful) day" many will entreat him but he will "ignore them" (see 25:12). The second section that starts with 24:36 ends up, in fact, with the majestic portrait of the last judgment by Christ (25:31-46), that marks the close of man's history. Between the destruction of Jerusalem and "that fateful day," the history of the Christian community unfolds; it is condensed in a few parables of which the "leit motif" is watchfulness.

It is to this second section that the passage we consider today (24:36-44) belongs, and its predominant teaching is precisely watchfulness. In point of fact, this passage is an introduction to the parables that follow (24:45—25:30) and to the closing description of the last judgment. To those who will happen to be alive at the end, the same thing may happen as happened to those on earth at the time of Noah's flood. The time of the "parousia" (coming) of the Lord will be like the "days of Noah"; the idea being that the Lord will come unexpectedly, he will appear suddenly. The evangelist himself stresses that "you do not know at what time your Lord is going to come" (v. 42), and hints at the traditional idea among Christians (v. 43) that the Lord will come like a thief in the night. The character of suddenness in the Lord's coming is strongly emphasized.

Tied up with this is the idea of unpreparedness. The coming of the Lord may catch men unprepared for this important meeting, just as the men of Noah's time were wiped out by the surging waters of the flood when it was least expected. Their unpreparedness consists in their exclusive concern with the things of a day-to-day life: "they were eating and drinking, marrying and being married" (v. 38); thus they gave no thought to any other dimension of man's existence, such as some security measures for an emergency of this sort.

This leads us to another aspect of the problem. The question was not just unpreparedness, but something worse besides, namely, false security. Noah's contemporaries felt secure in their own world; the idea of a possible catastrophe did not even cross their minds. They were completely committed to the pleasures of life, as if these should last forever, and nothing could prevent those men from enjoying them to the last. False security is a trait of those who fall into God's punishment; man likes to hide evil from himself and to indulge in self-deceiving. In his day, the prophet Jeremiah saw this very clearly, when in view of the impending Babylonian invasion, false prophets and priests kept telling the people to go ahead enjoying their immoral and materialistic life, since there was "peace, peace" (i.e., everything is perfectly all right), whereas the prophet knew that "there is no peace" (Jeremiah 6:14). In 1 Thessalonians 5:3, Paul applies Jeremiah's words to the coming of the Lord: "You know very well that the day of the Lord will come exactly as a thief in the night. When they may say 'peace and security,' then all of a sudden destruction will come upon them—as birth pangs do on a woman with child." In biblical thinking, this sense of false security is itself a characteristic sign of the last misfortune and doom. The generation of Noah's contemporaries remains in the bible the prototype of an evil and irreligious generation, which certainly sheds a less than bright theological light on all those who will have to face the coming of the Lord.

So it will happen that, among those involved in everyday life tasks, some will be prepared to meet the Son of Man, and these will be "taken along" with him. Others, completely immersed in worldly affairs, will be left (v. 40f.); they will not be chosen. This is the "separation" of sheep and he-goats (25:32f.), wheat and weeds (13:40ff.), and good and foul fish (13:49). In view of all the elements pointed out, the Lord wants his Christians to "stay awake" (v. 42) and to "get ready because the Son of Man is coming at the time you least expect" (v. 43). This need for watchfulness and preparedness is the reason why "the Son" was not supposed to disclose the time of "that day and hour"; it remains God's secret.

Second Sunday of Advent

Matthew 3:1-12

John the Baptizer proclaimed a message: "the reign of heaven is close at hand." It is God's rule or reign that he preaches and not the kingdom because what is intended here is not a particular area or society belonging to God, but a new order in the world; a new order brought about by God's intervention and grounded on God's rule or will. We say God's rule, for the term "heaven" is just a respectful substitute devised in order not to utter the sacred name. John's message is exactly the same as

Christ's (4:17). John, however, does not imply that God's rule is being brought about through himself, that is, by his ministry. He meant that the Messiah was about to make his appearance, and that through him God would establish his rule on earth. It is in this sense that John, in the wilderness, admonishes the people to get ready for the coming of the Messiah by "preparing the way for the Lord, making the paths straight for him."

John understood that this had to be done by a sincere "conversion," which has nothing to do with repentance or penance. The notion of conversion was common to contemporary Judaism and derives from the Old Testament prophets. It is a complex and multi-sided concept and implies more than what the Greek word (*metanoia*) suggests, namely a change of mind. This is certainly included, but beyond that, it includes a total and sincere "return" to God in a practical life of religious commitment to him and of a living in accordance with the demands naturally flowing from that commitment. John refers to "bearing the fruit worthy of conversion," and this is precisely what he means, namely, a human activity and human living that expresses the reality of an internal return to God. In 7:17ff. the evangelist knows that "you can tell a tree by its fruit," as he also knows that "a sound tree cannot bear bad fruit." The tree is the person who returns to God; the soundness or unsoundness of the tree depends on the soundness or unsoundness of one's return to God, and they will show this in the quality of the fruit.

The ax is already laid at the root of the tree; and the tree that does not bear fruit, the expected fruit of sincere conversion, will be cut down and thrown into the fire. John the Baptizer proclaims to the Jewish audience the absolute necessity of honest and sincere return from worldly things to God's "thing." The other alternative is punishment or judgment, namely, being confronted with God's wrath which is to be revealed. God's wrath is not a passionate outburst of bad temper, dissatisfaction or impatience. It is rather God's withdrawal and distance from those who withdraw and keep away from him. It is a non-help; it is denial of his gifts, grace, and loving assistance in general. Thus many "trees" in the Jewish community face God's withdrawal and disfavor, and as a result they will be cut down because they will be cut off from the Messianic community with everything it implies. This would open the way to many other evils which would follow when God abandons man to his own wishes and fate. Fire is the expression of every kind of destruction and punishment. The ax is already laid at the root; there isn't any time to waste by putting off one's conversion; things are about to happen; God's intervention through his Messiah is around the corner.

The Jewish people were not receptive to such ideas. Of course, they knew from the prophets that God can also discipline his own people. Many voices of contemporary Judaism had proclaimed the need of deep and serious conversion. In the last analysis, however, the conviction that God could punish his people remained more theoretical than vital and realistic. The notion that God might reject his own people was just inadmissible. That God could exclude anyone in his people from the Messianic community was just unthinkable. They put a great stock on their blood connections with Abraham: being a "child of Abraham" was a guarantee of divine favor because God could not render his promises to Abraham null and void. They were correct in their understanding of God's faithfulness, but they forgot that God had the power to raise children for Abraham from the very rocks, just as at the beginning he raised Adam from the dust of the earth. After all, sonship is not only nor mainly a matter of biological connections, but also of spiritual kinship and factual following (John 8:33-44; Romans 4). God can be faithful to Abraham and still reject a great majority of the chosen people. Thus, being a Jew and boasting that "our father is Abraham" are of no avail; they are no guarantee of being received in the Messianic community.

This was a message for the pious Jews. Sadducees and Pharisees find it harsh to hear, because they are a "brood of vipers." They are afraid of God's wrath; they know what their religious condition is; and yet, they try to accommodate both God and their own interests, even when both are in open conflict. They attempt to deceive themselves. Their conversion, expressed in receiving John's baptism, may not be sincere and wholehearted; and they may deceive John, after all, "I baptize you in water." But they will not be able to deceive the Messiah. He will clean the threshing floor by separating chaff and grain with accurate precision; the grain being brought into the "messianic" barns and the chaff burnt with fire. Or, according to another metaphor, he will separate the dross and the good metal in the people by fire (see Isaiah 1:22, 25; Jeremiah 6:29). Without metaphor, the Messiah, "the mighty one," being in possession of the fullness of the Spirit, "shall not judge by appearance; shall not decide by hearsay; but he shall judge the poor with justice and decide aright for the land's afflicted; he shall strike the ruthless with the rod of his mouth, and with the breath of his lips he shall slay the wicked" (Isaiah 11:2-4). The Messiah will flood man with his, "Spirit of knowledge and insight"; he will be able to pass judgment on their conversion and choose or reject them: "I baptize in water...he will baptize you in Spirit."

Third Sunday of Advent

Matthew 11:2-11

John the Baptizer was in jail. There he had heard about the "works of the Messiah," and sent a delegation of his own disciples to hear from Jesus himself whether or not he was the Messiah. If he had heard of the miracles performed by "the Messiah," what else did he have to ask about? In his answer (v. 6) Jesus hints at a possible "scandal" that he may be to John. Furthermore, at the time of Jesus' baptism, had not John been told that Jesus was the Messiah? These observations show that in the "works of the Messiah" we have to deal with an expression of the evangelist that prepares Jesus' answer in vv. 4-6. The evangelist speaks of the works by which the Messiah was supposed to be recognized because such were the works he was expected to perform.

Of course, John wanted to know whether or not Jesus was the Messiah, but he describes him as "he who comes," he who was supposed to come. This sort of description goes back to some prophetic passages, such as Isaiah 40:10; and Malachi 1—3:1 (see Matthew 3:10, 12; 11:10; Luke 7:27; Mark 1:2), where the reference is to God's coming in power and sovereign lordship. The concept of power and sovereign rule in a ruthless judgment is very prominent in John's convictions about the coming Messiah, according to the traditions of his ministry reported in Matthew 3:1-12, where he describes him as "the mighty one." The meaning of all this is that John the Baptizer was perfectly Jewish in his ideas, hopes and expectations concerning the Messiah; it had not crossed his mind that the Messiah could be a humble, inglorious, suffering man. When he asks Jesus whether or not he is "he who was to come," the question amounts to this: are you the powerful, universal judge that passes ruthless judgment on sinners in order to exclude them from your community and throw them into eternal torture? It was about such a person that he had preached to the Jewish crowds.

This explains the question of John to Jesus, Jesus' enigmatic answer to John, as well as the reference to a possible stumbling block to John in Jesus' answer, the stumbling block being, oddly enough, Christ himself. The question of John was prompted by the conflict he saw between his convictions about the Messiah and the actual performance of Jesus. John expected a powerful Messiah who could wipe out sin and sinners from the face of the earth; whereas Jesus keeps company with sinners of all sorts, with irreligious people, surrounded by the poor, the sick, those who suffer, the powerless; whereas no influential person of those who really count is around him. Jesus himself seems to be powerless against his opponents; John himself, his herald, friend and relative, is in jail under the power of a sinful, unjust and oppressive king; and yet it seems that Jesus couldn't care less or was in no situation to help him. Can this be the man he had talked about?

Jesus sends back John's delegation with a code answer. Jesus does not answer the question with a straight "yes." He refers John to Jesus' own performance. But the reference is not just a listing of his miracles. It is the language of Jesus' answer that is significant: the reference to Jesus' miracles is made in words taken from several prophetic passages (Isaiah 35:5f.; 26:19; 61:1; see Luke 4:18) where "the works of the Messiah" were pointed out. In so doing, Jesus refers John to the Scriptures and to see for himself that the works he does are, in fact, those the Messiah was supposed to do and expected to do. Both the Messianic oracles of the Old Testament and Jesus' deeds show that a dutiful dimension of the Messiah was his association with the poor, the sick, the outcast, the helpless, etc. This is the kind of messianic projection that had so far escaped John's attention. But he had to learn it and live with it. This is why Jesus concludes his message to John by saying that "blest is the man to whom I am not a scandal," scandal being a stumbling block upon which one can stumble and fall. John is blest, i.e., to be congratulated, if he does not lose his faith in Jesus. In his answer to John, Jesus brings to the fore his soft and delicate approach to the problem of how to teach one's friends. But the message is clear: I am the Messiah, but not the Messiah of your dreams. You had better change your mind and believe in me.

Once John's delegates were on their way back, Jesus addressed the crowds and taught them the saving significance of John, which is very great indeed; but even this praise of John is at the service of Jesus' significance as Messiah. John was held to be a prophet by the crowds, and Jesus couldn't agree more, only he goes even beyond that. The very outfit of John shows his prophetic quality. In his austerity, John reminds everyone of Elijah, the great prophet of old; and the mention of "fine clothes" that John does not wear is a clear reference to his "garment made of camel hair with a leather belt around his waist" (Matthew 3:4), which is to be compared with 2 Kings 1:8. Furthermore, John is not "a swaying reed" that the breeze can bend. In his confrontation with Herod (Matthew 14:3ff.), he showed himself to be an uncompromising man of unshakeable firmness (see Jeremiah 1:17-19).

Above all, John is more than just a prophet. The text of Malachi 3:1 that applies to John shows that he is the "angel" of the prophetic oracle in the sense that he is the "messenger" (this is what "angel" means) who goes before the Lord, heralding his coming: he is the messenger of Exodus 23:20 who leads the community of Israel to the promised land of the messianic kingdom. John is more than just a prophet because he not only foretells the coming of the Messiah; he points out to the people who the Messiah is, thereby showing that the Messiah is here, and he, John, had prepared the people to welcome him. By describing John as the "angel before" the Lord, Jesus describes himself as the Lord/Messiah that was to come and who is now here. And by his message to John about the association of the Messiah with poverty and misery, Jesus discloses the nature of his messianic career: the Messiah has to walk humble paths "first"; his glory must come later (Luke 24:26; 1 Peter 1:11).

Fourth Sunday of Advent
Matthew 1:18-24

At first sight, it would seem that Joseph is the true center of the evangelist's interest in his narrative of Christ's "origin" (Matthew 1:18-25). This is a wrong reading of the gospel message. The narrative was not written for the sake of Joseph, but for the sake of Jesus himself. It is not the psychological anxieties of Joseph that the evangelist wants us to know. His purpose is to teach us something about Christ; he writes a narrative which is "gospel," namely, good news or saving news, not an irrelevant episode in a man's private life or history.

The evangelist states very clearly his intent right at the beginning of the written episode: "the origins of Jesus the Messiah (see vv. 16 and 17) were in this way," which means that the purpose of the narrative is to describe how Jesus, the Messiah, came to be; how his existence started. The prominence of Joseph in the narrative is a device precisely at the service of this overriding concern. Through his own role in the episode, he must tell the reader of the gospel that he has nothing to do with the "origins" of the child, even though he has something to contribute to the saving significance of Jesus.

Mary was betrothed to Joseph, but she appeared to be with child before they came to live under the same roof and, therefore, before marital relations were established. This is certainly the concern of the evangelist; the evidence for this being that the remark is added that Mary was with child "of the Holy Spirit," i.e., by God's power and intervention. The remark is important in itself because, according to the author's intent, it shows what Jesus' origins are—he originates from God, not from Joseph. For the correct understanding of the narrative, however, it is even more important to take note of the placement of the statement at the outset of the reported episode, even before Joseph came upon the stage.

From the start the reader knows how Jesus came to be, and he is supposed to read the remainder of the narrative in the light of this knowledge; namely, the knowledge that God, through his Spirit, was active in Mary and was developing a human life.

Obviously, if Mary "was found with child" it is Joseph's awareness of this development that the evangelist intends to point out as the unfolding episode serves to prove. But the evangelist links such awareness to the explanation that the begetting power was "the Holy Spirit." The key to understand Joseph's reaction to such a state of affairs is the angel's address to him: "Do not be afraid to take home Mary, your wife." One wonders why Joseph should be "afraid" to take Mary home. This "fear" is neither psychological, juridical or other; it is rather religious, we may say "theophanic." According to the biblical perspective, whenever the human being comes too close to God's active presence he must be afraid (see Isaiah 6:5; Daniel 8:18, 10:8; Revelation 1:17; John 18:6, etc.). This explains why Joseph was afraid to take home a woman in whom God's active power was so manifest and who, therefore, had conceived a child in this way. The evangelist's remark about Joseph's fear is at the service not of Joseph's personal history, but of Jesus' supernatural origin. Joseph's fear was prompted by God's active presence in Mary; Joseph is portrayed as respecting God's work.

It is for this reason that he acts as the evangelist reports. He refused to "investigate her," Mary, (this is what "auten deigmatisai" means), i.e., to "have her case tested-and-proven"; to probe her (as any husband would); and to divorce her quietly, without any publicity, with a minimum of juridical requirements if any. It is also on account of Joseph's respect for God's action that Joseph is characterized as "righteous." He cannot be called "righteous" in the sense of a person who complies with the law, because the episode reported in John 8:1-11 shows that compliance with the law in similar cases demanded a quite different course of action; and if it is contended that in New Testament times that law was not enforced, then there was no law to comply with in acting as Joseph did. Joseph is said to be righteous because he was pious and God-fearing. The passage of Luke 2:25—which also is in a Jewish setting—shows that the Greek term "dikaios" (righteous) does convey this notion. Symeon was a "dikaios" and pious/religious ("eulabes") man, where the latter term is a variation/explanation of the former, especially because Symeon is not said to be involved in any legal situation. More particularly, Joseph is described as righteous from a Christian viewpoint, namely because he cooperated in the Christian event. Surrender to God, as well as respectful and obedient cooperation with his will and plan, is the supreme righteousness. Joseph's cooperation started with his respect for God's work and active presence.

The evangelist still insists that Joseph has nothing to do with Jesus' origin. The angel tells Joseph that "it is true" (as stated in v. 18), what was begotten in her is of the Holy Spirit; "but" she will bear a boy "and you will call his name Jesus." Jesus' virginal conception is pointed out again. This time, however, the emphasis of the statement falls on the second part: it is a conception of the Spirit (as stated), but it is a boy that Mary will bear, and the name you will give to the boy is Jesus. The quality of "boy" is emphasized because of the dynastic rights involved (see "male" in Revelation 15:5). Here the particular role of Joseph is brought up. He had to give to the child, not so much, the name Jesus as the family name "son of David," as it appears in Matthew 1:1. After all, the evangelist is reporting the origin of Jesus "the Messiah" (vv. 18, 17, 16), and the angel was careful enough to identify Joseph as Joseph "ben-David" (son of David). It is to this that the entire genealogy in 1:2-16 should lead, first of all, because of the "formular" break in v. 16. It is through Joseph that Jesus becomes "son of David," and that the dynastic promises to David come down to the child.

The narrative closes with a new reminder that Joseph respected Mary as the bearer of God's presence. Joseph took Mary home, but he did not touch her "until she bore a boy." At this point, the reason for Joseph's respect for Mary is not related to Jesus' conception, because it had already taken place; the observation can only mean that Joseph really respected God's work and, therefore, respected Mary herself as the support of God's activity. The remark "until she bore a boy" does not imply or suggest that after that the statement is no longer true. Both the Hebrew and the Greek idioms connote just what happened—or did not happen—up to this point, without any implications or innuendoes for the time after that (see 2 Samuel 6:23; 1 Samuel 15:35).

Christmas Season

Christmas (At Midnight)
Luke 2:1-14

The narrative of Christ's birth in Bethlehem (Luke 2:1-14) has its focal center in a confessional formula in v. 11: the child born in Bethlehem is "savior," but he is a savior "who is Messiah/Lord." This definition of the child as "Messiah/Lord" fits uneasily in the sentence to which it is attached; the connection of these two concepts without any declensional coordination or joining particle is difficult. It certainly expresses one of the basic concepts of the Lukan theology (see Acts 2:36), and there is every reason to believe that it represents an idea of the evangelist inserted into a previous context. This is a clear indication that the writer's concern in the entire narrative is to demonstrate the thesis that the child just born is "Messiah (and) Lord."

The child, however, is not just one more "anointed" (messiah) king; he is rather "the" Messiah of the Jewish hopes, and this is why the Messiah is born "in the city of David," a description that now, for the first time, applies to Bethlehem, whereas in the Old Testament, the city of David is Zion/Jerusalem. The detail stresses the connections between the new-born child and David himself, whose home village was Bethlehem (see John 7:42). Evidence of this intent is the explanation of why Joseph went to Bethlehem: "because he was of the family and of the lineage of David." The insistence on Bethlehem as "the city of David," and on Joseph's connections with Bethlehem and with David's family, constitute a discreet but sufficiently clear reference to Micah's messianic oracle: "you Bethlehem-Ephrathah, too small to be among the clans of Juda, from you shall come forth for me one who is to be ruler in Israel; whose origin is from of old, from ancient times. He shall stand firm and 'shepherd his flock'...he shall be great to the ends of the earth, and he shall be 'peace' " (5:1, 3f.). Obviously, for Luke, Bethlehem is no longer "too small," it has become "the city of David that is called Bethlehem." It is not Bethlehem that identifies the city of David; it is "the city of David" that identifies Bethlehem. In Luke's narrative the motives of "peace," "shepherds" and "flock" also point to the prophetic passage. The whole context should show that Jesus is the Messiah of whom Micah spoke.

Jesus is also "Lord." Luke knows that the humble child of Bethlehem has by now been enthroned in heaven as the supreme ruler of the universe, as the Lord whom all tongues proclaim and "to whom every knee in heaven, on earth and under the earth bends" (Philippians 2:10). But of course, the child is the father of the man; this is what Jesus was from birth: Lord. This is why the angels and the splendor of the divine world surround this birth and proclaim the "greatness" and the transcending significance of the "Lord," whom all angels serve and to whom they "bend their knee"—they are at his service from the very start. It is as Messiah and Lord that Jesus is also "savior." The old priest, Zachariah, blessed God because "he wrought 'redemption' to his people as he raised up a strong 'salvation' for us in the house of David his servant...'salvation' from our enemies and from the hands of all our foes...that, rid of fear and delivered from the enemy, we should serve him" (Luke 1:68ff.). It is a Jewish atmosphere that is breathed here. The terms are nationalistic, and the "salvation" connotes national independence and total religious freedom. The concepts of redemption and salvation will evolve, but at this stage it is the Jewish notion that prevails.

The messianic dignity of the child, his "lordship" and his salvation, are a "gospel"; they are good news. It means that deliverance is near, that the Messiah is here, and that God is intervening in the world's affairs on behalf of his people. On behalf of his people, because the "joy" proclaimed by the angel is not just "for you," for the shepherds, but "for the entire people," for the entire nation of God. The shepherds, after all, play a representative role; they represent the entire "flock" of the messianic people, namely of the humble, the poor and outcast. It is this kind of people that will receive and believe the message of the "Good Shepherd," and it is to them that the very first "gospel" is proclaimed.

The fact that the shepherds "return glorifying and praising God for all they had heard and seen" (2:20) is evidence that they "believed" the message from heaven, in spite of the fact that the "sign" of a baby in a manger did not seem to square very well with the current Jewish ideas about the Messiah—the Lord and the Savior. From the very outset, the Jesus of Luke is the friend of the friendless and is in the company of the poor and destitute. The poverty of the entire episode is in sharp contrast with popular messianic concepts and with worldly conventionalisms.

It is in this connection of ideas that the mention of the Roman ruler, "Augustus" (divine), adds to the sharpness of the picture. The world ruler gives orders; and the Messiah, the Lord, the Savior, finds himself obeying these orders just as he enters the world; and as a result of this he is born in a sort of exile, out of his parents' home, and for all comfort he has to be content with a "manger" for a cradle "because in the lodging they had no (better) place." The contrast between God's ways and the world's ways cannot be stronger. As usual, it is in the midst of poverty and humility that God makes his salvation known and offers the gift of messianic "joy" to the world. The Messiah is born "for you," for mankind; he is a gift of God to the "entire people," to the world.

The angelic beings, halfway between God and man, disclose the saving meaning of the event. The birth in Bethlehem is a saving intervention of God; it is a redeeming feat that God has decreed and brought about from his sovereign throne "in the highest." This is why the angels give "glory to God" for his gracious gift and supreme intervention: "He has visited his people." God's gift, however, means "peace" to mankind, to those men who open up to God's love and saving care. It is not the peace of the "pax Romana" of Octavianus. It is the Hebrew greeting "shalom" that conveys a message of integrity and perfectness in one's life and being; it is a message of wholesomeness and wholeness in one's relationship with the loving God, who in the child of Bethlehem, presents mankind with their Savior, their Messiah and their Lord.

Christmas (At Dawn)

Luke 2:15-20

Jesus was born in Bethlehem, and the news was disclosed to the shepherds by an angel who gave them a sign by which to recognize the Messiah, Lord and Savior: "You will find an infant in swaddling-clothes lying in a manger." At the same time, a host of angels revealed the meaning of the event; it is a glorious event of God's power for which he is glorified and praised; it is also an event that brings "shalom"/peace to man.

The shepherds believed. They believed that a child in a manger could be the Messiah and Savior. The idea of lying in a manger was not very reassuring from a "messianic" standpoint, and in this sense that "sign" given by the angel was not particularly indicative of the glory and splendor of the Messiah the Jews visualized. That is why the shepherds' response to the angel's message is brought into relief. The first message of the "gospel," good news (v. 10), is addressed to them, and they gratefully received it.

Because they believed, they became the first heralds or apostles of the gospel. This is why their trip to Bethlehem is reported by the evangelist. In point of fact, obedient to the message of the angel, the shepherds went all the way from the fields to the town of Bethlehem and, of course, with their own eyes they saw the factual reality of the event. The evangelist notes that they set out for Bethlehem "in haste," which indicates diligence, eagerness and joy. Mary's attitude in her visit to Elizabeth is the same (1:29). What they found was, first of all, Mary and Joseph; and the baby lying in the manger. Not only the child was there, the shepherds find also Mary and Joseph. Nor is it only the inglorious cradle of the child that does not appear messianic and demands great faith; the appearance of Mary and Joseph does not look very royal, very "Davidic," either (see 2:24 and Leviticus 12:8). In spite of everything, the shepherds believed, because the Lord had "made known" to them the meaning of the event and the high importance of the child. It was on the assurances of God's revelation that the mystery of the "manger" was credible to them. Now, in their turn, they have to hand down their faith to others.

The presence of a child in a manger, and accompanied by two not uncommon-looking parents, was a too ordinary sight to impress anyone and suggest ideas of messianic power and glory. At this point, the evangelist refers to "all those who heard" the shepherds speak; the shepherds, therefore, had an audience that had not been mentioned so far. At the sight of the event and the circumstances surrounding it, the non-enlightened onlookers could not grasp the meaning of this birth. It is in this context that the shepherds become the heralds of God and hand on their faith in the message they had received: they become apostles of the "gospel" and of the "joy for the entire people" (2:10). They "make known" to their audience the meaning and significance of the unimpressive, everyday event their eyes are witnessing. Just as the Lord spoke to the shepherds, the shepherds in turn "make known to others what they had been told *about the child*," namely that the newborn child is "Savior, Messiah and Lord" of "the house of David." The audience heard the message of the Lord, and in spite of all appearances, they "were impressed" by what the shepherds had to say. They pierce the mystery of the child in the manger. This is how God works and makes his revelation known. He sends heavenly messengers to proclaim to men the meaning of what he does. Then these men explain the meaning of the same event to others; thus revelation is handed down. The audience is struck with "admiration" and they may eventually come to faith.

The shepherds played the role of the announcing angel as "evangelists" to the crowd gathered around the manger. They play also the role of the angels who sang the *Gloria in excelsis Deo*. The shepherds departed from the manger and the child "glorifying and praising God for everything they had heard, and then seen, in complete agreement with what they had been told." Just as the angels, the shepherds also give "glory to God in the highest" for his great gift to mankind. The main subject of glorification is not the privilege of having received a message through angels; it is rather focused on the child in the manger. They "saw," and what they saw with their physical eyes was not much; but their faith in the heavenly message discovered in that child the Savior and Messiah, and the fulfillment of all the promises to David. It is for his splendid gift that they glorify God, the source of all perfect gifts. The conduct of the shepherds is a triumph of joyous and obedient faith over evidence.

Mary, too, heard what the shepherds had to say about the apparition of the angel to them; about his message of "good news"; and about the "glory/light of the Lord that shone all around them." She heard them say that, on the word of the heavenly messenger, this child was a "great joy to the entire people"; that he was the heir of David, the Savior, the Messiah, the Lord. This was what the voice of God had to disclose about her child. Every mother pays attentive heed to any hint that may unveil, however imperfectly and tentatively, the future and the greatness of her child. The message of the shepherds was astounding news, and the source of the message was reliable beyond question. Mary "was keeping all these things" in mind, not just the message of the shepherds but also the angelic appearance and the "glory of the Lord shining around them." She not only kept these things in mind. With affection and loving interest, in her motherly heart she was "comparing" all these happenings and words with the events concerning the child in the past; and in that light she also "compared" these events with the facts of the future as they unfolded. The result was a better understanding of the mystery surrounding the child. Interestingly, the same thing is not said about Joseph, even if he was there—just as Mary was. Mary "was keeping all these things" in mind, not only for herself, but also for the writer, who first put down the infancy account. She became a source of the writer's historical knowledge and theological insights. (See other reflections on the feast of Mary, Mother of the Lord, January 1.)

Christmas (During the Day)

John 1:1-18

The prologue or introduction to St. John's gospel (John 1:1-18) discloses the deepest meaning and the theological significance of Jesus' birth. The climax of the entire theological reflection is the solemn statement that "the Word became flesh and dwelt among us." The reality of the Word becoming flesh is the Bethlehem event. But the significance and transcendence of such an event cannot be grasped in any depth, unless one comes to the realization of what the Word really is and of his "history" before his becoming flesh. That is why the evangelist sketches such a history before his thought lands on Bethlehem and comes to rest in the cave.

The being who now becomes flesh is someone who by his own nature has no flesh, nor does he belong in the realm of the flesh. He is precisely the Word of God. The Word of God is not an articulated sound. He is the thought of God; he is God's idea spoken to himself in the overpowering and deafening thunder-clap of his silent stillness. He is the expression of God's thinking mind, and as such, the expressive revelation of his sovereign and irresistible will: "God 'says' and things come into existence." The Word of God is his operative and active Wisdom of the sapiential literature in the Old Testament, Wisdom who knows the secrets of God and is an inseparable collaborator of God in everything he does (Proverbs 8:22-36; Wisdom 8:3f.; 9:4, 9).

Precisely because of his essential relationship to God, the Word of God "was," that is, was existing and acting at any point in "time" one can think of, even before the existence of the time that the interrelationships of created things brought about. As a matter of fact, the Word was *en archei* (in the beginning). The Greek term means much more than a chronological starting point. It is a highly philosophical notion which conveys the idea of principle, source, and origin. It is in this sense that the Johannine school of thought uses the term in Revelation 3:14, of Christ as being the *arche* of God's creation. In *arche*, therefore, the reference in John 1:1 is to the absolute Principle of everything; the Principle without principle; the Godhead who is source and origin of everything else, including the Word and the Holy Spirit; whereas he has no origin or source. At any point in "time" one can think of, or even beyond time, the Word's existence was already flowing from and within the Principle or Origin—namely the Godhead. Such is the understanding of the passage by authoritative Greek Fathers of the early Church.

His existence could not be in isolation. As the Word that he is, he existed in reference to the Godhead, as the Word being spoken to God. Given his origin from God himself, he shares his very nature; and very naturally, the evangelist stresses that at any moment of the Word's existence "the Word was God." Being God's thought or Wisdom, the Word was instrumental in God's creation since it was from his thought or Wisdom that God received his ideas concerning the things to be created and the conducive methods, etc., to create them. Furthermore, it was by speaking his Word to himself that God gave and implemented his order of creation: "He 'said' and things came to be" (Psalm 33:9, 6; Genesis 1:3, 6, 9, etc.; see Psalm 104:24). Nothing came to be except through this intervening contribution of God's Word.

God is the "living" One; he is the source and reservoir of all amount and quality of life. By sharing the nature of the Godhead, the Word partakes of his very life, and this is why there is life in him—as there is water in a spring: "Just as the Father has life in himself, so also he gave the Son the gift of having life in himself" (John 5:26; see 6:57; 11:25; 14:6). In reference to men, however, the life of the Word comes to them, first of all, in the form of "logical" light, i.e., of truth and revelation. But this is true even before the Word became flesh. He is the light of man's mind, that is, if man is going to be "logical" or rational; or if man is going to know the truth, no matter how imperfectly and fragmentarily. Whatever "light" man gets in his mind, and whatever amount of truth man "conceives" in his mental, logical "word"—they are a share of the Word's light, even at a natural level. As a matter of fact, in the darkness of logical and moral error in the world, the Light/Word shines steadily and powerfully; darkness can never overcome his splendor. The evangelist sees in the Word the archetypal light of the platonic categories. The authentic light is not the faint copy we know and experience, but the Light that knows no end; the Light that lights up the entire world at the same time that it enlightens, and not just man's physical eyes, but man's spiritual/internal "eyes." Such is God's Word, who inasmuch as he is Light, "enlightens every man," giving them, first of all, a rational mind, and then, beams of truth coming into man's mind.

The Word of God was in the world shining in the beauty and order of creation ("the world had come to be through him") and in man's "light." But "the light which is in you" (Matthew 6:22f.) can become darkness (Romans 1:21f.; 2 Corinthians 4:4); and then "the world," the mob of mankind mobilized in defiance of God's love and power, fails to recognize the Word of God (see 1 Corinthians 1:21). There is more. Through the divine revelation in the Old Testament, God's Word came to his own, namely, to God's people; but they paid no attention to him (see Acts 7:51; Thessalonians 2:15; Matthew 23:37). Still it is through him that man can become a true child of God: by faith in the Word and by "receiving" him as a genuine gift of God.

This Word of God, who is himself God, life, light, creative power and revealing truth, is not only in the world to enlighten it; but he also becomes a human being, lives among us, and makes his own the bitter experience of man's history and institutions. The notion of "flesh" indicates the human nature and the human condition. It does not suggest the idea of humiliation or slavery, but it certainly is in sharp contrast to the divine, and points out the weakness and powerlessness of the human condition. And yet, it was through this condition that God manifested to us his own splendor: in a man's works/miracles, in his love in a human heart, and in his very "Word," his truth, spoken with a human tongue and in a human language.

(See other developments on the Second Sunday after Christmas.)

Sunday After Christmas (Holy Family)

Matthew 2:13-15, 19-23

In the earlier episodes of Jesus' infancy narrative, the first evangelist teaches us the virginal origin of the Messiah, his dynastic right as "son of David," and his significance as "king of the Jews," to whom the gentile world pays homage by presenting him with gifts of gold, frankincense and myrrh. In the later episodes, however, the evangelist gives us a foretaste of the actual messianic projection in Jesus' life. Jesus is the heir, not only of his people's glory and promises, but also of its history of sorrow and suffering. In this regard also, Jesus appears ingrafted in the history of his people and of its leaders, particularly Moses. From his childhood, Jesus projects himself as the best synthesis and expression of his own people.

The flight of Jesus and his family to Egypt is a re-enactment of the stories about the Exodus of Israel from Egypt. Jesus has to go down to Egypt and live there as a stranger in a foreign land. From Palestine he went down to Egypt just as the people of Israel did, and he also comes back from Egypt as Israel did. It is because of this return to Palestine that the oracle of Hosea 11:1 applies to Jesus: "I called my son out of Egypt." The prophet spoke of the people of Israel of whom Yahweh says: "Israel is my firstborn son" (Exodus 4:22). Jesus lives out the history of his people. The episode of the Exodus is connected with the persecution of the Israelites—more specifically, with the persecution of Israelite boys, in Exodus 1:16—by a pagan (non-Israelite) ruler, the Pharaoh of Egypt. Pharaoh's counterpart is Herod, the non-Jewish ruler who motivates Jesus' sojourn in Egypt. More particularly, Jesus emulates the glories of the great leader of the Exodus, Moses: "When Pharaoh heard of the matter he would have killed Moses, but Moses fled from Pharaoh and made for the land of Midian" (Exodus 2:15). Jesus had to flee his own land "because Herod intends to search for the child and do away with him." Jesus follows in the footsteps of the great men of Israel.

The story clearly shows that the new-born "king of the Jews," son of David and Messiah, is not the glorious conqueror of popular Jewish Messianism. From the outset, Jesus is a suffering Messiah who attracts the hatred and jealousy of the powerful in the world. His life is sought in his own land; he finds a foreign country more hospitable than his own. The same concept is stressed by the episode of the Holy Innocents massacred in Bethlehem. On the other hand, both episodes show that Jesus enjoys God's protection, as he delivers him from all dangers until the appointed time. It is God who watches over Jesus' life and guides his existence (v. 13bc).

God's protection over Jesus' life appears even more clearly in the closing episode of Jesus' return from Egypt. The biblical tradition concerning Moses reports that "during this long period (of his sojourn in Midian) the king of Egypt died" (Exodus 2:23). Thus "Yahweh said to Moses in Midian: go, return to Egypt, for all those who wanted to kill you are dead" (Exodus 4:19). In clear reference to Moses' story, the evangelist writes that "after Herod's death, the angel of the Lord appeared in a dream to Joseph in Egypt and said: 'get up, take the child and his mother with you and return to the land of Israel, for those who wanted to kill the child are dead.' " Every step of Jesus' life is guided by God. But the multiple references to Moses' history intend to show that Jesus is another great leader of God's people, a new Moses, a new legislator who gives rise to God's definitive community.

The new Moses returns to his land, but he cannot go and settle in his own hometown in Judea because Herod's son, Archelaus, was as cruel as his father. Again, like another Moses, Jesus had to forget about his native Judean land and move to another area, to Galilee, and settle in Nazareth. The evangelist's term is that Jesus "withdrew" to Galilee. The concept of withdrawal refers the reader to the notion of persecution. He came to Nazareth because he was not secure in Bethlehem.

The settlement of Jesus in Nazareth gave the evangelist an opportunity to theologize on Jesus' familiar name "Nazarene" (in Greek *nazoraios*). Unfortunately, his theologizing is not altogether clear to us. He says that the Messiah's name "Nazarene" is attested to by the prophets, but contrary to his custom, the evangelist does not quote any scriptural passage or the name of any prophet. He may have thought of no particular passage, but of a general idea contained in the "earlier" or "later" prophets of the Old Testament. Obviously, the author connects the name Nazarene with the name of the town, Nazareth, which is never mentioned in the Old Testament. We have to deal with a popular etymological derivation. It is not unlikely that the evangelist established a relationship between the name of the town and the Hebrew term *nezer*, which means bud or twig and appears as a description of the Messiah in Isaiah 11:1: the bud or twig of the old Davidic stump. Thus the name Nazarene may be interpreted by the evangelist in the sense that Jesus is the "twig" of the Davidic dynasty, i.e., the son of David. But it is also possible that a connection be established between the name of the town, Nazareth, and the Hebrew word *nazir*, which indicates a man consecrated to God (Numbers 6:1-21; see Judges 13:8). If so, Jesus is "Nazarene" because he is a *nazir*, a man consecrated to God. The concept would agree with Luke's definition of Jesus as "holy" (1:35; 2:23), a man consecrated to God and to his service.

Second Sunday After Christmas

John 1:1-18

(See Christmas during the day, and B, Second Sunday after Christmas.)

The process through which the Logos of God "became flesh and pitched his tent among us" enabled man to become a child of God: "all those who did accept him (the Logos) he empowered to become children of God, those namely who were begotten not by blood, nor by carnal desire, nor by man's willing it—but by God" (v. 12f.). Man's divine sonship is a fairly prominent theme of the Johannine theology, but it is also found in other writers of the New Testament (Romans 8:14ff.; 1 Corinthians 4:15; James 1:18; 1 Peter 1:23).

One day, or rather "one night," a "Pharisee," who, furthermore, was "a leader of the Jews," came to Jesus. His name was Nicodemus and he was impressed by the "miracles that you worked" (3:1f.). At once Jesus steers the man into the right track; faith in miracles is short-lived; it disappears as miracles stop. Nicodemus came to him with the mind of all those Jews in Jerusalem who "believed" in Jesus "seeing the miracles he performed," but Jesus could "not trust them" (2:23ff.). That is why, right at the start, Jesus teaches Nicodemus to forget about miracles and realize that what is needed is a "rebirth from above." Judaism has become "old"; it cannot be brought back into the womb and "regenerated"; it has become the "old" garment that cannot be patched up with a "strong" piece of cloth, and the "old" wineskin that cannot contain "new" wine (see B, 8th Sunday in Ordinary Time).

Something new is needed. In view of the fact that "what is born of flesh is itself flesh, and what is born of spirit is itself spirit," it is a (re)birth from "water and spirit" that is now needed if anyone is going to enjoy the kingdom of God. Therefore, being a Jew is no privilege; a birth originating from motherly "blood," from human genetic drive and from man's will to beget a child is of no avail here, as it is only a birth "from the flesh." Jews, of course, regarded themselves as God's children, but in the new religious order divine sonship is something more and better than just being a "son of Abraham." Only a "rebirth" from above or "from water and Spirit," i.e., "by God," can render man a child of God.

The Old Testament knew that Israel at large was God's son (Hosea 11:1); that the king could be addressed by God with the words: "You are my son, I have begotten you today" (Psalm 2:7); that the righteous man had God for his father (Wisdom 2:13, 16, 18). But it is not in this sense that John (and the New Testament) refers to man's divine sonship: "See what love the Father has bestowed on us, that we be called children of God—and we are!" (1 John 3:1) The writer means it. In the bible one is called what he "is," in one way or another; this is why Christians are not just called children, they are so called because that is what they are. God has loved man to the extent that he made him his own child; and as his fatherly gift, he bestowed upon his child that particular token and guarantee of his love, namely, the donation of the Holy Spirit.

Of course, man's childhood is related to God's fatherhood; it is the "Father" who has such love for his children. In point of fact, it is not through the Holy Spirit that God begets his new children. In John 1:12f. the author suggests that it is by "receiving" God's Logos and by "believing" in him that man is reborn; not by blood, desire or will, but by God himself. In 1 John 5:1 it is he who "believes" that Jesus is the Messiah that "has been begotten of God, and everyone who loves him who begets loves also him who has been begotten by him" (the Father). In this text, he who is begotten is another fellow Christian, as the context, which urges mutual love among Christians, serves to prove. Thus it is through faith that God acts as a father who generates his new children.

In the same first letter, in connection with those who have been born of God, the Johannine writer emphasizes that "his (God's) 'seed' (Greek, *sperma)* is immanent in him," namely, in the child born of God. The concept is clear: man's rebirth is caused by something of God himself, which the author calls "his seed," and this seed is instilled into and implanted in the Christian man, where it remains "immanent," as the starter and perennial source of his new being. John discloses that God's seed has to do with faith in Jesus and with "receiving" him through faith. Some other parallel passages illustrate the idea further.

In 1 Corinthians 4:15, Paul tells the Corinthians that it is he who has begotten the Corinthians "through the gospel." Paul, of course, was instrumental in this process of generation; and that is why he can say that he begot the Corinthians "in Christ," i.e., as Christians, even though the ultimate and real "father" is God himself. The center of our interest, at this point, is that this generation happens "through the gospel," which is the "word" that the "sower sows" (Mark 4:3, 14). In a passage deriving from a baptismal liturgy, the first letter of Peter (1:23ff.) maintains that "the newly born infants" (2:2) "have been 're-generated,' not by a perishable 'seed' (Greek, *spora),* but by an imperishable seed (see John 1:13) *through the living* (see Hebrews 4:12) *and immanent word of God";* and that is why he exhorts the newly born babes to long for the "logical/rational milk" (2:2), which is their further instruction in God's word (see 1 Corinthians 3:1-3; Ephesians 4:12; Hebrews 5:12ff.). The imperishable "seed" is "the word that has been proclaimed among you as good news" (1 Peter 1:25). Similarly, in his letter (1:18, 21), James states that the "Father of luminaries...by his will gave birth to us through the *word of truth,*" which is an "implanted word with power to save you" and which the Christian man has to "receive."

This theological line develops the germinal notion contained in the parable of the "sower," who sows precisely the "word" which is "received" with more or less enthusiasm, or is "not received" at all. The Johannine theology marks the peak of this development. In Johannine theology, what the Christian man "receives" is not just the preached "word"; it is the "Word"/Logos himself (John 1:12); the Logos who existed from all eternity, who was Logos to the Father, who was God; creator, life, light, etc. It is the divine Word who is "received" whenever his divine revelation is "believed" and accepted. This is the "seed" through which God "begets" his new child because, as Jesus himself maintains, "the words I have spoken to you are 'spirit' and are life," namely, vivifying power (John 6:63), and they are the means by which the "branches" have been attached to the Vine (John 15:7).

Epiphany

Matthew 2:1-12

(See B, *Epiphany.*)

The view of the New Testament is that the gospel is a light that appeared on the earth "through the 'epiphany' of our Savior Christ Jesus" (2 Timothy 1:10). Another perspective is that "the grace of God our Savior has had its 'epiphany' for the benefit of all men" (Titus 2:11), an epiphany connected with Jesus' first appearance on earth, whereas now "we are waiting for the blessed and hoped-for 'epiphany' of the great splendor of our God and Savior Christ Jesus" (Titus 2:13)—a clear reference to the second coming of the Lord, which is also called his "epiphany."

The word "epiphany" is a loan from the Greek, where it means a bright and radiant appearance or apparition, a shining manifestation. Every epiphany implies the concept of light and brightness in either a proper or metaphorical sense. In the bible, the term applies to the radiance of God's light when, in one way or another, God manifests himself to man and irradiates his "light" so that man may perceive his invisible presence and his saving grace which are offered to man. In reference to Christ, epiphany means the resplendent manifestation of "our Savior Christ Jesus" to a world immersed in darkness and to a world that, having no light, was unable to "see" its goal and the path leading to it.

The light this world was lacking was the light that enlightens man's soul, spirit and intelligence, and which concerns the basic issue of his relationship: to God, to his own destiny, to religion and to moral life. The world was darkened by the prince of this world (2 Corinthians 14:4); the light that is in man (Matthew 6:22f.), i.e., his natural reason, was utter darkness, as it was plunged in the gloom of religious ignorance, error, superstition, idolatry and immorality. The world was tyrannized by slavery to religious ignorance and error. The Israelite community had enjoyed the light of God's revelation in the Old Testament; and this is why they regarded themselves as "guides of blind men, light of those who were in darkness" (Romans 2:19), precisely because they could irradiate God's light contained in the Scriptures. But the pagan world, namely "the blind" and "those in darkness," had not been given such a grace before the "epiphany" of Christ. They were deprived of the light that enlightens man's eyes, spirit, life and ultimate destiny, as well as man's religious and moral path through this world.

Christ appeared in the world; he was the "light coming into this world" (John 2:19) because he is, in fact, "the light of the world" (9:5) and the "light of life" (8:12); he is "the true light enlightening every man" (1:9); and he always "shines in the darkness" (1:5). There were some, "his own," who refused to come to "the light" because their deeds were evil (3:19). But then, Christ's light made its resplendent appearance, his "epiphany," in the pagan world; it was then that the non-Jewish men perceived and were given God's light to see (i.e., to know) the direction and purpose of man's existence.

It was by the preaching of Christ's person, work and message, and by the proclamation of his gospel, that the world was bathed in God's light, in God's revelation, and began to emerge from the gloom of religious and moral ignorance and error. At his time, the author of 1 John 2:8 could write that "the darkness is over and the real light begins to shine." The Lord Jesus, the bearer of God's revelation, is the radiant star that shines in the sky of God's saving plan. The Lord Jesus is the true, genuine light that enlightens every man coming into this world of darkness and gloom (John 1:9). The Lord Jesus is the light that unceasingly shines in darkness because darkness cannot overpower this powerful light (John 1:5). Darkness cannot overpower that light because it is the "radiance of God's very splendor" (Hebrews 1:3), it is the "refulgence of God's eternal light," and an "outflow of the Almighty's splendor" (Wisdom 7:25f.). It is the light which is God's Wisdom herself; "she is fairer than the sun, and surpasses every constellation of the stars; compared with light she takes precedence, for that, indeed, night supplants, but wickedness does not prevail over Wisdom" (Wisdom 7:29f.).

This is why, when the Lord Jesus started his missionary preaching in Capernaum, the perception of Matthew 4:15 was that the oracle of Isaiah 8:23—9:1 acquired a new depth: "Land of Zebulun, land of Nephtali along the sea beyond the Jordan, heathen Galilee: a people living in darkness has seen a great light; on those who inhabited a land of deadly gloom light has arisen" (see A, 3rd Sunday in Ordinary Time). This is the light of the Gospel irradiated by Jesus through his proclamation. St. Paul maintains that the unbelieving minds have been blinded by the god of the present age, so that they do not see the splendor of the gospel showing forth the brightness of Christ, who is the "image" of God; for God, who said, "let light shine out of darkness," has shone in our hearts, that the apostles and Christians in turn might make known the splendor of God shining on the face of Christ Jesus (2 Corinthians 4:4-6).

It was in this way that the grace of God, held out to man in Christ Jesus before the world began, was made manifest through the "epiphany" of our Savior; he has robbed death of its power as he "irradiated" life and immortality through the Gospel (2 Timothy 1:9f.). This is why, according to Ephesians 5:14, in the rite of Baptism in the early Church the candidate for Baptism was addressed with these words: "awake, O sleeper, arise from the dead, and Christ will dawn on you." Such is the light of Christ's epiphany that the world received because such light was "given" to it.

Lenten Season

First Sunday of Lent

Matthew 4:1-11

Christ's temptations represent a struggle between Jesus and Satan; Jesus has just been proclaimed Messiah, "my Son" (see Psalm 2:7), at his baptism and he is preparing for his messianic ministry. In Matthew the third temptation marks the climax of the unfolding process. It is here that the meaning of the entire episode becomes clear: the burning issue is "service," to serve either God or Satan. Basically, Christ's temptations are those of Adam, at the beginning, and of every human being throughout history.

Christ is the Messiah, and this is why his temptations are not ascetic but messianic in character. Satan's purpose is to drive a wedge of disobedience (to "serve" him, not God) between God and his Messiah in order to render Jesus' messianic mission void and ineffective. Satan's suggestion is that the messianic path of suffering, chosen by God for his "Servant," is doomed to failure; Jesus has the power to change this and be a successful Messiah, accepted by all. The unwavering answer of Jesus is that he is determined to remain the "Servant," obedient to God's will, even in those circumstances that by human standards would seem unbearable. Putting God to the test, in whatever manner, already implies a certain distrust. The Servant prefers the darkness of a complete and unconditional faith in God.

There is a clear relationship between Christ's temptations and his baptism. Both are a sort of introduction to his apostolic ministry and a summary of it; both disclose Christ as the subject of the Gospel; he is the bearer of the Spirit's power to cast out devils, i.e., to conquer Satan. The Spirit of baptism leads Christ to the desert where he is tempted: it is God's will and plan that his Servant be put to the test. This is what happened throughout his career up to Gethsemane, to Calvary. It is common Old Testament and rabbinic teaching that the righteous man will always be put to the test (Wisdom 3).

The temptations open with the suggestion that Jesus can do wonders "if you are Son of God," which is a reference to the baptism episode. The point is not that Satan wants to know whether Jesus really is the Messiah, nor to make Christ doubt his messianic character. His messianic dignity is granted: this is the basic assumption that underlies the whole narrative and makes it understandable.

The first temptation consists in suggesting to the Messiah that he use the powers he enjoys for his own benefit in a way contrary to God's will and purpose. For Jesus, God had chosen the career of the "Servant," of a suffering Messiah. Jesus' refusal to follow the suggestion declares that he (and every man) is supposed to live according to God's orders ("the word coming from God's mouth"), and God's order/word can support man's life even without the ordinary means. Satan's suggestion of turning stones into loaves is projected against the background of the miraculous bounty in the Jewish messianic expectations. Christ was tempted throughout his ministry to yield to the ideas of popular messianism (Matthew 12:38; 16:1; Luke 9:54; John 2:18; 6:30, etc.). But Christ decides to accept the path of God's will ("not my will but yours") and remain the suffering, obedient Servant.

The second temptation consists in "putting God to the test," that is, in requiring God to perform an unnecessary miracle in order to rescue his Messiah from harm or death. The temptation does not imply that God is not willing to rescue "his Son"; rather, it intends to drive Christ to disobey God by a misuse of his power to do wondrous and miraculous things. The setting of this temptation is the temple in Jerusalem, where the crowds gathered to worship. A rabbinic tradition maintained that "when the King, the Messiah, will reveal himself, he will come to the top of the temple" (see John 2:18; 7:3f., 28, 37). Again, the temptation requests Jesus to yield to popular Jewish messianism. Christ's answer ("not to put God to the test") is that he trusts God; he is confident that God has his own ways to make him successful and to have him recognized as Messiah; he would not resort to his superior powers in disobedience to God. He is God's Servant.

The third temptation is the most direct, and it is clearly linked with the reference to Psalm 2 ("you are my Son") at Jesus' baptism, in which the rule of the world is offered to the Messiah (Psalm 2:8f.). It consists in the attraction of worldly concepts such as glory, splendor, pleasure, and above all, power and authority. The assumption is that Christ is aware of being the ruler and master of the "nations," but how to achieve this rule? The suggestion is, by surrendering to the spirit and to the "prince" of the world. Jesus could achieve messianic success and recognition by political and military power displayed in the deliverance of Israel. This, too, was a problem throughout his ministry (Mark 10:37; John 6:15; Acts 1:6). Christ's answer sheds light on the entire narrative: he declares that he is resolved to be the "Servant" of the Lord described by Isaiah and to serve "him alone," no matter how demanding this may prove to be.

Second Sunday of Lent
Matthew 17:1-9

(See B, Second Sunday of Lent, and Transfiguration, August 6.)

The theme of light, or brightness, is the mandatory requirement of the Transfiguration narratives. It is found, in fact, in the three synoptic gospels (Mark 9:3; Luke 9:29). But the emphasis of Matthew on this theme is striking. Mark says that Jesus' clothes turned resplendent, exceedingly white, but no observation is made concerning his face; Luke points out that the appearance of Jesus' face turned different, and his raiment became dazzlingly white. Matthew not only insists further on the notion of light, but also uses a stronger language, even when he parallels the other two evangelists.

In the first place, it is not just the clothes of Jesus that become bright: it is "his face that lighted up," and it lighted up "like the sun." His clothes not only turned white and resplendent, they became white "as light" (in Greek with the article: like "the" light). Later on, whereas the two other synoptics have no descriptive detail of the cloud, Matthew points out that the cloud was a "shining" cloud; and it is, of course, from the shining cloud that the voice comes and speaks of "my Son." Interestingly enough, the "shining" cloud "overshadows" the people present there.

The insistence on the light element is tied up with another detail that is exclusive to Matthew in this narrative. After Jesus' "metamorphosis" ("change of form," v. 2), and after the voice speaking from the shining, overshadowing cloud, "the disciples who heard it fell forward on the ground and were very much afraid; but Jesus came to them and as he touched them he said: "Get up, do not be afraid."

The second episode, of the disciples falling to the ground, refers the reader to a similar episode in the gospel shows for a while. For this reason also, the disciples are in awe and fall to the ground in respectful adoration.

Both the declaration of Jesus' divine sonship and his divine splendor point to the order of the heavenly voice: "listen to him." They provide the grounds of his teaching authority and the obligation to believe what he teaches. Notably, in the fourth gospel, the "light" of Christ is first of all a revealing light, a light that reveals God's teaching splendor. Before John, Paul had already written about "the splendor of the gospel showing forth the splendor of Christ, the image of God...that we (apostles) might make known the glory/splendor of God shining on the face of Christ" (2 Corinthians 4:4, 6; see 1 Timothy 1:11; 2 Timothy 1:10). In the "face" of Christ, God's light of revelation shines with all the brightness of "the sun," and the gospel "irradiated" by Christ is the radiance of God's very light; this is why, "listen to him." When Moses received God's revelation "the skin of his face became radiant" (Exodus 35:29, 35); it was a dim reflection of God's splendor. In the case of Christ, "his face lighted up like the sun"; even his clothes became white "as light." It is this light, or revelation, that the apostles of the New Covenant "reflect" in their preaching (2 Corinthians 3:18). In reference to Moses' radiance, the Israelites "were afraid to come near him"; in regard to Christ's splendor, his disciples "fell face downward to the ground and were very much afraid." But with his gentle "touch" Jesus causes them to get up—and live without fear.

Third Sunday of Lent

John 4:5-42

The fundamental notion in Jesus' dialogue with the Samaritan woman is water. The key to the meaning of the entire episode is the comparison between Jacob and Jesus suggested by the woman in v. 12; in her view, Jesus of John. In John's gospel, when the Jewish security forces came to arrest Jesus in Gethsemane, at Jesus' declaration "I am he" they "backed up and fell to the ground" (18:5): they backed up and fell to the ground precisely when Jesus uttered the unfathomable, awesome formula, "I am he." It is one of the devices the evangelist uses to convey the message of Jesus' divinity; the soldiers are overwhelmed by the fear of the divine presence in Jesus. Furthermore, the episode reminds the reader of another passage of the Johannine school that refers to the *risen* Lord: the risen Lord, "whose appearance was like the sun when it shines in all its power," called John to be a prophet; and John "fell at his feet as though dead, but he laid his right hand on me and said to me: do not be afraid" (Revelation 1:16f.). In this passage, Jesus' self-definition is highly relevant: "I am the first and the last, and the living one" (v. 17; see 2:8; 22:13), which are attributes of God himself in the Old Testament; and the expression, "I am the first and the last," is taken from Isaiah 44:6 (and 41:4), where it applies to God. It is the divinity of Christ that the writer brings into bold relief. It is the divine presence that frightens John and strikes him down to the ground.

That is the message that Matthew wants to convey through his narrative of the Transfiguration. The whole event of Jesus' "metamorphosis" is a transitory display of what Jesus really is in the depth of his being. The voice from the "shining" cloud, which obviously is the voice of God himself, has just declared that Jesus "is my Son, my beloved." The declaration/"profession" of God himself is a confirmation of the profession of Peter a few verses earlier (16:17), when the apostle, "by a revelation of my Father in heaven," declared that Jesus is "the Son of the living God"; all the disciples had professed the same faith in 14:33: "you are the Son of God, really." The imposing presence of the divine in Jesus strikes the disciples with awe and they fall to the ground. This is a functional device to bring out the divinity of Jesus and the worship due to him.

The episode of the disciples' fear and worship of the divine, however, marks the end of the entire episode and is its conclusion. The transcendent personality of Christ is disclosed, not only by the voice from the cloud, but by all that light and the brightness that Jesus' nature irradiates. For the biblical mind, "God is light" (1 John 1:5) and God's world is a world of light (see 1 Timothy 6:16). It was in the form of light that God appeared to Moses in the burning bush which, although on fire, was not consumed (Exodus 3:2f.). All manifestations of God are surrounded by and shrouded in light. In his description of the heavenly city, the author of the Apocalypse can say that "the city has no need of sun or moon to shed light on it, for the splendor of God lights it up, and the Lamb is its lamp" (21:23), because in the Lamb the splendor of God himself shines. It is along this line of thought that the Logos is "the true light" (John 1:19), and Jesus can say that "I am the light of the world" (John 9:5; 8:12; 12:35), and that "the light came to the world" (3:19).

Such is the idea that Matthew wants to emphasize when he so strongly insists on the abundance and brightness of the light that accompanies Jesus' transfiguration. The cloud itself is a "shining" cloud because it is the vehicle or support of God's very presence; it is from the shining cloud that God speaks, and so his "splendor" brightness permeates the cloud with its light. God cannot be seen, but he can be perceived by the radiance of what he is, namely "light." The radiance of Christ's face and clothes come from within himself; it is the light of divinity which is released for a while and permeates the external dimension of Christ. In a sense, this external dimension of Jesus, his body and clothes, becomes the "bush" where the splendor of the divine light shines and cannot be greater than "our father Jacob"; he cannot offer anything better than Jacob did. However, the comparison goes beyond personalities and is aimed at two religious systems. Jacob is the patriarch of both the Jews and the Samaritans and stands for their religious systems, also represented by Jerusalem and Mount Gerizim (v. 21f.). Jesus, of course, represents the Christian system. Within this perspective, the "water" of Jacob is the water of a well; it is not running water; it is somewhat stagnant, still and stale; it does not have the freshness and moving power of running water. Also, it is difficult to reach. The water that Christ offers is "living water." It is not only running water: in John's understanding of life, it is something that contains life, lives, and conveys life.

The term water stands for what a religious system gives to its followers, or for what a believer gets from the "sources" of his religion. The source of the Samaritan (and Jewish) religions was the Torah or Law, and this system had become stale and old-fashioned in what it offered to the believer; it is stagnant. It is the "old man" of Nicodemus (John 3:4); it is the wine, which in comparison with the "good wine at the end," is like "the water of the Jewish purifications" (John 2:6ff.); it is the "old" garment or the old wineskins of the synoptic tradition. That is why the time has come when both Jerusalem and Gerizim must be replaced as symbols of a given worship, and a different kind of worship is ushered in (4:21-24). To his followers, Christ offers something else, the same thing that he offers to the Samaritan woman: "his" water, namely a messianic water which happens to be a "living" water, that in addition, becomes a source within the believer—a source that unceasingly leaps up in strong jets of water. It is the freshness, abundance, steadiness and dynamism of Christ's gift that is portrayed.

An obvious question is this: in concrete terms, what is the water that Christ offers? The answer is that there are no concrete terms. The notion of water, like many others in John, is a metaphor that describes, from a particular angle, the entire gift of eternal life or salvation brought about by Christ. In fact, it stands for the sum total of God's messianic gift to mankind, with everything it entails. It can be added, perhaps, that in this and other Johannine passages, "water" is a sapiential metaphor (see above all Sirach 24:22-31; 47:14f.; 51:24) that stands for the gift of divine wisdom which comes to man as the Spirit or as the "Spirit of Truth." This is why Jesus' water becomes a perennial source. Since the gift of the Spirit is given through baptism, there can be little doubt that a reference to Christian baptism is included in the messianic water. The sapiential character of this water is further supported by the fact that the woman expects the Messiah to "disclose to us everything" (v. 25), and the Messiah happens to be Jesus himself, who impresses the woman with his knowledge about her five husbands; she tries then to call the attention of her neighbors to a man who may be the Messiah, by letting them know that the man has told her everything she had done (v. 29).

The new worship "in spirit and truth" (v. 23) leads us in the same direction. The point is not an internal worship versus an external worship. It is rather a spiritual/superior worship compared with an earthly/inferior worship. The worship of the new religious system established by Christ is "spiritual" because it is according to the truth of Christ's full revelation of the Father, according to the freshness of a new supernatural/divine knowledge and wisdom imparted to mankind by the "Word" of God. Only those who worship the Father, according to this revealed knowledge, please God because the new revelation of his will requires such worshipers. The worship performed in Jerusalem and on Gerizim must come to an end because it does not reflect the updated worship required by the Father's revelation in and through Christ. God is spirit in the sense that he is also love (1 John 4:8, 16); this sort of definition is not essential but functional.

God is love because he loves unceasingly with generous, infinite love. Likewise, God is spirit because he lavishly dispenses his own spiritual/supernatural wisdom and knowledge to man in the revelation given through the words and deeds of his incarnate Logos and unceasingly develops it by the gift of his own Spirit (John 16:12-15; 1 John 2:27).

Revealing the Father is Jesus' pressing task: it is his "nourishment" (v. 34). Pouring the water of revelation is the "work" the Father entrusted to him (17:4). His revealing work, as John understands, has been very successful: "the fields are shining for harvest," the crops are ahead of time. It is laborers that are needed to harvest the abundant crops. Christ always is the real "sower" of the Christian seed; the laborers just gather the fruit. Jesus entered the Samaritan village and "many" recognized that he was "the Savior of the world" and believed in him.

Fourth Sunday of Lent
John 9:1-41

The episode in John 9 is well known. As Jesus went by, he comes upon a man who was blind from birth. His disciples call his attention to the question debated in the theological schools: is physical sickness or disability always divine punishment for one's sins? The Pharisees maintained that it was (v. 34). There is a controversial point against the Pharisees throughout the narrative, and the Lord is determined to prove them wrong.

The debated question had to do with God's justice, and the case of a man born blind posed the problem in burning terms: his blindness cannot be a penalty for sins he had never committed (or else the injustice is blatant); and if he is punished for his parents' sins, how can God be said to be just? These are the two alternatives that the disciples brought up. They could not imagine that there was a third alternative. Only Christ, in his wisdom, could know of it. Physical evil—be it sickness, poverty, disaster, or suffering—can also be an opportunity intended by God to show his love and compassion for men so that they can discover what God really is, namely Love. This is how God manifests his "glory," his splendid bounty and goodness; and this is how physical evil can be intended for God's glory.

The overriding concern of the entire narrative, however, lies elsewhere. The episode is reported to demonstrate two things: a) the Lord says, "While I am in the world I am the light of the world" (v. 5); b) "It is for judgment that I came to the world: that those who do not see may see, and those who see may become blind" (v. 39). The Lord is light, but he is also judge.

The Lord is the light of the world: he demonstrates this by the fact that he gives sight to the man born blind. There could be no doubt that the man is utterly blind; he had never had sight. As usual with John, the factual miracle becomes a "real" symbol pointing in the direction of unfathomable depths in Christ's interventions. The miracle of "enlightening" man's physical eyes leads John to discover that Jesus is "the light"; the light not just for a man, but the light that enlightens the frightening darkness of the whole world; he is the light, not just for darkened physical eyes, but the light enlightening man's darkened spirit, intellect and soul. That is why, at the end, the man born blind not only receives the sight of his eyes; he also receives the light of his spirit: he "believes" in the Son of Man and comes to recognize his God in him; he "adores" him. The wonderful light that Christ irradiates is such that it reaches the deepest recesses of man's heart, if man's heart opens up to him.

The symbolism also extends to other areas; such as the man washed in the pool of "Siloam." It is a real pool that can still be seen in Jerusalem and which even today, as in ancient times, receives its running water from the other side of the hill through an underground channel. The water is "sent" from the other side (this is what Siloam means, "sent"). But for John the pool where men receive sight is the pool of the "Envoy" sent by the Father to enlighten this world. This is why the pool of Siloam is a symbol of the baptismal font where men receive their light as they are "washed" in the sacramental bath (see Ephesians 5:14).

The presence of the Light in the world is a disquieting factor: it calls for a decision for or against the Light. Either you open your eyes and "see," or you close your eyes (or keep them shut), and then you cannot see. But the fact of closing or opening one's eyes is in itself a value judgment; it discloses an internal attitude, a basic disposition towards the light. Man is free to close or to open his eyes, but he is not free to change the nature and the value of his "openness" to the Light or of his aversion to it. Your attitude towards the Light certainly reveals your disposition towards everything the Light stands for. The mere presence of the Light in the world passes a judgment on the world (and condemns it). By the mere fact of his presence, the Light is a judge. This is exactly what John writes in 3:19-21 (see 12:46-48). This is why the Lord came to the world—for judgment: his mere presence in the world leads some to adhere to him, and others to oppose him.

This is how the Pharisees experienced the judgment of the Light. Confronted with the Light, in the form of a powerful miracle, they close their eyes and prefer to entrench themselves in the pettiness of their own "pharisaic" religiosity. They thought they were "enlightened," that they had sight: they held "the key of knowledge" (Luke 11:52) and imparted religious legislation (Matthew 23:1ff.). This is why, in the presence of the Light, they became blind. They opposed the Light and thus manifested their real attitude toward the Light.

The "blind" man did not know anything about all the subtle reasonings of pharisaic religiosity, but he used his good and sincere judgment: sabbath or not, this was a great miracle; Jesus must be a prophet at least. This is as far as the man could go by his natural light. Eventually, the Light supplements his deficiencies and leads the man all the way to a pious and humble faith in the Light. It is a matter of sincerity in regard to the Light: love for or hatred of the Light (John 3:19ff.) makes all the difference in this judgment conducted by the Light in the world.

Fifth Sunday of Lent
John 11:1-45

Just as all other miracles in the Fourth Gospel, the resurrection of Lazarus in John 11:1-45 is a "sign." It is not just an impressive happening which strikes those who witness it, both for its unusual nature and the tremendous powers of him who performs it: it is much more than that. It is a pointer, "signifying," and to some degree expressing, something far greater and sublime. Besides its factual reality, the resurrection of Lazarus becomes a "symbol" of something else: it must serve as evidence and as an "empirical" demonstration of some higher and absolute principle. This is, in fact, the reason why the miracle is reported. It is not its actuality, its historical eventuality or implications, nor its scientific aspects that prompted the evangelist to record it. Its force as a "witnessing" work (John 5:36; 14:11) was the determining factor for the evangelist to choose it as one of the few signs (John 20:30f.) which prove the point he makes in his gospel.

The climax of the narrative, therefore, is the actual resurrection of Lazarus—only insofar as it provides the evidence supporting the point of the evangelist. From a logical or conceptual standpoint, the climax and the nucleus of the entire literary unit is the Lord's utterance in his answer to Martha (v. 25): "I am the resurrection and the life; whoever believes in me, though he should die, will come to life; and whoever being alive believes in me will not die for ever." One of the basic tenets of the fourth evangelist is that Jesus is "life," just as he is the way and the truth (14:5); he has life in himself, and this is why he can give life to others. It is for this reason also that he is the resurrection: he causes the resurrection because he instills life into dead bodies or members. The difference between Jesus and other miracle workers, as John sees it, is that others do something that God may give life, whereas Jesus releases a flow of life from himself, and through it starts or stirs life in others.

The practical dimension for men deriving from Jesus being the resurrection and the life is that man receives the flow of Christ's life while he is alive on this earth. This is how the evangelist explains the relationship between man's inescapable death and his vivification by Christ: of course, man undergoes physical or biological death any way, but in spite of that, if he has given his faith to Jesus, he will come to life. In other words, whoever, while he is physically alive (before his physical death), believes in Jesus will not die for ever; his (physical) death is not definitive. Other elements of the same basic thought are provided by John in 5:21-29 on the occasion of the healing in which Jesus gave life to the dead members of a man crippled for thirty-eight years: "Just as the Father raises the dead and grants life, so the Son grants life to those to whom he wishes...I solemnly assure you, the man who hears my word and has faith in him who sent me possesses eternal life. He does not come under condemnation, but has passed from death to life. An hour is coming, has indeed come, when the dead shall hear the voice of the Son of God and those who have heard (the word, v. 24, in their lifetime) shall live. Just as the Father possesses life in himself, so he has granted it to the Son to have life in himself...an hour is coming in which all those in their tombs shall hear his voice and come forth. Those who have done right shall rise to life, the evildoers shall rise to be damned."

The instance of Lazarus exemplifies and proves this truth, empirically as it were. Lazarus had believed in Christ; he had "heard (listened to) his word" when he was alive; he had, therefore, received "eternal life": he had passed from death to life because the Son has life in himself and gives it to whomever he wishes. Then Lazarus underwent biological death, but the "eternal life" was with him. All that he needs now is to hear the "voice" of Christ that gives an order to that life to release its full power and vivify even the physical dimension of the man who was dead (and in decay). As soon as Jesus gives that order ("Lazarus, come forth"), the power of Christ's life permeates the corpse ("swallows mortality" in the dead body: 2 Corinthians 5:4) and Lazarus comes out alive. This is how Christ gives a demonstration that he is indeed the resurrection and the life.

The texts quoted show that in this case faith is not just an intellectual assent to what Christ teaches. It is a total commitment to Jesus and his interests. It is intellectual assent plus loving attachment and devotion, not only to some theoretical principles, but to a living, concrete Person, Jesus; and it is an unswerving and tireless endeavor to honor that assent, that attachment and that devotion: "He who obeys the commandments he has from me is the man who loves me" (John 14:21, 23). This is why the resurrection to life is only for those who "have done right." It is a resurrection to live, because a resurrection to be damned is not "life" according to the biblical mind. Life is not just the operational functioning of a life principle: it requires fullness and enjoyment in one's living existence. In John's language, survival in condemnation is not life but "the second death" (Revelation

2:11; 20:14; 21:8). There is no second resurrection—there is only one, and this occurs when, through faith, a man "passes from death to life."

Passion Sunday (Palm Sunday)
Matthew 21:1-11

The passage of Matthew 21:1-11 is, like the remainder of the gospel, written from the viewpoint of the evangelist's Christian faith. The episode of Palm Sunday is described in terms of a proclamation of Jesus' royal dignity. Jesus comes to Jerusalem, the Holy City, in his capacity of messianic sovereign. It is as messianic Lord and Master that he is now rejected by the leaders of his Jewish people. It is in this perspective that Jesus' triumphal visit to Jerusalem is a prelude to his redeeming sacrifice: the initial triumph should strengthen the faith of loyal souls through the disappointing events of the coming week, until its resounding reassurance in Christ's resurrection.

In order to bring the royal aspect of the Palm Sunday event into a sharp relief, the evangelist systematically confronts the various incidents of that day with some messianic passages in the Old Testament. It is this confrontation that discloses the theological meaning of otherwise irrelevant happenings. In point of fact, parting company with the other evangelists, Matthew not only reports that on that day the Lord used the colt, but also its mother. The evangelist was keeping an eye on the prophetic passage of Zechariah 9:9f., which just mentions "a colt, the foal of an ass"; but Matthew's concern is not exegetical or chronicle-like. He wanted to illustrate Christ's deeds by referring them to the text of Zechariah: "Rejoice heartily, O daughter of Zion...see, your king shall come to you: a just savior is he. Meek and riding on an ass, on a colt, the foal of an ass." The same purpose is served by a reference to Psalm 8:3 in Matthew 21:16. Not the adults, but the children of Jerusalem acclaim the messianic king, to the disappointment and fury of the religious leaders who ask Jesus to silence them. Instead, his answer shows them that the children's acclamation should be regarded as one more messianic sign, because it gives fulfillment to an Old Testament oracle: "Did you never read that 'from the speech of infants and children you have framed a hymn of praise'?" Psalm 8, particularly v. 7, was a messianic psalm in the view of early Christians (see Ephesians 1:22; Philippians 3:21; 1 Corinthians 15:27; Hebrews 2:6ff.). Thus it also provided the right explanation of the children's acclamation as a praise of God for the glory he gives to his Messiah. The triumphant event itself and the gesture of spreading cloaks on the road refer the reader to a similar episode in 2 Kings 9:13.

The evangelist also mentions that blind and lame people came to Jesus in the temple area, and he cured them. As he does in 8:16f.; 9:35; 11:5; 15:30f., the evangelist also points out here, that Jesus' healing miracles indicate that he is the messianic king and the "Servant of the Lord," because of the relation they bear to messianic passages such as Isaiah 35:5-6 and others. The healings show that it is Jesus who brings the messianic blessings, foretold by Isaiah, to mankind. As such, they counterbalance and somehow legitimize Christ's rough attitude towards the merchants in the temple area: Christ is the real benefactor of man. Even the dealings of Jesus with the merchants are viewed from the standpoint of their relation to the Old Testament texts: Isaiah 56:6f. sees that in the eschatological restoration, "my house shall be called a house of prayer for all the nations." Matthew deliberately omitted the words "for all nations," because he is thinking of the temple that Jesus will rebuild "in three days" (Matthew 26:61), which in fact, is the body of him "who is greater than the temple" (Matthew 12:6). After all, the evangelist knew that the Jerusalem temple had to be destroyed, so it could not be the temple of Isaiah 56. The addition coming from Jeremiah 7:11 ("you are turning it into a den of thieves"), puts the blame on any religious superstition anchored on material buildings and intends to lift religious endeavors to a higher level of purity, where religion and worship are supposed to be conducted "in spirit and in truth" (John 4:24), according to the principles of the messianic revelation.

Above all, the Palm Sunday event is characterized by the acclamation of Christ as "Son of David." This is clearly a royal and messianic title which describes Jesus as the Davidic king of olden prophecies and as the eschatological king: the goal and end of the royal dynastic line of Judea. Thus, this proclamation anticipates the title "Jesus of Nazareth, king of the Jews" nailed to the cross above Jesus' head; it marks the end of a development started with the coming of the Magi, who asked about the newborn "king of the Jews."

But the messianic king is not the mighty warrior and political deliverer of the Jewish expectations. He is "meek" and mild; he rides a donkey and not a horse, the symbol of war times; such is the vision of Zechariah 9:9f. (see Genesis 49:10f.). His mildness had been stressed by Matthew in 12:18-21 with words from Isaiah 42:1-4. In fact, his caring attention goes to the blind and lame.

Beyond all that, Jesus' messianic entry into Jerusalem is a sign of future hope. It presages and sketches out Christ's final and saving coming in glory at the end of time: it points to the final salvation by the redeeming king. In this sense Christ's triumph on Palm Sunday becomes a promise and a security of his second coming. This is why Matthew does not refer to the Davidic kingdom but to the Davidic king, namely to the "Son of David." It is not the coming of the messianic kingdom but of the messianic Sovereign that he wants to portray. The authentic inauguration of the kingdom will happen later on. Before the Son of David ascends the throne of the ruler, he has to carry out his saving mission by "serving," i.e., by giving his life as a ransom for all.

Holy Thursday

John 13:1-15

The time for Jesus to pass from this world to the Father was imminent. The evangelist insists that Jesus was aware of that. In this awareness, he is about to give to his beloved disciples the "supreme proof of love," the "greatest love" anyone can show: "to give his own life for his friends" (John 15:13). The reference is to the passion and death, to which the section of the fourth gospel, starting with chapter 13, is an introduction. The devil, in fact, had already put into the mind of Judas to betray him: Jesus.

Still, in the perspective of the evangelist, the first move of Jesus that should disclose his supreme love is the washing of his disciples' feet. Washing someone's feet was a very lowly service. It was so humiliating that the Jewish law exempted a Jewish slave from providing this service to his master. Such a service was regarded as the lot of a "slave," and a pagan one at that. It is this that Peter's amazement brings into sharp relief: *"Lord!* (not slave) You washing my feet?" The true meaning of Jesus' gesture can be perceived only when it is projected against the screen of Paul's teaching in Philippians 2:6-11: Jesus, being in the condition of God and being equal to God, "emptied himself" and assumed the condition of a "slave"; he was humbled to death on a cross—but God exalted him. The washing of the feet is a symbolic action—or a dramatic performance—that acts out the teaching of the Pauline passage. The basic meaning is that Jesus is the humblest slave or "servant."

Just as in Paul, so also in John, Jesus is perfectly "aware" that he is the supreme Lord over the entire cosmos ("everything is given into his hands"), and even more: he is aware that his origin is divine and that he is about to resume his divine status (see 17:5-24; 6:62). In the fullness of such awareness, however, he removes his outer garment ("empties himself") in order to put on a towel round his waist, pour water into a basin and start washing the feet of his disciples: He "assumes the condition of a slave." In the same direction, the evangelist notes that, as they were at supper, it is Jesus who "got up from the table"; whereas the disciples, of course, remained seated. In the parallel passage of Luke 22:27, the Lord asks his disciples: "Who is greater: the one at table or the one who serves? The one at table, right? Yet here am I among you as one who serves!" Jesus portrays himself and acts as the "servant" of his disciples.

By this "service" the Lord wants to get across the message that he is the "Servant of the Lord" described in Isaiah 53. In the washing of the feet he acts as the humblest, lowliest servant; but this is just a symbolic action that brings out his quality of "Servant" and points to an even far more painful and humiliating service, namely his passion and death on a cross, where he has to be the real and genuine Servant of the Lord, who gives his life in ransom for all (Isaiah 53:10-12; Mark 10:45, etc.). The washing of the feet should prepare his disciples for the shock ahead by making them realize that "the Lord and Master" is also "the Servant" and has to discharge the duties of the Servant.

Jesus' gesture, however, also has an exemplary dimension and contains a stern lesson. At the end of his performance, he "puts his external garment on again"; he resumes his glory and dignity, and reasserts that he truly is "the Master and the Lord." And as such, as Master and Lord, he sits at table again and, in his full authority, explains what his performance should mean to them; he does not want them to miss the point: "I, the Master and the Lord, have given you an example that you yourselves do exactly what I have done to you." At this moment,

Jesus addresses himself to the Twelve; they are the only ones present at the supper. The Twelve are the future leaders of the Christian community, and he wants them to know what being "a master and lord" in his community means; namely to be "servants" and to be servants to the point of doing the supreme service: "If anyone wants to be at my service, he must 'follow me' and where I am, there my servant, too, must be" (John 12:26). In other words, a shepherd of the Christian community must be a "good shepherd": "the good shepherd gives up his life for his sheep" (John 10:11).

The exemplary dimension of Jesus' performance explains why a significant dialogue has to take place with Peter, and precisely with Peter, or "Cephas" (1:42), whom Jesus wants "to tend my flock" (21:15-17). As on other occasions (see Matthew 16:22), Peter would prevent the Lord from discharging his duties as "Servant of the Lord" ("do you mean to wash my feet?"). This is true even in John 13:36f.: "where are you going, Lord?... Why can't I 'follow you' right now? I will give my life for you." Later on, John reports how Peter brandishes his sword in Gethsemane (18:10). Peter just can't understand that "the Lord and Master" could or should be "the Servant" who has to suffer all kinds of humiliation—to the point of death. Jesus tells Peter that the apostle does not understand Jesus' performance "now," "but you will 'know' later on." For understanding and knowing, the evangelist uses two different words; the notion of knowledge connoting the concept of experimental knowledge or knowing by one's own experience. By his own experience, Peter will know what Jesus is doing "now." In point of fact, a few verses down the same chapter, Jesus has a prediction for Peter: "you cannot follow me 'now' where I am going, but later on you will." The "later-on" time came when, "meaning the kind of death" Peter was to endure, Jesus told him that against his will "somebody else" would put a belt around him and take him where he would rather not go (John 21:18)—as a "slave" doing somebody else's will and dying on a cross. This prediction comes right after Peter was entrusted with the task of "tending my sheep." At that moment, by his own experience, Peter will "know" what Christ did; he will know what being the chief shepherd of Christ's flock means: it means to be a "servant," to be "the good shepherd who gives up his life for the sheep."

Furthermore, in his dialogue with Peter (13:8ff.), the Lord wants the apostle to understand that Jesus must perform his duties of "Servant" and go all the way down the rugged path of service. It is his service that will bring about a tighter "communion" with Peter at the level of the vital oneness between the Vine and the branches. It is through Jesus' "service," that a perennial source of cleansing power will be opened in the Christian community, where those who have already adhered to him through a sincere conversion and baptism ("bath"), will be able to cleanse their "feet" from the occasional defilement contracted by walking the paths of life in this world. Only those who reject Christ will be unable to avail themselves of the source of purity provided through the cleansing death of "the Servant."

Easter Season

Easter Sunday

John 20:1-9

(See B, Easter Sunday.)

The resurrection of Christ is not only history. It is not something that belongs only to the past; nor is it a mere fact, something that just happened or was caused to happen. The resurrection of Jesus of Nazareth is an eschatological event; that is, an event projected against the screen of a distant future, indeed to the end of history. It is, furthermore, no mere factual anecdote; but a mystery: it is the tip of the iceberg which emerges from the ocean of God's hidden but purposeful design into the contingent world of man's perception.

The resurrection of the Lord is, first of all, an eschatological event. It marks a powerful and decisive intervention of God in the fortunes and eternal destiny of mankind. The writers of the New Testament are at one in stressing that the resurrection is an achievement of God's power. The forces of disintegration and dissolution are an ingredient of man's composite being in its natural existence. At death, body and soul break up; then man's body turns into dust, since it was out of dust that it was first molded. This is the law of nature in its present existence. No one but God can stop this process of nature as it now exists. Almighty God alone can either prevent the dust of man's body from breaking apart, or gather this dust again into an animated body. Only God can break the power of death.

It was through a particular display of his power that God intervened in the normal fortunes of mankind; and that is why the resurrection of Christ is an eschatological event. Through God's intervention, something absolutely new was "created"; a new perspective opened up for mankind. The state of mankind will never be the same again: in the resurrection of the Lord, man not only knows but also experiences somehow that death is not the final, inexorable fate of man. God has "created" or devised a means to keep man alive, even after the normal process of death has occurred.

The resurrection of the Lord, however, is much more than just a case of resuscitation—a return to the same kind of life that was enjoyed before death. Resurrection is a supernatural process by which God's life within a given person releases its effectiveness to the point that "mortality is swallowed up by life, corruptibility is clothed over with incorruptibility" (1 Corinthians 15:53f.; 2 Corinthians 5:4). This is a process which can be illustrated by the converse natural process of a living body which is being consumed by cancer or gangrene until death swallows up life and reigns supreme. Likewise, in the process of a life evolving towards a fullness of life, God's life gradually invades and conquers the entire being of man, to the point that this divine life "eats up" whatever is mortal and corruptible in man's being, even in his body, and permeates man's body with an imperishable life, with the result that no focus of mortality or corruption is left "unsterilized"—let us rather say "unvivified."

It is obvious, in this perspective, that a true resurrection implies not only a return to life after death. It also includes, by necessity, a real change in the very nature of man's being: the life man enjoys after being resurrected by God is not the same kind of life he had before; it is of a superior order. The life principle of a resurrected person is no longer the "biological" life principle; it is God's life in man, so that man lives the life of God himself, a condition which the New Testament calls "life of the Spirit." This implies a deep transformation, let us say uplifting, of man's natural capabilities; it is a supernatural change, which is supernatural precisely because it is beyond nature's means: only God can bring it about. This is an additional and decisive reason why the resurrection necessitates an exercise of God's power. This mode of existence for a "body," can never become real, without a powerful and supernatural intervention of God which renders "what is inglorious glorious, what is powerless powerful, what is 'biological' spiritual" (1 Corinthians 15:42f.).

This is something God never did before Christ. The resurrection of Christ is the first instance in which God engaged his power in order to change or upgrade man's make-up to supernatural proportions. Again, this is why Christ's resurrection is an eschatological event. Man's future is " full of immortality." After Christ's resurrection man knows, in a certain sense by experience, that he can transcend, by God's power and donation, the bounds of corruptibility and mortality; he can live free from fear of death; he can live in a condition in which he cannot die. This is the perspective that Christ's resurrection opens up to man. But above all, Christ's resurrection is an eschatological event because this kind of vivification of the dead was God's promise for the end of time: this is why all the dead wait for the end of time, to be raised and to be divinely vivified by God. In the case of Jesus of Nazareth, however, God anticipated His own promise; or rather, he anticipated the end of time: the end of time was ushered in with Christ's resurrection, when Death began to lose power. The most powerful and dreadful enemy of man suffered its first defeat. That is why Christ's resurrection is a source of joy and hope for mankind: "He who raised up our Lord will also raise us up through his power" (1 Corinthians 6:14); "He who raised up Jesus from the dead will also vivify our mortal bodies through his Spirit who dwells in us" (Romans 8:11).

Christ's resurrection is, furthermore, a mystery; it is the indicator of what God will do at the end of time. Christ's resurrection is not a "solitary boast" which is to remain the one exceptional occurrence in God's dealings with mankind. It is rather a guarantee of what God has in store for *all* the faithful. Christ's resurrection is an experimental proof of what God's power is able to do and what he is resolved to do at the end of time. "How can the dead rise? With what kind of body can they emerge?" (1 Corinthians 15:35) These questions haunt the minds of many so-called theologians today; but they are very old. In these precise terms, the question was put to Paul by the Corinthians (1 Corinthians 15:35). Though the terms were different, the question of the Sadducees was the same when they tried to ensnare the Lord with an academic trick (Matthew 22:23-28). Paul finds the question "silly," while Christ discovers in such a question an inexcusable "ignorance of the Scriptures." Both of them also feel that it indicates "ignorance of the power of God." Neither Christ nor Paul ever attempted to provide a philosophical explanation for the resurrection of the dead. Their only explanation is the unlimited power of God and his will to carry out his plan of salvation, which also includes the resurrection of the dead.

There is more. St. John records the Lord as saying that: "Unless the grain of wheat falls to the ground and dies it remains alone; but if it dies it brings forth much fruit" (12:24). Some time before, St. Paul had written that God "has vivified and raised us all together with Christ" (Ephesians 2:5), as he had also written that Christ "was raised for our justification" (Romans 4:25). What all this means is that the resurrection of Christ affects all Christians in various ways. Christ's resurrection is not just an individual thing which concerns him alone. It is rather an event of universal, cosmic and a-temporal, or rather trans-temporal, significance and efficacy.

The physical death of the grain is necessary, because its life has to be multiplied in the life of many more grains, which draw their life and energy from the one life of the original grain. This is how that life "rises." The death of the grain is not the disappearance of its life; rather it is in death that this life bursts and releases the vivifying power it contains. This was Christ's death and resurrection. The divine life contained in him "burst" and overflowed as he died, and, besides transforming the "shell-body" in which it was contained, released all its vivifying power, bringing forth the entire harvest of the Christian faithful who are, in other biblical variations of the same basic image, the branches of the one Vine or the various members of the one Body. This divine life in Christ is the Spirit of God, who dwelt in Christ and vivified his risen body which, as St. Paul puts it, results in a "vivifying spirit." It is through and from this "spiritualized" body that the Spirit is given to us as one of the gifts—indeed the main gift—of our justification by God. Christ's body becomes, at his resurrection, the source of the Spirit. It is by means of this transformation that Christ's life comes to us, through his spiritual body. That is why Paul says that we "were vivified and raised together with Christ." When Christ rose from the dead, God tapped the source, so to speak, of our eternal life and effected our own resurrection.

Second Sunday of Easter
John 20:19-31

(See considerations on B, Second Sunday of Easter.)

In today's reading, among other things, the evangelist emphasizes that "blest are they who did not see and yet believed." Obviously this is the lesson he wants to teach his readers; in fact, it is the conclusion of the entire episode in which Thomas is involved; it is in view of such a conclusion that the entire episode is reported and it is to this conclusion that the several elements in the narrative had to lead. In the narrative, the blessedness of those who believe without seeing is indicated to Thomas, who had his doubts about the resurrection of the Lord until he "saw." But it is aimed over Thomas' head at many, many—as a matter of fact to all—Christians of John's time and beyond who had and have no material evidence of the Lord's resurrection as the apostles and Thomas were given. After the first generation of witnesses, all Christians are blest because they have not seen and yet have believed that the Lord Jesus is risen, that he has overcome death.

In point of fact, the resurrection of the Lord is always an object of faith and can be firmly accepted by man only on the basis of faith. This was true even of those who had some material or experiential evidence of the fact. It is John himself who teaches us this: the beloved disciple came to the tomb, entered it, took good note of all the evidence available (empty tomb, stone removed, bandages still there, the face cloth laid somewhere by itself), and after "having 'seen' he 'believed' " (20:8). Vision, as such, is not compatible with "faith" in the proper, theological sense of the term. In point of fact, the factual evidence can only prove that the man is not there in the tomb; it can even prove that the man was alive when he left the tomb, and that he left the place by his own means, and, to that extent, it can prove that the man came back to life.

But the resurrection of Jesus is much more than that: it is his coming back to a superior, glorious life that is an authentication by God of all his work and a reward for his obedient and "loving" passion and death. In other words, the resurrection of the Lord is a transcending "event" full of saving meaning and theological significance. This is something the material evidence will always be unable to prove. Only faith can grasp this dimension, which certainly is the most important in Jesus' resurrection.

In themselves, the apparitions are no compelling evidence of Jesus' resurrection. In the first place, the evangelists themselves had to deal with an interpretation of the apparitions that resorted to a "ghost," perhaps the ghost of Jesus himself (Luke 24.37, 39). It seems that, as in Luke 24, the evidence required by Thomas was supposed to answer such a question. Beyond that, the apparitions may prove that the man is alive and well; that he was victorious over death. But, this does not yet manifest that God was the real cause of this resurrection; and that the resurrection constituted Jesus in a transcendent mode of existence with everything that implies and means. There is an element of interpretation, let us say revelation, to the whole event that only faith can disclose and grasp. That is why faith in the resurrection is always necessary, in spite of all the evidence available.

From another point of view, the historical evidence written down in the New Testament is still less compelling than the material evidence that was available to the first witnesses and the personal experience of the apparitions. This does not mean that the evidence is not valid; it only means that the beloved disciple himself "believed" precisely after having "seen" and evaluated the evidence available. In another direction, we must be aware of the possible difference between the sound value of the historical evidence recorded and the stringent demands of the historical method: the recorded evidence can correspond to historical facts and be valid from a historical/factual viewpoint, but historical criticism demands too much from a type of evidence that was not gauged to stand the trial of modern criticism. The point is that historical criticism may not be able to discard the question as non-existent; but the available evidence, in its turn, is not powerful enough to elicit historical assent. Obviously, as good as it is, the historical evidence recorded in the New Testament did not intend to "prove" the fact of Christ's resurrection critically, but rather to inform about it and make it known. For us today, even the historical aspect of the event requires the will to believe. This is a problem, however, inherent to any kind of historical evidence.

It has been observed (Bonhoeffer), and correctly so, that by its very nature historical evidence is not—cannot be—absolute. Precisely for this reason, the apparitions of the Risen Lord, like that to Thomas, were not a game of surprises, but they had a saving meaning; they belonged (and belong) to salvation history, and were an object of kerygmatic preaching. Christ, therefore, not only provided the apparition but also the light for the receivers to know with all certainty that it was Christ who appeared and that he was really alive. This explains why Thomas "believed" even if he is not said to have made the experiential "proof" proposed to him. The example of Paul is perhaps the most instructive. His conviction that he had seen Christ (1 Corinthians 9:1; 15:8; Galatians 1:15) was overwhelming; he never entertained any doubts about that, and his conviction changed the life of a man who was not at all inclined to Christ or anything he represented. The reasons for Paul's "conversion" must also have been the reasons why all other apostles and non-apostles "believed" that Christ had risen, was alive, glorified and in command of the entire cosmos. A "revelation" accompanied the experience and disclosed its full contents. After all, the apparitions themselves are characterized as a "gift" of God; not given to all but just to a few (Acts 10:40). This is why even those who could evaluate the historical evidence and were "given" particular experiences grasped all the mystery of Jesus' resurrection only by "believing," i.e., through faith.

The foregoing considerations indicate that our faith in the Lord's resurrection basically is no different from the faith of the apostles. And this is why it is not irrational, just as theirs was not; but it takes a will to believe. The fundamental reason for our belief in Jesus' resurrection is our faith in God's "gift" of revelation, that revelation that made the historical evidence understandable in terms of salvation.

Through centuries-old generations of Christians the faith and the experimental evidence of the apostles and their contemporaries (see 1 Corinthians 15:5-8) has come down to us. The Christians of the present generation are one more link, joining past and future generations in the faith and proclamation of the resurrection of the Lord. This is part of our theological task as Christians; and this is the service that we are supposed to do to God, to Christ, and to the Christian community of believers.

It is not quite clear whether or not Jesus' answer to Thomas is a statement or a sort of doubting question: "Have you really believed because you have seen?" Even in the case of a statement, the idea is not necessarily different from the experience of the beloved disciple who "saw and (yet) believed." The reason for this is that the mystery cannot be grounded in merely experiential evidence. This is why only those who "believe" without seeing are blessed: because a faith that is grounded on experience is like a faith based on miracles (see John 1:23-25); it fails and vanishes when the experiential evidence is no longer there and, therefore, does not provide the powerful springboard that catapults man into eternal life. This is what blessedness means in this context. It does not mean that in those who believe without seeing, there is any right or merit to be rewarded. They are "blest" because their hopes of salvation and of reaching eternal life are very good; they are on the right and solid path.

Third Sunday of Easter

Luke 24:13-35

In Luke 24:13-35, the gospel narrative vividly portrays the powerful revival of a dead faith and a dead hope. The two travelers had abandoned Jerusalem for Emmaus. Their disappointment had been great: not unlike James and John (Mark 10:35), they probably had expected the messianic rule of Jesus to be established in the Davidic capital. At any rate, they certainly expected that Jesus would "redeem" (i.e., deliver) Israel from foreign domination (v. 21), but nothing had happened—or so they thought. Like Moses, the great leader of Israel, Jesus had been "a prophet powerful for his deeds and words" (v. 19; see Acts 7:22); the result being that he raised great hopes in the people. But he proved to be no match for the power of the Jewish high priests and leaders, his enemies (v. 20). Now the man is dead—and so are all the hopes he aroused. This was the third day after his death (v. 21); nothing startling can be expected any more: he is dead for good.

There were some rumors around that for a moment seemed to lift up a disintegrating faith (v. 22). Some women went to the tomb (Luke 24:1ff.), found that the body was not there and came back with the story that some angels even appeared to them and told them that Jesus was alive (24:4ff.). In view of these reports, some of the Christian group went to the tomb (a valid support of the authenticity of the controversial v. 12 where it is said that Peter went to the tomb, see also v. 34), and found that the women's report was right. "But as to him—they did not see him" (v. 24). The new hopes were short-lived; so the two travelers decided to go back to their village and forget the whole thing. They exemplified the general discouragement and disillusionment of the entire Christian group in the wake of Jesus' death.

They did not even suspect that the man who joined them on the way, to whom they were saying what a disappointment Jesus had been, was the one they were talking about. For a long time, they did not recognize him. The risen Lord was the same as before; but he was also different because he belonged to a new world and was leading a new, different existence. This is expressed by the fact that he is not immediately recognizable. But now it is the turn of the third, incognito traveler. He starts a catechesis that is directed to the two wayfarers, and through them, to the Christian community of all times. The catechesis is important not only for its contents but also for the method it employs in handling this kind of theological problem.

The disappointment pointed to a sickness and malaise in their spiritual conditions. Not only their nationalistic concept of "redemption" and messianism was wrong; it is particularly the shallowness and tardiness of their faith that is chided. They founded their faith and hopes on Christ's deeds and words, which would be correct if they had followed the right process, going into their real meaning and value. The nationalistic views of the two men had been their criterion of interpretation. It was a glorious Messiah that they had in mind. If they had paid attention to the Scriptures, they would have discovered that, before being glorified, the Messiah had to suffer: "Did not the Messiah have to undergo all this (see v. 19) so as to enter into his glory?" (v. 26). In fact, through the prophets, the Spirit had "predicted the sufferings destined for the Messiah and the glories that would follow" (1 Peter 1:11).

This research (i.e., this religious reflection on the sacred text) had not been done. That is why they are "slow to believe 'all' that the prophets had announced." The prophets had announced not only glory but also "sufferings" for the Messiah, and in that order: first sufferings, then glory. After all, their problem was that they did not believe the Scriptures (see John 2:22; 12:16; 19:8), even after the facts had taken place. For the same reason, they found it difficult to believe the reports about Jesus' resurrection "after" his death.

Admittedly, no text of the Old Testament refers to the "resurrection" of the Messiah by that specific notion and term. But this is evidence that the fact of the resurrection of the Messiah is not a fabrication based on some biblical text (v. gr., Hosea 6:2, which is never quoted or even hinted at in the New Testament); the opposite is true: the fact of the resurrection enlightens the biblical text. Both Luke and Peter stated that the Scriptures do not speak of the resurrection, but of the sufferings and "glory" of the Messiah. Obviously the resurrection is a "glory," and as such it is part of the glory of the Messiah; that is why the reports of Christ's resurrection should be confronted with the Scriptures, for such a confrontation would lead more quickly to belief in Jesus' resurrection. But the two travelers lacked the "intelligence" to know that this was the correct method; and that is why they are slow in coming to faith, in spite of their good, though somewhat incorrect, disposition toward Jesus. Now Christ "opened their minds to understand the Scriptures" (24:45).

He opened their minds by a biblical exegesis of the Old Testament passages regarding the Messiah (v. 27). Beyond this general remark, no specific passage of "Moses or the prophets" is mentioned by Luke. The New Testament writings quote many texts of the Old Testament as referring to Christ. But there can be little doubt that the text that best illustrates that "the Messiah had to go through all this (suffering) so as to enter into his glory" is Isaiah 53. This passage is explicitly mentioned in the New Testament (Acts 8:32; 1 Peter 2:22-25, etc.) and is the background of a good number of other texts where it is not quoted explicitly (v. gr., Philippians 2:7-11; Ephesians 4:9f.; John 13:3-6) and where the humiliation and subsequent exaltation of Christ are portrayed. The longest section of Isaiah 53 is devoted to the sufferings of the "Servant," but the second part (vvs. 10b-12) refers to his exaltation as a reward of his "sacrificial" death. It was by reflecting on this text that the early Christian community could justify before a Jewish audience the "scandal" of a Messiah who had undergone a humiliating death on a cross. It is a "Christian" reading of the text which reveals that the text refers to the Messiah's sufferings and glory; a glory that started with the resurrection, to which some other texts of the Old Testament were applied (see Acts 2:25-28).

Christ's catechesis through the Scriptures conveyed to his listeners, not precisely erudition and intellectual pride, but rather the warmth and fire that "inflamed our hearts inside us as he talked to us on the road and explained the Scriptures to us" (v. 32). Thus the flame of faith was rekindled and revived to die no more. The Scriptures convinced them that the Messiah had both to die and to rise. They could believe again in Jesus. Now they had to make an experience of the lesson they had just been taught—it would show them what a good teacher Jesus was. By some characteristic gesture or word in his breaking of the bread, Christ disclosed himself to them. They were convinced that he really was the Messiah of their faith; that the Messiah had to suffer first, and that his glory started with his resurrection. In the Christian liturgy, at the "breaking of the bread," Christians keep on proclaiming that "Christ has died," that "Christ is risen."

Fourth Sunday of Easter

John 10:1-10

The episode reported by the evangelist before the simile of the shepherd and the sheep in chapter 10 recounts the rough and even brutal treatment of a simple man in the Jewish community by the Pharisees. They were the religious leaders of the time, or so they thought. The simple man had been cured by Jesus of his blindness: in his sincere mind he was able to realize that a real miracle had been worked on his behalf, that Jesus was a prophet (9:15, 17) (at least), that God listens to Jesus (9:30)—and because of his openness to Jesus, he is given the gift of "sight" in his soul and he believes in Jesus (9:35ff.).

But the leaders, the Pharisees, share other convictions: in their religious pride, as disciples (John 8:28) and successors of Moses (Matthew 23:2), they know that God spoke to Moses whereas "we don't know about the origins of this fellow" (Jesus). The cured man may become his disciple; "you"—the Pharisees insult him—"you are steeped in sin from your birth and you are giving us lectures?"; they had already decreed excommunication from the Jewish community for those who believed in Jesus and, in point of fact, they ended by also excommunicating the simple man. This is how those shepherds tended their sheep. They were inflated by their canonical "sight"/knowledge of institutionalized religion, a religion that should lead them to Christ; but precisely when they are faced with the Light, they are shown to be utterly blind—more so than the simple man enlightened by Christ. It is against this background that Jesus conveys to them the message of the simile of shepherds and sheep in chapter 10. It should teach them that the position they hold and claim in the community of Israel had become absurd and impossible. Jesus contrasts the true and the false shepherds in both the Jewish and Christian communities. How can a good shepherd be recognized?

The image used by Jesus is that of a shepherd who has, next to his house, an enclosure where his sheep are kept at night. The wall all around the enclosure provides protection for the sheep; it can be entered by only one doorway, guarded by a watchman. In the morning, when the shepherd comes to his sheep, he comes to the door and the watchman lets him in to the sheep. If anyone attempts to reach them by climbing in some other way, it is evidence that he is not the shepherd: he is a thief and a robber. The sheep, in their turn, know the true shepherd by his voice, which they listen to and answer. Since they are his own property, he has a personal relationship with them: each one has its own name by which the shepherd calls them in order to bring them out of the fold. In full confidence they follow him, who puts himself at their head and leads them to pasture. If a stranger attempts the same thing, the result would be the opposite, since the common ground of confidence would be missing. In only a few words, it is a relationship of personal concern, confidence and trust between the shepherd and the sheep that is brought into relief. All this is missing in the case of someone foreign to the sheep.

In the simile, the doorway, the doorkeeper and the stranger are elements of a parable, brought in just to create a vivid picture and illustrate its meaning. It goes differently with the true shepherd and with the thieves and robbers. The true shepherd is, of course, Jesus himself. The thieves and robbers can be none but the Pharisaic leaders of Israel, the implication being that they got into that position unlawfully and that they misused it selfishly and despotically to the harm of those whom they were supposed to tend. The episode of the blind man is the evidence for this (see Matthew 23).

Though clear enough, Jesus' lesson is given through a comparison; thus it is not so unequivocal as the direct condemnation of the Pharisaic system in Matthew 23. A comparison always allows the fellow on the spot the outlet of pretending to misunderstand. The Pharisees did just that, which leads to an expansion and explanation of the simile proposed. However, instead of explaining who the true shepherd, and the thieves and robbers are, the idea of the doorway is applied to Jesus, whereby the focus of the image is shifted: the problem now is which shepherd is rightful. There is no legitimate access to the sheep (community) but through Jesus; only those who believe in him have the right to be shepherds "through him," by his authority. All those who do not fulfill this requirement are not legitimate shepherds; they are thieves and robbers. When Jesus refers to those who "came before me," it is not Moses, the Prophets, John the Baptist or God's other envoys that he has in mind: he speaks of those who presently "are" (present tense) thieves and robbers, namely of those who at present are acting as shepherds—but are not. These are those who came into position of leadership before he appeared, and still claim such leadership over the community now, without his authority and even against his own interests (later on, v. 11, Jesus openly declares, "I am the good shepherd"), and who lord it over the community for their own selfish interests. Mark 12:40 puts on Jesus' lips the reminder that the Pharisees "devour the savings of widows" (see Mark 7:11). It is the Pharisees who, far from being shepherds, are thieves and robbers.

Admittedly, they were the undisputed religious leaders in Israel, but theirs was a rule of imposition, power and selfishness. They had never won the heart of their sheep. On the contrary, to their dismay, they had to realize that "the entire world has run after him" (John 12:19)—after Jesus, the true shepherd, whose voice was easily recognized and with whom the sheep found themselves comfortable and at home. This is why the Lord says that "the sheep had not listened to them."

The doorway applies to Christ in still another manner. He not only is the doorway for any shepherd to have access to the sheep; he also is the doorway for the sheep to come through to safety and to find the pasture they need for their healthy nourishment. The doorway into the fold now becomes the doorway into God's kingdom, the doorway that leads into life and "to the sources of living waters" (Revelation 7:17), the "shining and crystal-clear river of living water flowing from the throne of God and of the Lamb" (Revelation 22:1). The beginning of that life is given on earth: by Christ's revelation, by his death, by his saving signs and by his Spirit lavishly dispensed to his sheep (John 4:14; 6:35, 40, 51-58; 7:37ff.). A thief-shepherd comes only to steal and slaughter in order to satisfy his own greed (see Ezekiel 24:2f.), but "I"—says the Lord—"I come that they (the sheep) have life and have it in abundance." One wonders if the lesson of this gospel passage has lost any of its value, just because the Pharisees of olden times are no longer here.

Fifth Sunday of Easter
John 14:1-12

Jesus has just told his disciples that he has to leave them shortly and that Peter will have to follow him, not right now, but later on (John 13:31-38). The horizon looks gloomy and dreadful. Obviously, the "little flock" is shaken and upset. When the storm was over, the disciples were still in the room where they had locked themselves "for fear of the Jews" (John 20:19). Drawing on biblical resources, Jesus tells his own that the only reassurance and defense against fear is faith: faith in God. But faith in God also includes faith in Christ, who is "one" and the same with the Father (John 10:30), and no one can snatch from Christ's hands what the Father has given to him. The disciples had been given to him by the Father (John 17:6, 9). Thus "you have faith in God, but have faith also in me." This is a faith that does not guarantee shelter from trouble, but promises a happy end: peace and joy in the Father's house. The eschatological perspective opens up (see 17:24).

The sentence related to the dwelling places in the Father's house can be understood in more than one way.

The meaning seems to be this: do not worry, "in my Father's house there are many dwelling places," there is plenty of room—not only for Jesus, who is about to leave, but also for his disciples; if this were not so, Jesus "would have told them so," he would not have deceived them and misled them into a life of sacrifice and "hatred from the world" (15:18ff.; 16:20ff.) without any hopes for the afterlife. As a matter of fact, Jesus is leaving, not because he abandons them (John 14:18), but because he goes ahead of them to prepare their glorious abode in the Father's house. Jesus' departure is not one without return, as when someone deserts his own. No, "when I shall be gone and made preparations for you, I shall come back and take you to my house, that you be where I am myself" (John 14:3; see 17:24). Christ is the "man who went abroad" and "after a long time" came back to reward his servants (Matthew 25:14, 19).

In John's usual style, the disciples miss the point of Jesus' reference. Jesus assumed that his disciples knew, not only the goal of his journey, but also "the way" there. Obviously he was assuming too much. Voicing the general puzzlement, Thomas speaks up and says that the goal itself of such a journey is unknown to them, and even more so the way leading to it—in spite of Jesus' reference to the Father's house. Jesus' answer is somewhat disconcerting because it discloses what Jesus wanted to teach and not necessarily what Thomas wished to learn.

Of course, the house of the Father—the goal of Jesus' journey—is there "where Christ was before" (John 6:62), where he will "enjoy the glory he had with the Father before the world came to exist" (17:5, 24); and the way for him to get there is his passion and cross (13:1; 16:28). But Jesus' answer is that "no one can come to the Father but through me," thereby teaching that what really matters for his disciples is not so much to care about Christ's final goal, but about their own coming to the Father. Christ does not intend to satisfy their curiosity but to teach them how they can reach the Father themselves and, therefore, to show them the way leading to the "house of the Father" and to the dwelling places that Christ is going to prepare for them. After all, the important thing is not to discuss the goal: if you hit the right route, it will surely lead you all the way to the goal at the end. The real question lies in getting into the right path —particularly when all else is in utter darkness—and, then, in traveling it all the way to the end.

Now, the way—"I am the way, and the truth and the life." There is an unfathomable depth to this statement that keeps a universal and absolute value. In point of fact, what it means is that Christ is the way because he is the truth enlightening man's path with the light of his revelation (12:35f.; 8:12; 1 John 1:6f.; 2:7), and because through his revelation, etc., he is the life that empowers and dynamizes man to "walk" in his light and reach his final goal (6:63, 40, 53; 5:21; 11:25f., etc.). In the present context, however, the concrete meaning of the statement derives from the "way" that Christ will travel, which is his passion and cross. Thomas and all the others—first of all Peter (John 13:7, 36; 21:18f.)—must learn that going to the Father is no tourist trip; it is a rough walk, a way through the hatred of this world, persecution and death as of a victim in sacrifice (15:18—16:3, 20ff.; 17:19). This was an essential part of Christ's message (John 12:25f.; Matthew 10:38; 16:24f.), and this was the lesson of his own example. Still he does not deceive his followers: even if the truth is hard to believe and still harder to live up to, the rough path is the true and real avenue to life; it can be traveled on the word of Jesus who, furthermore, gives the living power to travel it: "after a while the world will not see me any longer, but you will see me because I will be alive and you also will be alive" (14:19).

The text of v. 7 is not well established. Its meaning seems to be this: "if you have come to know me, you will come to know also the Father" in the future, the notion of "knowing," including a semitic flavor of experiencing, enjoying (Christ's and God's beneficial relationship). This knowledge of the Father, however, has already started in this life (with and through Christ, vvs. 9ff.), as a foretaste of what will happen in the "Father's house."

At this point, Philip points out that all this talk about the knowledge of the Father could be spared if Jesus "showed the Father" to them. Of course, Philip's intervention provides Jesus with a fresh opportunity to deepen his thought. Philip and all the others should know that seeing Christ implies a seeing of the Father, because in Christ's words and deeds the wisdom, power and authority of God are directly involved. Christ becomes a mirror (image: Colossians 1:15; 2 Corinthians 4:4) reflecting the true reality and activity of the Father: no one has ever seen God, but Christ reveals him (1:18). Faith can see that; a man without faith may conclude that Jesus is possessed by Satan (8:48, 52; 10:20), or that his miracles are worked by Satan's power (Mark 3:21). It is not a question of physical seeing but of faith-guided insight. Only the eyes of a soul enlightened through faith can distinguish God's power from Satan's, and thus perceive the true being of Christ and his relationship with God. Loving faith makes all the difference.

Sixth Sunday of Easter

John 14:15-21

Jesus had just promised his disciples that in their mission as apostles they would be able to perform astounding miracles, rivaling those performed by Christ himself. But they will be able to do so "because I am going to the Father," to the Father's house (John 14:2), so that "whatever you will ask for in my name, that very thing I will do" (v. 13). And the Lord explains: "if you ask me something in my own name I will do it." Of course, in their mission, the apostles said to the crippled man in the temple: "in the name of Jesus Christ the Nazarene, walk" (Acts 3:6), and then Peter comments that the healing was accomplished "in the faith of his (Jesus') name": it was "his name" that healed the man (Acts 3:16; see also 16:18; 19:13). The apostles ask Jesus ("in his name") to work a miracle; it is Jesus who does it through them, but the ultimate source or power is the Father. The Lord stresses that his disciples will do wonderful things "because he is going to the Father" and will obtain from the Father whatever his followers ask for—the Lord knows that the Father "always listens to him" (John 11:41f.). In a sense, Jesus describes himself as the "attorney" of his disciples at the Father's throne.

It is against this background that the Lord promises his disciples "another paraclete" (v. 16). Paraclete is a Greek legal term that means attorney, lawyer, advocate, or intercessor. In his function as priest, Christ can be defined as "paraclete" of sinners before the Father (1 John 2:1) because he defends them at the Father's court. In our passage of the gospel, the Lord is one "paraclete" because he pleads the cause of his missionaries/disciples with the Father; the "other" paraclete is the Spirit of Truth. The disciples, therefore, will have a helper in heaven and another on earth. Christ was their helper on earth, but now he has to go to the Father who "is greater than I" (v. 28, it is a promotion), but this is to the disciples' advantage because he will be in a position to send them the new helper they will need in their activity as missionaries (16:7). But even the gift of the new helper is the result of Christ's pleading with the Father: "I will ask the Father."

The "other" helper or attorney will never go away from them, from the disciples, "he will be with you for ever," and being with someone is to provide help and assistance as needed. The world cannot receive this helper, not because the offer is denied but because the world does not "accept" it, it refuses the gift, and the reason for this is that the world has no perception of the Spirit, it has never had an experience (this is "to know") of the Spirit, it doesn't know what he is like or how he works (see Acts 3:8, 13-22; 5:32, 40; 6:10, 51-50). But the disciples do have such vital experience, in fact he is at work within them; and now he will "be with them" permanently in order to help them, first of all in their missionary work when they will be confronted with persecution (John 15:18-26; 14:20-22) and, therefore, law-courts and trials (Matthew 10:17-20; Luke 12:11f.).

It is the setting of law-courts, trials and forensic defenses that gives specific and concrete value to the definition of the Spirit as the "Spirit of Truth": in the law-courts "do not worry about how or what you are going to say in your legal defense, for the Holy Spirit will 'teach' you at that very moment what must be said" (Luke 12:11f.), and this will be "an opportunity for you to proclaim the gospel" (Luke 21:13-15; Acts 6:10). It is through this assistance and help of the Spirit that the Lord does not leave his community, first of all his apostles, in the condition of orphans: "I come back to you," He promised.

He will certainly come back at the end of time (Jn. 14:3; 16:22). But this is not the return contemplated in 14:18. After the total "black-out" during his passion and death, Jesus "comes back" to "be with you (his disciples) till the end of time" (Matthew 28:20) in the life of his community. His physical presence is denied to his own; but he will be present by his action, light, vitality and love—through his Spirit, the "helper" he promised to send. That is why the world will not see him after a while, after his death, because the world can perceive physical things only; it has no perception to discover the spiritual presence and power of the Risen Lord. But it is different with those who can perceive the mysterious "fourth" dimension of man's life and of the world, namely, the spiritual dimension or the dimension of the Spirit (see v. 17). Christ's disciples were given the secret key to discover and enjoy this mysterious dimension.

In their lives as Christians, "you—not the world—will 'see me.' " This is not a physical seeing, but it is much more powerful, persuasive and evident than physical sight: it is a vital and vitalizing realization and experience that Christ is present and at work around myself, but first of all, within myself, and through myself he reaches others; it is an invisible and dazzling light; it is an inaudible, deafening thunder-clap; it is an unintelligible evidence that overwhelms man's intellect and brings it to an unshakable firmness that no scientific reasoning or experimenting could ever produce. It is the certitude of God's reasoning—who, as in many other aspects, creates powerful evidence out of nothing, nothing in terms of man's scientific requirements and controllable data.

A highly significant conclusion of this vital experience, of this "seeing," is that "I (Christ) am alive." By his action and activity they will "know," see or experience that he is at work; he is as active and powerful as ever; he did not vanish after his death (see Revelation 1:17f.). This opens up an encouraging certitude to his disciples under persecution and dangers of death; after death there is life: "You, too, will be alive," even after death. Such is the promise and the power of the Risen Lord. Another extremely relevant realization for the disciples will be that "on that day (when they will 'see' Christ) you will know/experience that I am in the Father, and you are in me and I in you." In their living interrelation and interaction with the Lord, Christians, and particularly Christ's missionaries, will come to the living awareness and experience of the unfathomable depth of the Christian mystery: that Christ subsists in God; that the Father's very being is involved in Christ; and then, that there is an intercommunion and inter-exchange between Christ and his own (John 6:56; 15:4; 17:26; 1 John 3:24), which draws the Father himself into the living mystery of the Christian "communion" (1 John 1:3f.). "That all (Christians)"—the Lord prayed—"may be a oneness: as you, Father, are in me and I in you, that they also may be in us...that they may be a oneness as we are a oneness: I in them and you in me, that they may be totally processed/integrated into oneness" (John 17:21).

This is a oneness that is brought about by an internal and "closed" circuit of life flowing from the Father through Christ to Christians and reflowing through Christ into the Father in the form of vital and vitalizing love springing up from the common bond of the Spirit, of "the" Love: so "that the Love with which you (Father) have loved me may be in them and (so) I also may be in them" (John 17:26). In Christians this love will blossom in obedient and loving compliance with Christ's commandments, which, in turn, will draw more love from the Father and from Christ himself, in the form of new insights into and disclosures of God's and Christ's mysteries: "I will reveal myself to him." Even the Paraclete is Christ's and the Father's gift in exchange for a love displayed in obedience to their commandments (v. 15); above all, the missionary commandment.

Ascension

Matthew 28:16-20

(See B, Holy Trinity.)

The fundamental contents of the Ascension of the Lord are disclosed in the initial words of the risen Christ: "all power in heaven and on earth has been given to me." The risen Christ receives from God full power over the entire cosmos, over everything outside God himself; he is constituted supreme and sovereign Lord. This is, of course, the basic truth upon which everything that follows rests.

Understanding, however, Christ's sovereign lordship as a sort of "honorary" title or position would be far off the mark and miss the point completely. As a matter of fact, Jesus' lordship is nothing static or ceremonial. It is dynamic, active, effective and powerful. This is the message of the Lord's words which follow in vv. 19f., but more particularly of those in the last sentence of v. 20: "know that I am with you day by day until the end of the world."

In the Bible, "being" is not a philosophical notion, and still less something static and removed, something to be contemplated from afar in its unchangeable essence and existence. It is rather functional, existential, practical and operative. Yahweh is not Yahweh ("he who is") because he has "the" being in its fullness, that others may contemplate, admire and meditate upon from the distance of man's almost insignificant being. Yahweh is such because "I will be there such as I shall be there." He will be "there": at the right spot, at the right time, when his help is needed, when he decides to act and "be" there for real, not for himself but for others. He is Yahweh because he is always "there," furthering his plan in his elect or confronting his opponent; but he is there because he is active, he is doing something. Jesus, the supreme Lord, promises that he also "is there with you."

Jesus' being there is not a matter of happening to be there, or of just keeping someone company, or of being close to someone or something so as to be able to see the film of world events unfold under his eyes. Christ is "there" because he is active in man's world; because he intervenes in the world's affairs, shapes them and guides them. Christ is there as an active ruler and driving power who steers the events of history with absolute and undisputed leadership. It is dynamism, action and power that characterizes his leadership as he drives the world to its end and to its goal.

Such is the vision of the New Testament in regard to Christ's lordship. The author of the letter to the Hebrews understands that everything created was put under Christ's feet in the sense that everything must fall under his control: "but at present we do not yet see the universe subjected to him" (2:8). St. Paul saw Christ's lordship in the fact that he "has to reign until he will have put all his enemies under his feet," which will come about by "defeating every sovereignty, authority and power" (1 Corinthians 15:24f.). In other words, Christ's royal quality consists, not in his being respected and worshiped by all, but in actively conquering the kingdom that he will surrender to the Father, by overcoming every resistance and crushing any opposition. It is a matter of active and "aggressive" conquest. Everything "has been created for him" (Colossians 1:16), and he has been constituted the "heir of the universe" (Hebrews 1:2); but what belongs to him is now under the rule of a usurper; a "war" of conquest or liberation is needed to bring his own kingdom under his control. Such perspective obtains its highest expression in the Apocalypse, where, after the "official enthronement of the Lamb with 'seven horns' " (full power) (Revelation 5), the "Lion of Judah" and the "Root of David" enters upon office and starts bringing God's secret plan (scroll) into execution by breaking open the seals of the scroll (ch. 6). Towards the end of the book, the Lamb "stands" on Mount Sion at the head of his armies (ch. 14) and, followed by his own, fights against the "kings of the earth" and defeats them (17:14), because he is "the King of kings and Lord of lords" (19:16).

In the letters to the Ephesians and Colossians, Christ's kingship transcends man's world; and he appears as "the head of all principalities and powers" (Colossians 2:10), since God's definite plan was to "bring all things in heaven and on earth under Christ's headship" (Ephesians 1:10; see 1:21f.; Philippians 2:10f.). But again, this is an active lordship that "disarms the principalities and powers and exposes them publicly by leading them on in his triumphant train" (Colossians 2:15). It is always a matter of conquest and active, "aggressive" rule.

This is how the risen Lord "is with" his disciples. He is with them, leading them in their work in the world. He "is there": displaying his activity, using his power, "destroying stongholds, demolishing sophistries and every proud pretension that raises itself against the knowledge of God" (2 Corinthians 10:4f.), crushing every opposition to his rule and conquering the kingdom that is his by right. Christ is "there" with his disciples and followers carrying out his plan of salvation through them; in the "militaristic" imagery of the Apocalypse, Christ's followers are his "armies": the forces of evil "will fight against the Lamb but the Lamb will conquer them, for he is the Lord of lords and the King of kings, and *those who are with him are professional, chosen and faithful*" fighters (Revelation 17:14; see 19:14). All power in heaven and on earth is given to him, and the exalted Lord is determined to use it and does use it in his rule of man's history and of the cosmos at large.

The text of Matthew 28:19f. stresses Christ's conquest through the missionary and teaching activity of his followers. This certainly is an aspect of the Lord's active and "aggressive" conquest of man and of history. But Christ's existential, dynamic "being" with his own goes far beyond that. To his disciples, who were confronted with all the hatred of the "world," with full assurance and confidence Christ says: "in the world you are in plight, but take heart: I have overcome the world" (John 16:33). He has been seated at God's right hand in heaven, "high above every principality, power, virtue and domination, and every title that can be given in this age or in the age to come" (Ephesians 1:21). His "kingship has no end" (Luke 1:33), it extends from age to age, and his ruling authority will span the whole of man's history "to the end of the world" (Matthew 28:20).

Seventh Sunday of Easter
John 17:1-11

The "hour has come," the hour that throughout his lifetime Christ knew was to mark the peak of his activity as Savior and Redeemer. The "high priest" draws closer and closer to the time of his liturgical offering, collects his thoughts and spells out for himself, for the Father and for others, the intentions of his sacrifice.

In the first place, Christ's sacrifice/death on the cross is his glorification or exaltation by the Father and, in turn, a glorification of the Father by Christ. The reason why his death (apparent humiliation and defeat) is precisely a glorification of both Father and "Son" is that through this death Christ attains the highest honor and dignity: he becomes the universal, unique and absolute source of "eternal life" and salvation for "all flesh," for all mankind: past, present and future. No one can obtain salvation except from this source; Christ becomes an absolute necessity for all human beings to be saved. This is why the Church of the New Testament gave "glory and power for ever to him who loves us and with his blood washed us from our sins and made us a kingdom and priests for his God and Father" (Revelation 1:5f.), "from among all tribes, languages, peoples and races" (5:9f.). Conversely, Christ's saving power will enable many to put his salvation to good use and thank God for it—this is how God will be glorified in Christ's passion. Another dimension of God's glorification, however, is pointed out in v. 5: Christ's absolute surrender to God's will, and his disposition to carry out the work of salvation entrusted to him. Christ's supreme obedience is a homage to God's supreme sovereignty and rule. But it is from this glorification of God that the former aspect necessarily follows; it was the former effect, after all, that God intended: "God so loved the world!" (3:16)

In point of fact, it is not only at the last moment that Christ glorifies the Father: "I have glorified you on earth"; throughout his life and ministry Christ always surrendered to the Father's will. He always did what God wanted by carrying out God's saving plan in the way and by the means that God wanted, even if they led to an apparent defeat and failure. The cross merely marks the highest point of a life of obedience at God's "service," a service that now comes to a climax. In turn, God also had glorified Jesus throughout his ministry, through the wonderful wisdom and power given to him in order to convey God's revelation and to work impressive miracles (John 12:28) through which people were attracted to Jesus and saved.

Now, the glorification of Christ by God points to the resurrection, through which Christ will go back to the splendor of his divine life with the Father—which is his from all eternity—but with the added dimension of his priestly "promotion," as source of universal salvation. Before God's throne in heaven, "the Lamb appears slaughtered" (Revelation 5:5) and he is worthy to open the scroll of God's secrets "because you were slaughtered"; therefore praise, honor, glory, etc., are given to "the Lamb that has been slaughtered." In other words, Christ's glorification is connected with his priestly office that in 1 John 2:1f. is understood as that of an attorney/intercessor who offers "atonement" for the sins of all mankind (see Hebrews 7-9).

The eternal life given to man through Christ starts with the "knowledge" of the Father as "the true God" and of the Son as his messianic envoy. God is the true, genuine God, in opposition to the "many gods and lords" (1 Corinthians 8:5) of the pagan world; Christ is God's messianic envoy, in opposition both to all who pretended to be the real Messiah and to all other true envoys of God in the Old Testament who, however, did not have the full messianic authority that Jesus enjoyed, as the plenipotentiary delegate of God.

Life eternal, though, does not consist in an intellectual knowledge of God's and Christ's existence and work. It is an existential knowledge that consists in "not ignoring" them and their principles in man's practical life and activity. It was Christ who taught these principles in his preaching ministry. That is why part of his "work" consisted in "disclosing your name (Father's) to men you gave me from the world" (v. 6). What Christ disclosed was God's plan, will, ideas, instructions; above all, he "disclosed God" himself (John 1:18), not what he is in himself, but what he is for man, namely "love" (1 John 4:8, 16), since even God's commandments and revelation were prompted by his love for man. But he wants his fatherly love to be reciprocated in filial obedience.

The community of Christ is regarded as a "gift" that the Father handed to him. It was the Father who drew them to Christ (John 6:44, 65); he helped them with his grace to surrender to Christ's calling initiative. It is the Father who gave them the grace of faith to accept a difficult teaching and life-style; it is God's grace that they "kept the Father's word" revealed by Christ; they kept it because they did not abandon it under the pressures of persecution. In their faith, lived out amidst the hardships of a hostile world, they came to know/realize by a certain experience that whatever Christ has and offers is in fact an involvement of the Father himself (v. 7); that even the teaching of Christ is a teaching of God himself. Above all, they came to the living awareness that Christ draws his origins from the Father and that, as a result, it was the Father who sent him (v. 7f.). John points out the essentials of the Christian faith; in his own way, he formulates a condensed confession of faith that, as a matter of fact, goes beyond a confession and, remaining faith, grows into a living awareness or "knowledge" of the Christian mystery.

It is for these men "from the world" given to Christ that he prays at this moment—for them, "not for the world." It remains true that "God so loved the world" (John 3:16); that Jesus "came not to condemn the world but to save it" (12:47; 3:17). The salvation of the world (world being man's establishment hostile to God) was an enterprise common to God and Christ. It is precisely for this reason that both of them are so interested in preventing the loss of the gift taken "from the world." This is what God could obtain or choose from the world and give to Christ; viewed from another angle, these are the men "from the world" who let themselves be drawn by the Father towards Christ. They are not only Christ's, "they are yours" also, or better "they are for you" (v. 9), since Christ is not the final goal of redemption. These men from the world represent God's and Christ's common interests, "what is mine is yours, and what is yours is mine" (v. 10). These men are, so to speak, the hope of success of God's and Christ's enterprise. It is through them, as missionaries first of all, that "glory" is added to Christ (v. 10). This is why at this point he prays for them and not for the world. It is not disregard of the world that is implied, quite the opposite. To a great extent the salvation of the world—the success of God's and Christ's initiative, hinges on them, on their faith and fortitude. Aware, by his own experience, of the dangers involved and of human weakness, Christ prays for them when he is about to part company with them: "I come to you, but they have to remain in the world" (v. 11).

Pentecost

John 20:19-23

(See B, Pentecost.)

The Holy Spirit was given to the Christian community. Even if it transcends History, such an event took place in this world of ours at a definite moment of time. It was a saving event that has ever since involved the life of Christians and constituted the atmosphere in which the life and existence of the Christian community unfolds. That which began to be on the day of the first Christian Pentecost has never ceased to be a saving reality. It has been a living and operative truth through the centuries; and it is true also today in our own age, in our own lives and in our personal existence.

The vital and saving fact consists in this: that the fullness of the Holy Spirit was given to the Christian community by God as a permanent endowment that the Church always has at her disposal in order to administer it as she deems fit. The Spirit is a real gift, a free donation from God (Romans 5:5). Only God can make such a precious donation; and no man, no human community can lay claim to it. The Spirit is a permanent endowment of the community of Christians, since he represents in the Church a sort of quality or habitual, "natural" condition of her existence. The Church possesses the Spirit as a "personal" possession, so to speak; the Spirit is, as it were, something she has at her disposal at any time.

Not only the "individual" Christ—Jesus of Nazareth—enjoyed and enjoys the fullness of the Spirit as a very personal gift. The "full" Christ also, the Body with all its members, has been given this special possession of the Spirit. During his lifetime on earth, Christ baptized, ordained priests, consecrated the Eucharist, healed sick people, forgave sins, gave others the power to do so on a temporary basis, etc. All this is now done by the Christian community on its own right, according to its judgment.

The community possesses a comparative fullness of the Spirit and, as a matter of fact, the community administers the Spirit for the most varied effects. Such is the sanctifying power, the saving power at the disposal of the Church.

The prophetic oracle (Isaiah 11:2) had established that the Messiah would be given the Spirit in the fullness of his gifts: wisdom, understanding, counsel, strength, knowledge, fear of the Lord (and piety, LXX). The messianic/Christian community is an extension of the Messiah himself, and John 1:16 explicitly says that "of his fullness all of us received" a share. This is Paul's point in 1 Corinthians 12:4ff. when he discusses the "Charisms of the Spirit" in the Church and, in a clear reference to Isaiah 1:2, speaks of the gifts of "wisdom" and "knowledge," besides the other gifts that are displayed in more or less miraculous activities that are specifications of the messianic gift of strength or power. The message of Paul is obvious: the fullness of the Spirit that was at work in the Messiah himself is now at work in the messianic community that is the "Body of Christ," or "the fullness" of Christ (Ephesians 1:23).

Just as the community has been given the same endowment of Christ, it has also inherited the "messianic" obligations. After his glorification the Messiah comes back to his own: "as the Father has sent me, I also send you." And for such a mission he equipped them with the gift of the plurivalent Spirit, even if the emphasis is laid on the forgiveness of sins. It was on the day of Pentecost that the Christian community founded by Christ became the missionary Church. Besides being the covenantal community and the worshiping community, it became also the *witnessing* community. The bestowal of the Spirit upon it truly was the "confirmation" of Christ's community. It was at that time that the Church of the Lord received a new "character," a new seal for all the world to see: a particular share in the "prophetic" projection of the Messiah, with all the authority and power to exercise it.

By the power of the Spirit, the Church is not only strengthened in her faith and Christian life, but also prompted in various ways to bear witness to Christ, to bear witness of the Christian truth in a sweeping missionary undertaking, the bounds of which are none other than the bounds of the whole world.

The day of Pentecost establishes a real relationship between the confirmation of each individual Christian and the "confirmation" of the Christian community. Those who through baptism were made members of the covenantal and worshiping community, through the sacrament of confirmation become members of the witnessing community.

Through individual confirmation, the Christian person is given a new share in the fullness of the Spirit in possession of the Church, and he is made an official delegate of the witnessing community to the world, with the effect of proclaiming and defending the common truth and faith in Christ the Lord. It is a share in the prophetic function of the Messiah and of the messianic community. Thus the Christian is given the commission of being a missionary who proclaims the Christian teaching in the face of the whole world. This is what the Messiah and the messianic community expect him to do. Being a true Christian implies, of necessity, being a Christian missionary.

The missionary dimension of each individual Christian is no academic question. It is a duty that a Christian assumes the day he commits himself to Christ and to his saving purpose. The day of his confirmation is his personal "Pentecost." And Pentecost, both for a Christian individual and for the Christian community, means missionary commission and missionary effort.

Most Holy Trinity
John 3:16-18

A firm principle of the Johannine theology is that "everyone who has faith in the Son has eternal life" (John 3:15). It may seem incredible—it was incredible to a legalist Pharisee—that salvation could come from somewhere other than man's accomplishments, his "good works"—salvation through faith would seem to be all too easy. It is easy indeed, but it is easy, credible and possible by God's power and goodness—and "love." Salvation through trust and reliance on Jesus ("faith") is not the result of hypnotic suggestion or some sort of magic achievement; it is not just a nice idea grounded nowhere.

The evangelist knows that a gift of such a magnitude and transcendence is grounded on a solid basis, namely God's love: "God so loved the world...." It is God's love that makes things easy for man, easy to the point of appearing too good to be true. It is on God's love for the world that man's salvation through faith in Christ is grounded. God loves his creatures; in fact, it was out of love that God created them (Wisdom 11:24—12:1). But he does not want his creatures to perish; thus God is always driven to new excesses by his love in order to save what he has created.

Love is sweet, delightful—and painful. "Love is strong as death" (Song of Songs 8:6). It is strongest precisely when the lover's death is its result: "no one has greater love than he who gives his own life for those he loves" (John 15:13). In the bible and particularly in the New Testament, love is not just a matter of emotion and sentiment. Love is help, giving, assistance and sacrifice; it is weeping of one's heart and bleeding of one's soul. It is all this particularly when it is God himself who loves his creatures, first of all his human creatures. When St. John had his most penetrating insight into God's boundless being he made an astonishing discovery. What is God?

"God is love," he states (1 John 4:8, 16). God is a prodigious, inexhaustible generator of love, and it is this hypertension of overflowing love that dynamizes him and prompts him to action outside himself. But for him also, "love is strong as death," and his heart had to bleed dearly. When St. John gives us his definition of love, he also tells us where he discovered that love: "the love of God was disclosed in this, namely in that God has sent his only Son to the world that we may live through him; his love consists in this: that it was not we who loved God, but it was he who loved us and sent his own Son as atonement for our sins" (1 John 4:9f.). The dramatic point in St. John's thought is that God's love for the world cost him his one and only Son. This is exactly the thrust of St. John's consideration in his gospel (John 3:16): "God so loved the world that he gave his only Son." It is a Father's heart that is torn by his love for his servants/creatures.

The abysmal depth of God's great love appears even more poignantly when one takes note of John's terms. God loves the world, and to the world he sends his Son. But the world is not a geographic or cosmic notion; it is a theological qualification that characterizes man's enslavery to Satan (see John 8:34-44) in rebellion against God; it is, in fact, the mob of mankind mobilized in defiance of God's love and power. It is to such a peculiar "world" that God sends his Son: a lamb among wolves (Matthew 10:16). St. John would say that God sent "the good shepherd" who has to confront the wolves (John 10:11f.). He did so because God really loved that kind of "world." As a matter of fact, God did not expect any sort of reciprocation from the world; he was aware that he was "giving" his own Son: he sent him precisely that he become "atonement," i.e., atoning victim for our sins, which certainly implied the shedding of blood and sacrificial slaughtering. The sending of the Son to the "world" was weighed not on the basis of the Son's advantage but man's, "that we may have life through him."

That is why it was in Christ's passion and death that John made the great discovery that "God is love"; the cross was a "revelation" of God's love, and in this sense Christ's earthly life and death were a "theophany," something through which man could see God himself at work, and what he saw was that "God is love." This is the mercy/love that John saw in the incarnate Logos when he contemplated the Father's only Son as he appeared "full of mercy/love and truth" displaying the "glory" of the Father himself (John 1:14).

God "gave" the best he had, his "only" Son. Here the notion "only" does not just express a numerical notion but the tenderness of a unique love, the dearest attachment and what one treasures most (the bride of Canticles 6:9 is the "only one," the darling, the beloved of her mother). Such is the "gift" of God to the world: the delight of his heart and the pride of his divine fatherhood. Again, the notion of "giving" connotes the concept, not of giving up, but of sacrificing; of "not sparing" what is dearest to God (Romans 8:32). "God so loved the world." He did so, "that whoever believes in his Son may not perish but obtain eternal life." Such is the basis of man's salvation or vivification through faith. It is an easy salvation for me, because it was costly to God; it is easy for me, because it is grounded on God's love or, rather, on God who "is" love.

In point of fact, God's purpose in sending his Son to the world was not to pass judgment upon the world, but rather to save the world. This remark harks back to v. 14, where the evangelist referred to Christ as "the Son of Man" who, according to the background of Daniel 7:13, is the supreme judge of mankind, and as such has the power and the mission to "judge" the world (see John 5:27, 22). Before becoming the eschatological judge, Jesus is just the "savior" of the world through faith in him. What is more, he will not judge, not even at the end of time. The real judgment of man takes place in this life, and it is man himself who passes judgment upon himself;

his attitude here and now towards Christ decides his eternal future: he who does not believe in him is already judged (and condemned), because this is evidence that he refuses his own salvation, as well as God's love—and God himself (see John 12:46-48). In his final sentence, the Son of Man will just confirm this state of affairs.

Corpus Christi
John 6:51-58

The Lord describes himself as "the living bread" (v. 51). A bread, however, that others can "eat"; just as he refers to "my blood," and this is a blood that others can "drink." He spoke, of course, of the saving eucharistic mystery, the sacrament of the "body and blood of the Lord" (cf. 1 Corinthians 10:16). But the Lord also stresses that this "living bread" and "my blood" are indispensable means for anyone to receive "eternal life," and also to possess it "in oneself" as a personal endowment, with the result that the "bread" and the "blood" (no mention of wine!) are the only guarantee of our mortal nature to be raised from the dead on the last day (vvs. 53f.).

As a matter of fact, "my flesh is real nourishment, and my blood is real drink." They were intended to be eaten and drunk. This points to one of the many purposes of the incarnation, when the Logos of God became "flesh" (1:14). The divine Word took on human nature, not just in order to become a priest (Hebrews 8:3f.; 9:11, etc.) or to undergo a redeeming death (Hebrews 10:7ff.; John 12:24, 27), but also to nourish his "sheep." He points out that "he who eats 'me' will live because of me," just as he himself lives because of the Father (v. 57). The Lord wanted his flesh and blood to be "eaten" and "drunk" by man, to be received and tasted by man as he exists, namely by man's corporeal dimension. The evangelist lays great emphasis on this aspect, namely that man's body also touches and tastes Christ's salvation in the eucharistic mystery, and it is man's body itself that "eats" and "drinks," i.e., perceives divine life and will be raised on the last day. After all, at the institution of the eucharist, Jesus himself gives to those present the eucharistic bread to "eat" and the eucharistic wine to "drink"—which they did eat and drink—and at the same time that he explicitly states that they are "my" body, "my" blood.

The understanding of some biblical concepts can be helpful here. In the bible, the human being, rather than a composite of soul and body, is a compact unit, a single thing with two aspects or projections: spiritual and corporeal. In the bible there is nothing of the Greek conflict between human soul and body. The result is that man has to attain salvation in the fullness of his being. God saves whatever he has created; and man's body, too, is God's creation. Man's body itself has to be saved, redeemed, nourished, washed, etc., if the total man is to be saved. This is the fundamental principle of the entire sacramental system. Contrary to the biblical thought, the Greek mentality understood the salvation of man to consist in being stripped of one's physical body (see 2 Corinthians 5:1-4), so that man's soul may be free from "jail," from its body. The biblical system understands that the "external" factor in the sacraments is necessary in order to give man's body itself an experience of God's invisible grace, which is received by the whole person and saves the whole person.

This explains why the Lord wanted his eucharistic flesh and blood to be "eaten" and "drunk" by man. They are touched and tasted by man's body itself, in a manner natural to it; it "eats" and "drinks" the "living bread" that conveys that kind of life which will raise it on the last day. In a manner of its own, man's physical dimension also experiences that it is being nourished for eternal life; that it is actually getting this eternal life and being reached by God's saving work. To such an extent, God adjusts to man's frail nature, saving him in all that God has created, and including the whole of man in the mystery of his grace, of his love and of his power.

The evangelist shows that the eucharist was intended to be a "sacrament," namely a real sign or symbol consisting in elements of this cosmos with their cosmic appearance, through which saving effects are bestowed on cosmic realities—on our body, too, which belongs to this cosmos and is part of it. It is for this reason that Christ gives to his own the gift of the eucharist; the gift of his human flesh and blood as food and drink for human flesh and blood. This is, among other reasons, why he became "flesh," human weakness in cosmic elements: he wanted to reach man in the totality of his being and at his own (low) level. Such is the sacramental dimension of the eucharist in terms of its being nourishment for man. It is really food, and man understands and feels it to be so. Through faith, he perceives and somehow feels that he is being given eternal life—not only in his soul but also in his body. The eucharistic mystery attains the entire man, but is particularly related to his corporeal projection.

The biblical thought of a compact unity in man's reality also explains the biblical understanding that the body/blood of Christ can give eternal, and even divine (v. 57) life to man. Ever since the incarnation, the divine and vivifying Word of God cannot be separated from his "flesh" or human nature—they are intertwined in a "personal" relationship. His human nature is permeated by the divine Logos and turned into a suitable tool of the divine presence. Thus the divine life that dwells in the Logos (John 1:4; 5:26) flows through his eucharistic flesh and blood into the man who "eats me." The principle is illustrated in the gospels by several miracles that can be called sacramental miracles: Christ cures people by touching their bodies with his hand, life flows from him when he touches the bier of the young man in Naim, or smears someone's eyes or tongue with his saliva, or when the bleeding woman touches his cloak. Jesus' human projection is a suitable channel that conveys divine power and life.

In the eucharist, the life flowing into the receiver through Jesus' flesh and blood is the life of the Father himself. The evangelist understands that "just as the Father has life in himself he also gave to the Son the gift of having life in himself" (5:26); a life that he has received from the origin of all things, namely the Father. It is on these grounds that "just as the living Father sent me and I have life because of the Father, so the man who feeds on me will have life because of me" (John 6:57). The life reaching man through Christ is the life flowing from the "living" Father—living, in the sense that he "has life in himself" as in its ultimate origin.

In the eucharist, the body of Christ is a source of divine life and power; and through a real contact with man, the body of Christ gives life, divine life, to the receiver who now "is immanent in Christ and Christ in him" (v. 56), in a true "communion" of two persons in which, however, Christ remains the source from where everything flows in a one-way direction towards the man who is in need of everything he can get.

(See also B, Twentieth Sunday in Ordinary Time.)

Sacred Heart of Jesus
Matthew 11:25-30

(See A, Fourteenth Sunday in Ordinary Time.)

In the gospels, we find several self-definitions of the Lord: "I am the light of the world, I am the bread of life, the bread from heaven, the genuine vine," "I am the way, the truth and the life" (John 4:6), etc. Perhaps the Lord's self-definition which is dearest to man's heart is found in today's reading: "I am gentle and humble of heart." The real meaning is that "my heart is gentle and humble," or "I have a gentle and humble heart." Such self-evaluation would seem pretentious, if it did not come from Jesus himself.

In the bible "heart" is not just the seat and symbol of man's affections, tenderness or emotions in general. It is the innermost dimension of man's being; "heart" stands for the deepest roots of man's very reality; it is the source of man's personality and, therefore, activity. Jeremiah understood that "the sin of Judah is written with an iron stylus, engraved with a diamond point upon the tablets of their hearts" (17:1), meaning that sin has become part of their own nature. This is why at the time of salvation, "I (Yahweh) will place my law within them, and write it upon their hearts" (Jeremiah 31:33). Man's heart is that "nuclear" dimension of man that gives a spiritual direction and meaning to everything he does, thinks or desires: "it is from man's heart that evil thoughts, fornication... evil eye/envy, blasphemies, *arrogance*...derive" (Mark 7:21f.). The notion of "heart" stands for the entire person, for one's personality, for what "characterizes" an individual or a society. Jesus' "heart" is his personality; it is the grass-roots of his intimate and profound being. The heart is that mysterious, elusive "spot" in man that is neither the soul nor the body (nor divinity); it can refer to them as "my" soul or body, and it can refer to itself as "I," an "I" somehow distant and different from both soul and body. But his heart is the real source from which everything Jesus does, or feels, or thinks, or desires, or wants, flows.

In the passage of Mark just mentioned (7:21f.), man's heart is the source of, among other things, "arrogance" ("hyperephania"). In her canticle, at the same time that she speaks of her "humility" ("tapeinosis"), the Blessed Mother refers to those who are "arrogant ("hyperephanoi") in the thinking of their hearts" (Luke

1:51), i.e., in their own evaluation of themselves and, as a result, are arrogant in their conduct and actions. Such an attitude, arrogance of man's heart, represents the opposite of Jesus' heart. His heart is "humble" ("tapeinos"), he says, it is not arrogant. In another direction, humility, or a humble heart, is also the attitude of the Blessed Mother when she says: the Lord was mindful of the "humility of his *servant*." Humility includes an attitude of service, or rather, of being a servant; it is an attitude opposite to that of the "powerful" rulers and self-confident rich persons, i.e., of overbearing tyrants and self-assertive rich who look down and tread on the lowly. Humility implies both a lowly social status and, even more importantly, a spiritual attitude of surrender, of being a "servant" and acting as one.

A short poem (Psalm 131) was devoted to the biblical notion of humility, and it is in that poem that it is most aptly described:

> O Lord, my heart is not proud,
> nor haughty my eyes.
> I have not gone after things too great,
> nor marvels beyond me.
>
> Truly I have set my soul
> in silence and peace.
> As a child has rest in its mother's arms,
> even so my soul.

This is written with the understanding that peace comes from "hope in the Lord, both now and forever" (v. 3).

Close to humility is the concept of the "gentleness" ("praytes") of Jesus' heart. The characteristics of gentleness are mildness and kindness in manner, word and approach. The Messiah can be a "king" and powerful, and still he is "gentle" (Matthew 21:5; Zechariah 9:9). The opposite is the roughness and harshness that the arrogant and insolent display in their attitudes in order to make room for themselves in the world and have it their own way. It is to the "gentle" that "the possession of the land" is promised in the beatitudes (Matthew 5:5). Such is Christ's personality or heart.

What emerges in Jesus' self-definition or description is the spirit of the beatitudes (Matthew 5:3-13). Jesus presents himself as the embodiment of that spirit and, therefore, as the supreme exemplar of the Christian reality and of Christian behavior. As a matter of fact, such a spirit is what Jesus invites his followers to "learn from me." Such is the great lesson that all Christians have to learn from Jesus' heart. In the present context (Matthew 11:25-29), the humility and gentleness of Jesus' heart mark a dividing line between himself and the "wise and the learned" in the Jewish religious society, namely the Pharisaic leaders with all their arrogance and showy display (Matthew 23:5f.; Mark 12:38). This is why his invitation goes, first of all, to those who are "toiling and overburdened" under the "heavy loads" of legalistic impositions (Matthew 23:3f.; see A, Thirty-first Sunday in Ordinary Time; B, Thirty-second Sunday in Ordinary Time).

This is just part of the total spirit of the beatitudes, which also includes the pinch of real poverty suffered in respect and regard for God, mourning and weeping amidst the hardships of life without rebelling against God, gentleness and meekness, real effort for complying with God's law and wishes, a compassion that first of all means forgiveness of offenses, singleheartedness in man's dealings with God, the spreading of peace and concord among fellow humans—and "persecution" for justice, i.e., "for my sake." Christ wants his followers to learn this spirit from him, because he can say with complete assurance that he is the outstanding model to be imitated; and he also gives the complete assurance that "the Lord is close to the broken-hearted, and those whose spirit is crushed he will save" (Psalm 35:19).

The power of Christ's teaching and exemplary proclamation does not derive so much from his words as from his own example in his life. The "prohibitive" and alienating invitation of Christ gets its irresistible punch from the fact that his heart "was" gentle and humble, actively and dynamically: his life in obedience to God, in service to mankind, in submission to and at the mercy of worldly powers, in friendship with the destitute and outcast, in mercy and love for sinners, in gentleness with children and women, in patient love for his disciples, in total surrender to God's saving plan, in complete and absolute service to God as "the Servant of the Lord" to the point of death, "without returning any insult, or countering with threats, but rather delivering himself up" (1 Peter 1:23)—this life and "death" are the power that makes Christ's invitation imperishable, valid for all times, irrefutable and irresistible. He was aware of his own life, of everything he did, and this is why without pretentiousness or presumption he was sure that he could proclaim to the world that "I am gentle and humble of heart." And to his followers, he could propose an unsurpassable example that was he himself: "you call me master and lord, and you are right for this is what I am" (John 13:13). But his lessons are *supreme* exercises in "gentleness and humility." Jesus' teachings are not theoretical, they are eminently practical and real. They flow from his very personality, from what he really "is."

Ordinary Time

First Sunday in Ordinary Time (The Baptism of the Lord)

Matthew 3:13-17

The narrative of Jesus' baptism by John the Baptizer is designed to make Jesus' saving meaning manifest to the reader. The meaning of the entire account is disclosed by the proclamation of the "voice from heaven" at the end. The same purpose, however, emerges very clearly at the outset. When John sees Jesus coming to be baptized by him, he declares that Jesus is far superior to himself and, therefore, the roles should be turned around: "I"—John says—"should be baptized by you." The objection does not look backward to John's audience, but forward to the readers of the gospel; it should be understood as an answer to a thorny question debated among early Christians: who is greater, i.e., who is the Messiah—Jesus or John? The evangelist has John recognize openly that it is Jesus who is the greater and, therefore, the Messiah.

Why, then, was Christ baptized by John, and not vice versa? As far as Jesus is concerned, his conviction is that he had to do so in order to comply with God's will; he understood that he had to "give fulfillment to complete justice"; in other words, he felt and knew that receiving John's baptism was what the Father wanted him to do, and he is committed to comply with God's total will and wishes—this is "complete justice." The following shows, in fact, that God had chosen this opportunity to make an important proclamation concerning Christ who was about to launch out into his public ministry, his messianic career. God had determined to teach the Jewish crowds, and through them the entire world, who this unassuming and unpretentious man was, and to demonstrate in some way that he had the backing and support of "heaven" itself, namely God. This is why God wanted Jesus to honor the appointment and come to baptism.

God wanted men to know that Jesus of Nazareth "is my Son, my beloved in whom I take pleasure." Interestingly enough, the voice from heaven speaks the language of two important messianic passages of the Old Testament. The reader is thus referred to the entire context of these passages. The characterization of Jesus as "my Son" derives from Psalm 2:7, a messianic psalm, where the royal figure of the Davidic king is addressed by God with the words, "you are my son, today I have begotten you," and to him the promise is made that "I will give you the nations for your heritage, the ends of the earth for your dominion," because "this is my king, installed by me on Zion." In this manner, God declares before the entire world that Jesus is the "royal" Messiah of the ancient prophecies and of Israel's expectations and hopes.

The other characterization of Jesus as "my beloved in whom I take pleasure," refers the reader to the songs or oracles about the "Servant of the Lord" in Second Isaiah. Noticeably, in 12:18ff., the evangelist St. Matthew quotes *in extenso* from one of these songs where the words of the heavenly proclamation are found. This is how the author teaches his readers that this man, who has just been baptized and is about to begin a messianic ministry that will put him on the cross, truly is the "Servant of the Lord" who proclaims God's will, but who also has "to of fer his life as ransom for all." This dimension of Christ's person gives a deeper meaning to the "complete justice" that Jesus wishes to comply with and, therefore, to his baptism. John's baptism was a penitential practice or rite that signified "conversion" and was administered "for the forgiveness of sins"; it was a rite designed for sinners. Jesus, of course, had no personal sin of his own to be forgiven or to convert from. But just as at the end of his career he "died for 'our' sins"—not for his—so also at the beginning he received the baptism for the forgiveness of sins, as a penitential attitude through which he does penance for "our" sins, the sins of mankind. Just as his death on the cross was according to the Father's will, so also was his penitential baptism.

Related to the imminent beginning of his career as a herald of God's revelation or teaching is the detail that "the heavens opened." The author brings a motif of the "prophetic" ministry into the picture. When Ezekiel received his prophetic calling "heaven opened and I saw visions from God" (Ezekiel 1:1). The prophet of Revelation (4:1) says that "in my vision I saw a door 'open in heaven' and heard the same voice...saying: 'come up here, I will show you what is to come in the future.'" In the fourth gospel, the episode of the open heavens is transferred from the tradition of Christ's baptism to a few verses later, but placed just before Jesus' public career: "I tell you most solemnly"—Jesus says—"you will see heaven laid open and, above the Son of Man, the angels of God ascending and descending" (John 1:51). The concept is clear. The open heaven is a means for the prophet to get in touch with the heavenly world, where he is given the knowledge of God's revelation, which he then proclaims to men. It is all the more clear in the case of the fourth gospel, where Jesus himself is presented as being in touch with heaven (see John 8:29; see Wisdom 18:15f.) through a steady flow of "messages" (angels), a two-way traffic. In the baptism narrative (just as in John 1:51), the detail stresses that in the impending ministry of Jesus his message to the world is the pure and genuine revelation of God; he will speak God's word, revealed doctrine.

The coming of the Spirit upon Jesus points in the same direction. Being in possession of the fullness of the Spirit, the "Servant" will proclaim God's message to the world; it is a gift that will be set in action through Christ's ministry. The passages of Luke 4:18f. and Matthew 12:18ff. show that this mentioning of the Spirit refers the reader to several songs of the "Servant" in Second Isaiah. The Spirit is also that "power" of God that drives God's ministers to undertake their saving work, particularly when it is arduous. Again, this is what the passages of Luke and Matthew, just mentioned, suggest. Immediately after his baptism, it is the Spirit that "drives" Jesus into the wilderness. What theological ideas, if any, are associated with the dove as the symbol of the Spirit, no one knows for sure. References to Genesis 1:2 or Song of Songs 3:10, 14, etc., Deuteronomy 32:11 are of dubious and unconvincing value. Any reference to the myth of the origin of the world by a bird hatching an egg is still more questionable. That the idea of the text is that the Spirit came upon Jesus as smoothly and gently as doves usually fly is another unconvincing proposition.

The entire theophany at Jesus' baptism was not for Jesus' sake, but for the sake of the bystanders. This is what John 12:29f. serves to prove: "the voice did not come for my sake but for yours." The primary and perhaps only beneficiary of the heavenly witness to Jesus was John himself. It was he who had to reveal Jesus as Messiah to Israel (John 1:11), and God, who sent him to baptize in water, instructed him: "the man on whom you see the Spirit come down and rest is the one who is going to baptize with the Holy Spirit" (John 1:33). Some sort of internal visionary experience in John would account for all the elements in the narrative, and render the idea of a purely theological construction unnecessary.

Second Sunday in Ordinary Time
John 1:29-34

The fourth evangelist elaborates on the traditions concerning Jesus' baptism. But he never says that Jesus was actually baptized by John the Baptizer. Interestingly, Mark is the only evangelist who reports Jesus' baptism without reservations. In Matthew, John the Baptizer acknowledges Jesus' superiority: "how is it that you come to me for baptism when I should be baptized by you?" (3:4) In Luke 3:2, Jesus' baptism is just mentioned in an incidental sentence. In some very early Christian writings, Jesus' baptism by John is given as evidence to the effect that John was greater than Jesus. It seems that the discussion was already felt in New Testament times. That is why these various attitudes towards Jesus' baptism are found in the gospels.

In the fourth gospel, the notion that Jesus was superior to John comes through very strongly. As a matter of fact, John is viewed by the fourth evangelist as a "witness" to Jesus the Messiah, "to the Light," and so forth (1:6-7, 15, 20-27; 3:27-29). Even more: the entire ministry of John is understood as an opportunity for the Messiah to be "manifested to Israel" (1:30). This is why, John says, he administered a baptism of water. There is, in fact, a contrast between the baptism administered by John and that administered by Jesus: John administered a baptism of water, it is Jesus "who baptizes in the Holy Spirit" (v. 33). This, too, is evidence of Christ's superiority. To the same effect, John the Baptist stresses that he had started his career before Christ, but Christ ranked before him "because he was before me" (v. 30), an expression that, as in v. 15, seems to refer to Christ's pre-existence. It is another way of saying that "I have to diminish, he has to increase" (3:30).

Obviously, the evangelist is concerned about the real value of John's "witness" to Christ, just as he is concerned about the witness of anybody else in his gospel (5:31-37;

8:14-18; 19:35; 21:24, etc.). That is why he emphasizes that John's witness is grounded on a particular experience of his: "I have seen the Spirit coming down from heaven as a dove and remaining upon him." This experience taught him that Jesus was the one who was to baptize in the Holy Spirit, in other words, he was the Messiah.

There are some obscure points in John's "vision." In the first place, we do not know the background and origin of the dove as a symbol of the Spirit and, therefore, we do not know the theological concept conveyed by this symbolism. Various explanations proposed are far from convincing. In the second place, whether we have to deal with some real but personal, mystical experience of John himself or with some external event—and, if so, which event—is hard to tell. Importantly, the detail of the open skies/heaven is transferred to another place (1:51), where it signifies a free and steady communication of Christ with God's world, i.e., with God himself (see 8:29; 16:32). In 12:28 the evangelist points out a voice coming from heaven, and explains that the voice is heard by other people and that it is *for them* and "not for me" that this voice came. At any rate, from his experience John learned who Jesus was, and it is on the basis of his experience that John can bear a valid witness to Christ and teach others who Jesus really is.

Accordingly, John stresses that "I have seen and I have borne witness that this is the Chosen One of God." At this point, we have to choose between two readings. Instead of the "Chosen One," several textual witnesses read "the Son"; but the former alternative is generally preferred, not only because it is the more difficult reading but also because it points in the direction of the "Servant" oracles in Isaiah, in agreement with the synoptic traditions about Jesus' baptism. The reference to Isaiah and to baptism traditions is important because it characterizes Jesus as the Servant of the Lord who, this time, proclaims God's revelation (see Isaiah 42:1-4; Matthew 12:18-21).

The most significant characterization of Christ by John is found in v. 29: "Here is the lamb of God who takes away the sin of the world." The expression "lamb of God" is puzzling; it has been understood in various ways: a) with a sacrificial meaning—Christ would be either the paschal lamb (1 Corinthians 5:7) or the lamb of the daily sacrifice (1 Peter 1:19); b) as one of three possible translations of an allegedly underlying Aramaic term that can mean lamb or young man or servant—John meant servant, the evangelist understood lamb; c) the lamb in our passage should be explained in terms of the lamb in the Revelation (the Greek term is different), where it is the symbol of a ruling, powerful, conquering Messiah who crushes the forces of evil or Satan. The three positions do not necessarily confront us with a choice between exclusive alternatives. The sentence "who takes away the sin of the world," certainly refers us to 1 John 3:4-8 and, then, to John 12:31; 14:30; 16:11. The notion is one of confrontation between Jesus and Satan, in which the former comes out victorious over "the prince of this world," thus breaking the power of "the" Sin and of "the" Iniquity (1 John 3:4)—these Satanic forces that enslave the world and drive it into sinful acts (John 8:34).

Third Sunday in Ordinary Time
Matthew 4:12-23

Some eight centuries before Màtthew wrote his gospel, the prophet Isaiah (8:23—9:1) spoke of a bright light that would shine upon a land under shadows of death and upon a people in the gloom of oppression. The land was the northern end of the Israelite country; the people were the Israelites dwelling in these northern areas of Zebulun, Naphtali, Transjordan and especially Galilee—the name of the entire northern region, where many non-Israelites lived intermingled with the Israelites, or vice versa. The land and people had been plunged into gloom and oppression by the flooding "waters of the River (Euphrates), i.e., (the armies) of the king of Assyria and all his glory, and he shall come up over all his channels and go over all his banks" (Isaiah 8:7). The light was the radiance of deliverance from oppression, from exile and from tyranny.

At the beginning of his ministry, Jesus moved from Nazareth, in the hill country, to Capernaum on the shore of the lake Gennesaret, which marks the western and southern borders of Zebulun and Naphtali respectively. Capernaum was in the territory of Naphtali. A branch of the "Way of the Sea" (*Via Maris*) from Mesopotamia, through Damascus, to the Mediterranean and on to Egypt, ran through these areas. As Jesus moved to Capernaum, the evangelist had a new insight into the prophetic oracle, and the words of Isaiah acquired new dimensions and new depths. The light of deliverance is the light of divine revelation; it is the message delivered by Christ throughout his public ministry.

The present reflection of Matthew is a follow-up on the episode of the "epiphany" (shining, radiant manifestation or appearance) of the Messiah in 2:1ff. The "star in its rising" prefigured the light of revelation that Christ was in his preaching. This is why Matthew resorts to Isaiah's text when Christ starts his teaching ministry in and out of Capernaum, where he settled precisely for this purpose. The evangelist notes that "from that time on Jesus began to preach and to say: 'change your minds for the kingdom of heaven is at hand.' " The entire gospel of Jesus' public ministry follows. In Matthew it opens with the Beatitudes (5:1-11) and the Sermon of the Mountain (5-7) and closes with the commandment of the universal mission that carries Jesus' light to all the lands under "the shadows of death" and in the gloom of oppression. All this began when "Jesus toured all of Galilee teaching in their synagogues, proclaiming the gospel of the kingdom, and curing the people of every disease and illness" (4:23). It is in his teaching and preaching, first of all, that Christ is the bright light that shines in the darkness of a world plunged into religious and moral error.

It is through Christ's enlightenment that mankind obtains deliverance from tyranny. It is no longer political and military oppression, it is the tyranny of religious ignorance, error, and falsehood with its inevitable result of moral disorder, corruption and perversion. This is why Christ is the "bright light" shining on those who dwell in a world under the "shadows of death." He cures man, but the healing of physical illnesses is a real/sacramental symbol of the healing of man's mind brought about by Christ's enlightenment. Christ's deliverance rescues man from slavery to error, to sin, and ultimately, to Satan's rule and tyranny. Christ's deliverance brings light and joy to mankind—joy and deliverance are, in fact, the notions associated with light in the Bible. The miracles of deliverance from demonic possession reported in the gospel connote this tyranny and this deliverance from Satanic rule. Just three verses before (4:9f.), Satan is portrayed as the master of the world who can give all kingdoms, even to Jesus, "if you prostrate yourself in homage before me." Jesus was the only one who not only had not fallen into this slavery and refused to prostrate himself before Satan, but also undertook the task of rescuing those who had fallen under such slavery. He did so, among other things, by shedding the abundant and bright light of his revelation, his teaching and preaching, upon mankind. Every page, every word of the gospel is light of deliverance. This is true, of course, for Matthew, but it is John who turns this notion into one of the basic themes of his gospel about the "Word *who* is the true light enlightening every man" (John 1:9).

It was only fitting that the bright light of God's revelation and deliverance shone in Galilee—"Galilee of the gentiles"—by the "Way of the Sea" that connected the surrounding areas of the vast pagan world. The temple of the Lord, signifying his presence among his people, was in Jerusalem, where the national worship also was conducted and where the Law spoke more clearly through its authoritative interpreters and teachers. Galilee was a "mission land," far away from God's presence, with a pagan population in considerable numbers and with a somewhat lax approach to religion—a land where demonic possessions were no exception, whereas no possession in Judea is reported. It was in Galilee that the light of deliverance was needed most. It was through a missionary tour through Galilean towns and villages that, at the sight of the crowds, Jesus' heart was moved with pity: "they were lying prostrate from exhaustion, like sheep without a shepherd." And he realized that "the harvest was good but laborers were scarce" (Matthew 9:36f.). That is why right at the beginning of his ministry, in Matthew's presentation (4:18-22), the Lord chose some of those "laborers" whom he sent on a universal mission at the end of his career (Matthew 28:19f.). They also are "the light of the world" (Matthew 5:13), for those who receive light from the Light become light themselves—just as in the fourth gospel those who receive "water" from the Source become sources themselves (John 4:14; 7:37f.).

Fourth Sunday in Ordinary Time
Matthew 5.1-12

(See B, All Saints, November 1.)

Every time the reader of the gospel comes across the beatitudes, he is confronted with a shocking paradox. Everything the world values as a blessing and source of happiness is conspicuously absent from this page of the gospel. Instead, everything man regards as a failure and a non-value is proposed as a blessing and gift by Jesus. As one reads the beatitudes, the obvious question arising in anyone's mind is whether man can regard himself as "blest," lucky and happy in his sufferings, privation and persecution. One can understand Christ correctly only when he realizes that the beatitudes in the gospel look forward to the future; there is an eschatological dimension in each one of the promises attached to the beatitudes. Those who are poor, suffer, mourn, are persecuted, etc., will be consoled, satisfied, given the kingdom, etc., at some time in the future, a time which is the heavenly stage of the kingdom of God, when heavenly and eternal happiness will be the lot of those who have suffered on earth. They are declared "blest" by Christ, even in their sufferings, because their hope is good, a good and happy outcome is in store for them.

One should be careful so as not to misunderstand Christ's message and promise. He does not attach his promise to any sort of suffering; he does not bless suffering just because it is suffering. He blesses only that suffering which has a religious value, that suffering in which a spiritual dimension can be found; because such suffering is related to God, and man accepts it on religious grounds, i.e., without breaking God's law in order to obtain relief from this suffering and, to that extent and in that sense, accepts suffering in obedience to God, without rebelling against him. This is the kind of suffering that Jesus blesses.

After all, what Christ intends to teach in the beatitudes is that Christians should be Christians and live as such—always, and in whatever circumstances. If they do, if they are equal to their commitment to God, they are really blest because their sufferings, the expression of their loyalty and devotion to God, will be generously rewarded. The basis of that reward, however, is real suffering or privation that constitutes sacrificing devotion and commitment.

The question may be raised as to whether it is really necessary for a Christian to undergo suffering in order to be blest and, therefore, reach the eternal reward. Christ never appraises or evaluates things or questions from a philosophical standpoint. His message, therefore, should not be viewed as a rejection or condemnation of lawful enjoyment on earth. God, in fact, has created all visible things for man to enjoy. Christ considers man and all things as they act in the factual and existential situations of life. In practical terms, those who are rich, powerful, influential or hedonistic in their approach to life, tend to be self-assertive, or to disregard God and his commandments (1 Timothy 6:17-19; Matthew 6:20, 24). They trust in their power and wealth; they put their trust in themselves and not in God (Luke 12:15-21). On the contrary, those *religious* people who are in need, oppressed or downtrodden, know that they cannot trust in themselves, in their power or means, and they experience their own dependence; they trust in God and it is from him that they expect help and relief; they commit themselves to God, completely, in the conviction that, come what may, God does not fail them.

As a matter of fact, a *genuine* Christian, a committed Christian, will always be confronted with the ways and power of the "world" and, therefore, with suffering, opposition, if not oppression and even open persecution (2 Timothy 3:12; John 15:18ff.; 16:20). A truly Christian life, in which one always tries to keep God's commandments and answer his expectations, where one tries to give a positive witness to Christ and the gospel, will certainly run into social, economic and, perhaps, domestic problems. It is to this factual reality that Christ refers in his beatitudes.

In Jesus' view the beatitudes, like the entire Sermon of the Mountain, do not represent a utopian spiritual condition or attitude. They represent Jesus' radical demand of an absolute and unconditional surrender to God and his sovereign rule: he is God no matter the circumstances which may color man's relationship to him. Such is the basic principle of the new ethics proposed by Jesus. What he proclaims here is, not a list of unrelated items, nor a matter of more or less amount in good or evil deeds, but a radically new attitude of man towards God. He shifts the gravitational center of human religious projection from the Law and human evaluations, to God and his individual relationship with each man.

Jesus expects his radical demands to become the practical rule of man's life not because they are "his" demands, but because they are God's will and the basic expression of God's "otherness" or transcendence.

Jesus' demands do not derive from an overly optimistic evaluation of man; he rather points to the difficulties involved in complying with his teaching when he states that only few will enter the narrow and rugged path (Matthew 7:14). Still, he who listens to his words but does not make them the rule of his own life is a "fool" and his end cannot be but utter ruin (Matthew 27:26f.). Being God's will, Jesus' demands cannot be softened or watered down. They share, with Jesus himself, the character of "scandal" or stumbling block. Their formulation itself is radical and "unquestionable": Jesus does not speak to a "dialoguing" audience; he makes no efforts to win the intellectual agreement of those who listen. His demands make sense and are enlightening only to those who believe, to those who receive them in faith, and who in their faith find strength to undertake the strenuous task of complying with them. It is to these people that Jesus addresses himself.

Fifth Sunday in Ordinary Time

Matthew 5:13-16

Jesus had just declared that his followers would be persecuted for the new "justice" of his gospel, "because of me" (Matthew 5:11); in other words, for the new revelation of God's will in and through Christ. The prophets —he adds—were treated in exactly the same way (v. 12). This is a clear indication that, as bearers of his revelation, Christ's followers are compared to the Old Testament prophets who spoke the word of God in the world and made God's light shine in the eyes of mankind. It is this line of thought that is developed in a couple of metaphors that follow immediately afterwards in the gospel of Matthew 5:13-16.

Christ's followers—his community—the Lord says, are the salt of the earth, and if salt goes flat, its flavor cannot be restored—it is useless. A rabbi of the first century A.D. ridiculed the gospel, saying that talking of salt as becoming "saltless" makes no sense. Thus, his conclusion was that the Jewish people are the bearers of God's revelation and they cannot be stripped of this privilege. The reasoning of the rabbi gives valid support to the idea that the statement of the Lord transfers to the community of his followers a saying that was formerly applied to the Jewish community. Regardless of the transference notion, the rabbi's reasoning shows that the concept of salt applied to God's revelation—it is God's Word, his teachings, etc. That is the salt of the earth. The reference to the uselessness of a "saltless" salt is a serious warning of the Lord to his community: the community of Christians can render God's revelation tasteless, bland, insipid, weak, watered down and ineffective, just as the Jewish (Pharisaic, v. 20) system had done.

The Lord wants his followers to be genuine "prophets" who proclaim in the world the revelation that he brought from God; he wants them to be active in preaching the gospel that he entrusted to them. It is through the possession and proclamation of God's Word that the Christian community prevents "corruption" in the world and starts and sustains a process of "being antiseptic." This is why God, in this hope, can still put up with the world and put off his judgment of it—God still takes pleasure in the world: it is not completely "tasteless."

The metaphor of Christ's followers as "the light of the world" obviously conveys the same idea of revelation: the community of Christians bears the light of God's Word and of Christ's gospel in the darkness of the world. Not only that, they are supposed to proclaim it: no one lights a lamp and then puts it under a bushel basket; no, they set it on a stand where it gives light to all in the house. The parallel passages of Mark 4:21f.; 2 Corinthians 4:4; Philippians 2:15f., clearly show that "things are hidden only to be revealed at a later time; they are covered so as to be brought out into the open." The point is not the fact of putting the lamp on the stand, but this: that the light can be seen; that it gives light to all in the house or in the world. Christ is the original Light (Matthew 4:16), and it is he who has lighted the "lamp" of his community with his revelation; and now he wants this light to shine, to be in the open so that all may be enlightened by the proclamation of the Christian truth. No Christian should obscure Christ's light or gospel (Mark 4:22f.; Matthew 10:33); no Christian should be ashamed of what he believes so as to keep silent about Christ's revelation (Mark 8:38; 2 Timothy 1:8; Romans 1:16).

It is in connection with the proclamation of God's Word ("your light must shine before men") that mention is made of the Christians' good works or acts that all may see and give praise to your heavenly Father. It is not a question of "blowing one's own horn" or hiding one's own achievements; it is quite the opposite. The praise for the good deeds is not directed to those men who do them but to God; it is not a matter of putting one's own merits on display. The concept is rather that through the good deeds of Christians God's activity shines; it is he who appears as the driving force of man's good acts, and this is why, quite rightly, the praise goes to him. The good works of Christians are their initiatives, effort, suffering, patience, love, etc., which are required by the preaching of God's Word. Every privilege entails a responsibility.

The Christian community, furthermore, is "the city on a hill"—it cannot be hidden. It cannot be hidden because it is the bearer of Christ's light or God's revelation. Precisely because the Christian community must proclaim the truth of God's light and must, therefore, shine in the darkness of the world, it cannot escape the attention of those "who dwell in darkness": it necessarily attracts the attention of the world. Christ wants the "city" to attract this attention; it was for this purpose that he lighted the lamp; he wanted it on a stand, and not under a bushel basket. That is why the city cannot be hidden: it was set on the top of the hill deliberately. But here, too, the city—the lamp—will attract others' attention if it "shines." The real point is "saltiness" and brightness through an active proclamation of Christ's revelation in his gospel.

Sixth Sunday in Ordinary Time

Matthew 5:17-37

The Lord did not comply with the tenets of Jewish-Pharisaic religiosity. He performed miracles ("worked") on the Sabbath; he disregarded the rules of ritual fasting; he didn't pay any attention to dietary laws or purification rites; he, without any authorization from the Levitic priests and to their displeasure, made his own rule prevail around the temple, etc. Where does he stand in regard to the Jewish religious establishment? In his own time and in early Christianity, the question amounted to this: with his messianic authority did Jesus abolish the Law and implant a different religious order? Does the Old Testament Law have any authority for Christians?

The Lord addressed himself to this question when he solemnly proclaimed that his mission as Messiah, far from being to abolish the Law, was to give fullness to it. This was done in two ways: by fulfilling it, in the sense of complying with it according to its fullest and deepest meaning and true spirit; and by disclosing the full contents of the Law, or rather of God's full will, which was just initially suggested in the formulation of the Old Testament Law. The Law stands as long as this world—heaven and earth—will exist, and the slightest commandments retain their force even "in the kingdom of heaven" according to its new expression, the Christian community. The Law stands, but Christ realizes that the Old Testament Law was the minimal expression of what God really had in mind to achieve. It was just an initial draft, that had to be perfected and "completed" with further revelations of his total will or plan. With his messianic authority, Christ now discloses the complete and final will of God for mankind; he manifests what God's goal was even at that time when the existing formulation of the Law was written—he discloses what the spirit of God's Law really is. His disclosure consists in this: that "the entire Law and the Prophets hinge on two commandments," namely "love God, love your neighbor" (Matthew 22:40). In fact it is only one commandment: love, which is directed to two objects—God and one's neighbor. This is how St. John understood Christ's new rule (1 John 4:21). What this implies, in part at least, is the following: "do for others everything that you would like them to do for you" (Matthew 6:12). Paul grasped the new point of Christ when he fought against the Pharisaic legalism and stressed that the commandments "you shall not commit adultery, you shall not kill, you shall not steal, you shall not covet...are summed up in this sentence: you shall love your neighbor as yourself; love does not wrong one's neighbor. The conclusion is that love is the fullness of the Law" (Romans 13:9f.; Galatians 5:14). It is the fullness of the Law because it does more than what is specified in the Law, and does it better—out of warm love, not out of cold legal compulsion.

Obviously, if one "loves" God he does not change God for an idol; he respects his name; he worships God and respects his wishes even beyond the requirements of the written Law. If one loves his neighbor, he does not kill him; he does not covet or steal his property; he does not infringe on his marital rights; he does not wrong, in the first place, his closest neighbor—his marital partner, etc. If there is real love, man does not just stick to the literalism of the Law but makes efforts not to come anywhere close to the prohibitions specified in the Law; he tries to discover and to comply with the "spirit" of the Law. Furthermore, Christ's teaching and actions disclose that the Law is a gift of God's love for man, that man might be able to achieve the goal of a true and genuine "hominization," i.e., of a full human/spiritual development. Even the commandment of the Sabbath rest derives from God's love for man, that he may restore his vigor, both physical and spiritual; it was not intended to prevent the good from being done.

Christ gives fullness to the Law in the sense that he interiorizes the Law and radicalizes it. What matters is not legalistic compliance, but man's internal attitude toward God's will expressed in the Law; what matters is the loving attitude with which a person tries to comply with the spirit of the Law. By a reduction of the entire Law to the one commandment of love, far from rendering it any easier, Christ renders it all the more difficult. The question is not just to restrict one's obligations to those few statements in the Law, but positively and actively to engage one's love in all conceivable cases that this may be needed. The interiorization of the Law explains also why dietary laws and lustral rites lose their value: the external reminder of purity gives way to the real purity which derives from one's "heart," not from something external (Mark 7:15-23). Liturgical rules lose their force because God's worship also has been brought to "fullness," to a greater perfection: it is a "worship in spirit and in truth" (John 4:23f.), in the temple of Christ's body (John 2:19f.).

It is in this perspective that the "justice" of Christians, i.e., their effort to comply with God's will/law, must be greater than the Pharisaic justice, restricted to legalistic compliance. For a Christian, God's will is not the letter but the spirit of the Law, a spirit of true and generous love towards God and towards our fellow human beings. Justice is to act in the fashion that God himself does, to be perfect in the fashion that he is perfect.

Seventh Sunday in Ordinary Time

Matthew 5:38-48

The Law of the Old Testament stands because it is the expression of God's will. However, it is an incomplete or partial expression of that will. Christ completes the Law or brings it to its fullness, by freeing it from the strictures that an elementary religion attached to God's disclosure and unfolding of his plan of total revelation.

Thus, for Christ's followers, the old commandment "you shall not kill" keeps its force, but that is not enough. It is through wrath and hatred that all killings start (1 John 3:15); after hatred and wrath, insult (calling names) is a further step in the direction of venting one's anger by killing. In a religious society, a high expression of man's wrath and hatred is to call someone impious, which was a sort of curse, as if God's punishment were called upon someone. God's intent in the old commandment was to stress love and loving coexistence among men, but it was restricted to a minimum: murder. Now Christ teaches us that everything that disturbs this love is sin and falls under God's commandment.

When in the Old Testament Law God commanded "you shall not commit adultery," this was a minimal expression of his wish of complete purity in man. That is why Christ teaches that the old commandment stands, but now it is not enough. Lustful looks and everything that leads into impure actions are sins and contrary to God's will from the very outset. This may demand strong decisions and painful detachments (even from the dearest attachments: "right" hand and eye), but it is eternal salvation that is at stake. In the Old Testament, God put up with man's "hardheartedness" or wickedness, and went along with divorce. Besides imposing some restrictions on the practice of divorce (Deuteronomy 24:1-4; 22:19, 29; Malachi 2:13-16), he demanded only that the right of the Israelite woman be protected by giving her a document of divorce as evidence for her that she is free. Now God discloses what his goal was and is: no more divorce at all, except in the case of "fornication," i.e., unlawful union (1 Corinthians 5:1); and in this case also, even the dearest attachments have to be cut off and sent away (see Matthew 14:3f.; for "to cut off" in matters of divorce see Sirach 25:25).

Likewise, the commandment of God was "you shall not swear falsely by my name" (Leviticus 19:12, which was an interpretation of the commandment in Exodus 20:7), "but the vows you take under oath you must fulfill" (Matthew 5:33; Deuteronomy 30:3). God wanted his name to be respected and that is why it should not be used in false oaths. But now, Christ teaches that God's name should be absolutely respected: "I tell you not to swear—at all." One is not even to use substitutions for God's name: such as heaven, or earth, or Jerusalem —they represent God in his sovereign and majestic rule, or the place of his worship and special abode—or one's head/life since it is God's exclusive right to give and to take away our life. The basic reason for swearing is man's radical insincerity: if sometimes he decides to tell the truth, he has to stress his sincerity at this moment by swearing and making God witness to his statement. A Christian, Jesus teaches, is not only to avoid "false" oaths but to be radically and totally sincere at all times: merely to say "yes" to what is affirmative, and "no" to what is negative. Any emphasis beyond that, by the use of some form of oath, does not come from God, it comes from the Evil One.

In the Old Testament, as in any other legislation, the criterion to achieve justice was equal retribution in one way or another. In the Old Testament, the terms were "an eye for an eye, a tooth for a tooth." As a rule of justice, that principle is wanting. Now Jesus' commandment is this: "Offer no resistance to evil"; which is followed by the idea of turning the other cheek, giving up not only one's shirt but also the coat, and going along not one but two miles. Here Christ undermines the very foundations of man's justice; he is a revolutionary. But very few, if any, meet the challenge of "his" revolution. Substantially, man's justice tries to counterbalance an injustice (an eye, tooth) with another injustice (another eye, tooth). What Christ perceives is that two wrongs do not add up to a right. This is not how God in his justice deals with man's failings. Repaying evil "in kind" is another evil, another injustice; therefore, and in this sense, "offer no resistance to evil," but be just and perfect in the fashion that God is just and perfect. The non-resistance to evil does not imply weakness or complicity in it. When Christ was slapped on the face, he courageously called the attention of the offender to his wrongdoing (John 18:22); and Paul resorted to his civil rights when justice was denied to him (Acts 22:25; 25:11). It is Christian charity and justice to point out what is wrong and to use adequate means to prevent it. But countering evil with violence is adding a minus to another minus, which makes minus two but not plus one (right). The cheek, the coat, the extra mile are illustrations of the basic principle:

instead of violently defending your own right (1 Corinthians 6:7), point out what is wrong; then, if evil persists, put up with it wherever it may lead in terms of injustice. It is Christ who illustrates this principle with his own conduct: he pointed out that the slap was wrong and that Pilate was using his God-given authority in the wrong way (John 19:11), but then he went all the way down to his passion, cross and death: "no false word was found in his mouth; when he was insulted he returned no insult, when he was made to suffer, he did not counter with threats; instead, he delivered himself up to him who judges with justice" (1 Peter 2:22f.). Meeting the challenge of this "revolution" is the only effective way you have to convince evil-doers that they are wrong.

The old commandment of love was, "You shall love your neighbor and hate your enemy." In the biblical language, the notions of love and hatred are more dynamic and existential than conceptual or psychological: to love is to care and to do works expressing love; to hate is not to care, it is to disregard, to keep someone away from one's concern and effectual love. In the Old Testament Law the neighbor is one's Israelite countryman and, within this context, one's friend and brother (Matthew 5:46f.). It is to these that the Old Testament law of love (Leviticus 19:18) is directed. The second part ("hate your enemy") is not found in the Old Testament, but it certainly was the practice: pagans did not fall within the category of neighbor, they were disregarded; "enemies," i.e., those who wrong you, both pagan and Israelite, were the object of real ill-feelings and ill-treatment. Revenge is sometimes a legal obligation of the *goel* (redeemer, Numbers 35:19, 21, 24f., 27). The primary rule of the Qumran community was, "Love all the children of light and hate all the children of darkness." Christ removes all bounds from man's love: "Love your enemies and pray for those who persecute you." The illustration of Christ's law is, first of all, his own death and prayer on the cross, and the parable of the Good Samaritan (a non-Jew) in Luke 10:29-37.

In his caring love, a Christian must be a "son" who imitates God the "Father" of all: of both righteous and unrighteous, good and evil men; he cares for all, pouring his loving goodness upon all. The supreme rule of a Christian life is to act as God acts; this is the principle underlying all the improvements of Jesus on the Old Testament Law. The greatest "justice" is that of God. In other words, the Christian man, far from restricting his care to friends and brothers, as even pagans and sinners do, must be perfect in the fashion that the Father of Christians is perfect. We understand perfection in the sense of supreme completeness and accomplishment. In the Bible, perfection is rather a matter of integrity and wholeness, wholeheartedness (see Psalm 18:24-27). A Christian must be whole—as God is—in his thought, life and action; he must be wholeheartedly committed to God, as God is to himself, the absolute rule. In addition, a Christian man's caring heart, just as God's, must exclude none; it must go out to all: good and evil, righteous and unrighteous, Christian and non-Christian, friend and enemy. The emphasis falls on the non-exclusion of anyone from Christian care.

Eighth Sunday in Ordinary Time

Matthew 6:24-34

The passage of 6:24-34 in Matthew's gospel opens with a statement that, in fact, is the conclusion of the foregoing literary unit. Whereas the section in vvs. 25-34 is addressed to the poor, the section in vvs. 19-24 is directed to the rich and warns them against piling up wealth; it is a warning against greed. The warning closes with the solemn declaration that "no one can 'serve' two masters." The image is suggested by the social custom of the time: one and the same slave could belong to two masters; the question of divided and preferential loyalties was inevitable. This is what loving and hating means in this case: care or carelessness for either one's interests.

The "masters" of the gospel passage are God and possessions; and the point is loyalty to God or to one's possessions when their interests are in conflict. The biblical thought is that our entire life and being unquestionably belong to God. According to the "first" commandment of the Law, man is supposed to "love" God "with his whole heart, life, mind—and might" (Mark 12:30; Deuteronomy 6:5), which rabbinic interpretations understood as property. Whenever God is involved, both love and service become religious projections of man, and this is why a service to God or possessions becomes a religious service, worship. Such is the specific point of the teaching imparted in the biblical text. The letters to the Colossians 3:6 and Ephesians 5:5 regard greediness as "idolatry," the worship of some alternative to God (see James 4:4, "adulterers"). A moderate and restrained desire for possessions is not blamed, for such desire is no "service" to possessions. But when possessions replace God as the first concern of man's heart and, therefore, God is given the second—or any other—place but the first in man's priorities, man worships an idol and denies God a worship that is exclusively his. It follows, then, that man obeys the principles and rules of his "idol" and disregards the rules and wishes of God. In his insincerity, man would be able to strike a compromise; but the very nature of things is such that there is no possible compromise: either God or the "idol" of one's possessions. God does not settle for the second place: only the first fits him.

It is "for this" that the Lord goes on to say to the poor: "don't worry" about food, drink or clothing. The birds of the sky or the lilies of the field set an example for man to follow (vvs. 25ff.). Of course, everyday experience teaches man that he gets nothing for his livelihood, unless he plans and works hard to earn what is necessary for himself and for his dependents. But on the other hand, the gospel cannot be taken to teach fatalism or childishness in one's attitude towards the needs of life.

The key word in all this passage is "worry" with the clear connotation of anxiety, or better, overanxiety. A normal and natural planning for today and the immediate future is the common way of life; it includes a certain degree of anxiety, which being natural is not blamed in the passage under discussion. The real point at issue is a healthy balance between common and natural anxiety, on the one hand, and distrust in God on the other. The two ends of the comparison are man's "little faith" in God (v. 30) and a degree of anxiety that becomes anguish and agony because of the basic needs in man's life. It is this anguish that is not Christian, not even religious in general, because it implies a certain distrust in God, i.e., in what is usually called God's providence. A human being, still less a Christian, has no reason to distrust God.

On the contrary, many obvious reasons suggest that man can trust God. There is an order in God's creation, and some things are ordered to others; secondary things are in function of others that are more important. Now, by his creative power, God gave us our very being (body and life) and he knows that this creature of his has certain basic needs (food, drink, clothing) if it is to survive: and therefore, in his providence, God who provides the basic element provides also the secondary elements. This is what he does even with the birds: he created them and so he also provides for their food, according to their own nature. The example of the birds is mentioned, not to teach man that he should not work but rather to teach him that he should trust in the providence of God, who will provide for him according to his own nature. The same thing is true of the lilies of the field: they cannot earn all the beauty they display; and yet all the effort of man, even the effort of kings (Solomon), cannot achieve what God so lavishly gives to mere "grass" which is used by man as fuel for his own needs. Man must realize that in God's eyes he is much more valuable than both birds and lilies; the implication is that God's care or providence for man is even more compelling and, therefore, more dependable. On the other hand, can you change anything by worrying and being in anguish? You cannot add one single instant to your life span, which is determined by God; and abundant provisions do not lengthen it by as much as a second (or an inch, in a perspective of long measure). Anguish about what you cannot change doesn't make much sense, particularly when it implies a certain lack of reliance on him to whom you are indebted for your very existence and to whom you are supposed to devote the many or few days of your life.

The background of all this teaching is God's sovereign rule. A man is supposed to trust in God as well as to plan and work for a living. But this is no automatic guarantee or life insurance. God also cares for sparrows, and none falls to the ground without his consent; but with his consent (Matthew 10:29) they do fall. "Every hair of your head has been counted," i.e., they are in God's care and protection (10:30); but many people are bald. The point is that God rules with sovereign power, and everything, man included, is supposed to surrender its existence to him willingly, according to his wish. After all, if there is a difference between a pagan (v. 32) and a religious Christian it is this: a religious man tries to please God and knows that he can trust the heavenly "Father," wherever this confidence may lead. What really matters is one's compliance with God's "justice," i.e., his judgment, decision, will; such a compliance is the essential characteristic of his "kingdom," because he is really king where he is obeyed. All other needs will be supplied, as a secondary element, by God according to his plan and universal rule.

Ninth Sunday in Ordinary Time

Matthew 7:21-27

False prophets had been a poisonous evil in the community of Israel. The Lord warns that the same evil will infest his Christian community: there will be ravenous wolves disguised as sheep so as to be capable of causing havoc from within. They are rotten trees that bear rotten fruit. The "fruit" of their followers will unveil what they really are. Against this background, the Lord warns that "not all those who cry out 'Lord, Lord!' will enter the kingdom of heaven, but those who do the will of my heavenly Father." The reference is to those who share in the ministry of the Lord in several ways; in the first place by "prophesying" or proclaiming the teaching of Jesus. It is they who can easily become wolves in disguise or rotten trees. It is particularly they who can cause havoc from within or bear foul fruit.

The point stressed in these passages is that the real criterion to evaluate those devoted to apostolic ministry is not a profession of faith, nor an act of worship ("Lord, Lord!"), nor is it their ministerial quality through which Christ's power (teaching, casting out devils and miracles) was manifested. It is "doing the will of my heavenly Father" that is a valid criterion—doing, i.e., bringing into practice God's will as it was disclosed by Christ in general, and more particularly as it is formulated in the preceding Sermon on the Mount. Not doing God's will is "doing evil." Doing is the all-decisive element. It is decisive because it irreversibly seals the fate of man. The perspective is eschatological, as the reference to "that day" (v. 32) serves to prove. On that day, those who "do"

God's will, will enter the final phase of the kingdom; those who "do" evil will be ignored, i.e., disowned by Christ and "shoved away" from him (see Matthew 25:34, 41) to eternal damnation. It is salvation or condemnation that is at stake; both of them depend on "doing," doing God's will instead of one's own will.

In the same direction, doing is what matters—even in the case of non-ministerial workers (vvs. 24-27). The man who "does" is firmly grounded on solid rock; on "that day" he will not be shaken, let alone upset and overthrown: he will stand his ground. He who does "not do" will be turned down; he will fall. In this text, doing and not doing are directly related to "my words," which in this particular context are Christ's words in the Sermon on the Mount. At the end of this Sermon, in 7:24ff., the Lord passes a value-judgment on his own teaching. With complete assurance, he declares that eternal salvation hinges on "doing"—or not doing—what he teaches; it depends on compliance or non-compliance with his commandments and rules of religious conduct, disclosed in his Sermon on the Mount. Christ is aware that he has not just portrayed a utopian ideal to look at, but a goal to strive after; he is aware that his principles are extremely demanding, but he wants them to be complied with. His teaching does not depict a utopian society, but principles to be practiced in the real lives of real human beings. "Doing" is the word, and it is "these" words in the Sermon on the Mount that have to be "done."

The text makes a certain distinction between hearing and doing. The reference is to a man who "hears those my words and (moreover) does them" (v. 24), and to a man who "hears these my words but does not do them" (v. 26). Both of them hear, the only difference is that, beyond hearing, one does and the other does not do. Because of this difference, he who does is a "wise" man and the other is a "fool." The terms are sapiential and indicate success or unsuccess in one's life—in terms of reaching, or failing to reach, the final goal of one's entire life. In this kind of literature, hearing is associated with auditing and learning in the classroom. The implication is that just knowing a lot about "these words" is the lot of the fool; it is "doing" that is needed for someone to be wise.

Yet there is nothing of Pharisaic religiosity (doing) in this Christian teaching. At this point, the opposites are not faith and works (works: as the means of one's justification by God), but man's knowledge of a principle and his real commitment to that principle. In other words, the opposites are a "dead" faith and a "living" faith (James 2:14-26; 1:22-27). Christianity, and biblical religiosity, for that matter, have never divorced theoretical principles from ethical life. Christianity is a matter of wholeness, where man's thinking and living must be integrated into oneness.

The house grounded on rock or sand is a parabolic element. It portrays the concept of a lasting and unshakable success "built up" in one's life, or a "building" that cannot last because it does not stand the test of a real trial (see 1 Corinthians 3:14) on "that day." The sketchy parabolic figure of torrential rains and flooding waters buffeting (and sweeping away) the house, point to the judgment of the Flood (Genesis 6) and to the prophetic preaching concerning the destruction of the "house" of Israel. The Jewish "house" (community) that hears Christ's words but does not make them the rule of its life is doomed; but by Christ's word, a new community of "doers" is founded that will last and stand the test of time or trials.

Tenth Sunday in Ordinary Time

Matthew 9:9-13

In this reading, the calling of a tax collector as well as the friendship of Jesus for tax collectors and "sinners," as he socializes with them at a banquet, are reported —with the conclusion of the episode in mind. It is the conclusion that commands the entire narrative. The conclusion reads: "I did not come to call righteous people but rather sinners."

The trade of tax collecting was a real business, and it was leased to the highest bidder, who had to secure a given definite amount of revenue for the imperial authority or its delegates. His service was paid by whatever extra money he could manage to squeeze from the taxpayer. Understandably, justice was seriously offended; extortion and fraud were commonplace. On top of that, helping in tax collection was looked upon as collaboration with the foreign oppressive power—Rome— and therefore, as a betrayal of God's people. The fact that Herod, the ruler of Galilee, was a pagan (a non-Jew) and a protégé of Rome did not render things any easier. Obviously, economic and religious interests became natural allies to engender hatred for the tax collector, who, to the greater discomfort of the crowds, usually became wealthy (Luke 19:2, 8). Matthew was one of them, and he was conducting his business as usual when Jesus called him to be his follower and apostle.

Jesus accepted an invitation of Matthew, the tax collector; and in his house, he sat at table with many other tax collectors, the "natural" guests Jesus or anyone else could expect in those circumstances. Besides the tax collectors, however, there were also "sinners." Sinners and tax collectors were those who did not care too much about the Law and still less about Pharisaic religiosity. Jesus was sitting at table with this kind of people, which certainly was an expression of friendship and association. This attitude is one of the most fundamental characteristics of Jesus; he liked to associate himself with those who, in the eyes of the self-righteous Pharisees and others, were the outcasts of the Jewish society. Far from keeping them at a distance, he came close to them, enjoyed being in their company, and was fond of dispensing his favors to them. One can see in this a conscious reaction of Jesus to hypocritical self-righteousness and, ultimately, a rejection of it. But Jesus' behavior must also be viewed as a prominent feature of his human nature, which loved human beings and tried to understand and excuse their failings.

Jesus' close association with tax collectors and sinners was puzzling to the Pharisees. A rabbi, a Jewish religious teacher, or any pious Jew was not supposed to associate with certain people (v. 11: see Luke 7:39; John 4:27). Such an association led to the suspicion that Jesus was taking the law, the religious excellence of the Jewish people and the Jewish pride itself, as lightly, casually and carelessly, as all those tax collectors and sinners around him did. That is why the Pharisees, the religious inquisitors of the time, came, not to Jesus but to his disciples, and called their attention to the fact that "your teacher" or rabbi keeps company ("eats") with tax collectors and sinners. A pious Jew would refuse to share a table with such people (see Acts 11:2; Galatians 2:12). The suggestion is that one wondered how the disciples followed such a teacher, a man of no standing in the opinion of the true and authorized religious leaders and the judges of the established religion.

In spite of their pettiness, the Pharisees concerned themselves with the religious and spiritual health of the people of God, with their holiness or righteousness. In the last analysis, this is also God's concern (Psalm 103:3; Jeremiah 17:14; Ezekiel 34:16). Jesus takes up this principle, which underlies the Pharisees' intervention, and on the basis of the same principle, shows the Pharisees how wrong they are. Jesus stresses that his way is God's way of dealing with the "sick" and the "injured": as a good "physician" he tries to help and heal them. The mere realization that someone is sick or injured doesn't help much; keeping them at a distance and avoiding them helps even less. Only a sincere effort to help makes sense and is a realistic attitude. This is what the Pharisees would not do.

In this passage, Jesus' answer to the Pharisees is not necessarily ironic. They try to comply with the Law; they may even be in good health. But if they think that Jesus, like the other guests, is "sick" because he associates with the sinners, they are wrong: Jesus is the "physician" who heals those who are sick. The Pharisees may be in good health, but they are certainly not healers. Christ would not grant that his religious leadership could be called into question. It is not he who is wrong in his approach to sin and sinners; it is the Pharisees who keep away from sinners and hate, not only sin but also sinners. Such a pastoral approach may safeguard their personal pride and social standing among the people but does certainly not do anything for the sinner in the direction of rescuing him from his slavery to sin and of bringing him closer to God. Christ asserts beyond any ambiguity or possible doubt his religious leadership because being a religious leader implies by necessity being a physician, a healer; and it is among the sick that a physician must perform his job, not in the conference room where rules for liturgy and religious socializing and politiking are developed.

This is why Jesus tells the Pharisees to go and "learn" an important lesson which their unquestionable authority, the Scriptures, teaches them. Through the prophet Hosea (6:6) God himself had stated the pastoral rule he likes: "it is love *(hesed)* that I desire, not sacrifice." Jesus does not reject the sacrificial worship on which the Pharisees laid such emphasis; there are, however, greater values. Christ certainly stresses the first part of the biblical quotation: "it is love that" is really important, even in one's relations with sinners. The prophetic text is quoted again by Jesus in Matthew 12:7, against the Pharisees once more. The message of the text certainly expresses the basic rule of Christ's pastoral approach: "love" comes before all else. The text of the prophet uses the Hebrew word *hesed* which rather means steady and faithful love in general. But the Greek translation (used by the evangelist) *eleos* slants the broader original meaning in the direction of compassion and mercy. Compassion and mercy are what sinners need. They (not hatred and contempt) must direct any religious leader in his approach to sin and sinners. Compassion and mercy are two of the most valuable and genuine aspects of God's and man's love. Through the quotation from the word of God in the Scriptures, Christ teaches the Pharisees still another lesson, the most important one: his approach to sinners is correct and valid. He follows the very rule God himself has set. He is unquestionably right. Thus, it is the Pharisees who are unquestionably wrong. Beyond that, Christ's quotation of God's rule proves them to be ignorant of Scripture, and this is why he sends them back to school: "go and learn." Those who were all out to question Christ's teaching authority were exposed as proud but ignorant teachers of religion themselves. Surprise?

Eleventh Sunday in Ordinary Time

Matthew 9:36—10:8

In Chapter 10, the first evangelist puts together several instructions of Jesus concerning missionary activities in his community. The result is a composite literary and doctrinal unit where all the materials of Jesus' teaching related to this subject are integrated into a sort of treatise, the so-called missionary discourse. The section in Matthew 9:35—10:8 is intended by the evangelist as an introduction to the Christian missionary teaching. He wants us to understand that the missionary work and duty of the Church is engrafted into Christ's ministry of which it is the continuation, and is grounded on Christ's will and intention.

This is why Jesus is portrayed here as a real missionary, engaged in a large-scale mission as he tours all the towns and villages of Galilee. No place ("villages") was small enough to be disregarded by Jesus; he tried to reach wherever people could be found and saved. There were three main projections of His mission: a) he "taught" in synagogues on the sabbath; and in this case, His teaching focused on the proper understanding of the Scriptures, read in a new light, the "messianic" light (see Luke 4:16ff.; John 6:59); b) he "proclaimed" the good news of the kingdom, namely the news that "the kingdom of heaven was close at hand," which must be understood as a public proclamation, not in the synagogues, but wherever he could find an audience: this was a "message" concerning God's activity through Jesus himself; c) he "cured" every sort of sickness and disease (4:23; 8:16f.).

As his mission proceeded, Jesus became more and more aware of a sad situation, that no doubt prompted him to launch out into his missionary operation in the first place. He realized that the crowds, the poor people, "were harassed and dejected like sheep that have no shepherd." The key concept of the entire passage emerges at this point: Jesus is portrayed as a missionary who in all truth is "the" good shepherd; he really cares for people. It is John 10 that develops this theme to a considerable degree. In his turn, Matthew touches upon it briefly but with insight and sensitivity. The religious condition of the people was pitiful. Jesus was faced with a disaster area in religious terms.

The words used by Matthew suggest a condition of ill-treatment and weariness ("harassed"). Significantly, this same evangelist informs us that unbearable burdens were imposed on the shoulders of the people (23:4), and that Jesus addressed himself "to you who are tired and heavily loaded" (11:28)—they can find relief in his "light" burden. Furthermore, the people were lying down, prostrate, without energy or initiative; they had no religious/spiritual dynamism or enthusiasm, no liveliness; they were "dejected." Those responsible for such a condition are not hard to find; they are the religious leaders of the time, and first of all the Pharisees, who "were seated on Moses' (teaching) chair...and had bound up heavy loads hard to carry" (Matthew 23:2, 4). With their meticulous rules and legalistic observances, they had turned religion into a ritualistic practice: the result was a complete ignorance of the basic concepts about God on the part of the people, and a lack of fervor and initiative in religious matters. The crowds looked very much "like sheep who have no shepherd."

Their real and true shepherd made His appearance just now. "All those who came before me are thieves and robbers" (John 10:8). By a negative description of the situation, Matthew conveys the message that it is Christ who is the real shepherd of the harassed and dejected crowds. As a matter of fact, whereas the Pharisees did nothing to alleviate the burden they imposed on others' shoulders, Jesus was "deeply moved" at the sight of the people's condition. The term used by the evangelist, with its Hebrew background, signified a deep and tender loving emotion springing up from the very roots of man's being; He really cares. The comparison to "the sheep that have no shepherd" refers the reader to Ezekiel 34:5, 8 from which it derives and to the entire context. The prophet describes the state of affairs in which the sheep had "become food to all the beasts of the field, and were scattered." This is why Yahweh swears by himself that "I will set one shepherd over them, and he shall feed them, my Servant David; he shall feed them, and he shall be their shepherd" (v. 23). Jesus is, therefore, portrayed as the "messianic" shepherd of the prophetic promises.

Interestingly enough, the care and love of the messianic shepherd for his sheep does not consist in his missionary activity but in the fact that he sets up a group of "laborers" to bring in the harvest. The image has shifted;

the basic concept remains. The laborers in the fields are, in fact, shepherds whom Christ appoints for his flock. When Jesus leaves this world, he appoints Simon, son of John, as shepherd to "tend my flock" (John 21:15ff.; see 4:35-38). This is what Matthew describes in another way.

As a matter of fact, immediately afterwards, Jesus sets up the body of The Twelve, Simon being the "first," and he associates them to his missionary activity by first sending them to the "sheep" of the Jewish people, who were "lost." And he commanded them to "proclaim" the same message that he did: "the kingdom of heaven is at hand" and to do the same thing that he did, such as to cure sick people. Later on The Twelve and others will be sent on a universal mission that will include Samaritan and pagan territories. This is how Matthew teaches us that the missionary activity of the Church was devised by the messianic Shepherd as the continuation and perpetuation of his own shepherding care and love.

Twelfth Sunday in Ordinary Time

Matthew 10:26-33

The setting of this section of the gospel (Matthew 10:26-33) is the missionary activity of Christ's disciples in a hostile world, which implies trials as well as both popular and official persecution. That is why the encouragment "do not be afraid" is repeated no less than three times (vvs. 26, 28, 31) in a few verses; it is a fear of men, the fear of both individuals and human institutions, that will oppose the Christian message.

Christ's missionaries are requested to overcome fear because theirs is a divine commission which is grounded on Christ's right, truthfulness, and missionary duties. It is a divine obligation, and God's rights come first (Acts 4:19, 5:29), with the result that man's threats and ill-treatment must be disregarded. The commission they receive is this: "Nothing is concealed that will not be revealed, and nothing hidden that will not become known." This sounds very much like a popular proverb, "everything will come out in the open." But it becomes a commandment when connected with the following sentence: "What I tell you in darkness, speak in the light; what is whispered in your ears, proclaim from the housetops." Again, the expressions are proverbial and hyperbolic: the secrets disclosed in the confidentiality of the night will be made public in the lively activity of daylight; what is strictly private and, therefore, whispered in one's ears, will be shouted from high places, where one can get the attention of the crowds. The reference is to the more private teaching and confidential information that Christ imparted to his intimate disciples. They were told all this, not for their personal knowledge or use, but for the purpose that it might one day be proclaimed in the open places of the entire world with all available means of mass media, be it filmstrips, radio or TV. This is a commandment they received from Christ.

Such public proclamation of the Christian message will get the messengers into trouble. It is the loss of their life that is at stake; it is a martyr's death that is contemplated. But "do not be afraid of those who kill one's body but cannot kill one's soul." The choice is between what is less and what is more, what is good and what is best: between man's physical life (body) and his true, lasting life (soul). The Christian messenger is often confronted with this choice: the choice is inevitable; the right choice is all that is left. "What profit is it to gain the whole world and forfeit one's (true and real) life?" (Matthew 16:26) Such being the case, a man should disregard his fear and focus on the realization that his commission comes from God. What will God's reaction be if the messenger does not convey the message? The anger of God is much more to be feared. In his hands are both man's "body and soul," physical and true/lasting life. It is God, not man, who is to be feared.

The fear of God is very healthy; there is nothing un-Christian about it (Acts 9:31; Romans 11:20; 2 Corinthians 7:1; 1 Peter 1:17; 2:17). It is not the last word in man's relationship with God, but it is the "beginning of wisdom," and it is a part of man's filial attitude towards God and a part of man's love for God. Love without regard, respect and fear gradually degenerates into careless and negligent overconfidence. On the other hand, a healthy fear of God is founded on man's concern— that he may be unfaithful to a God who came so close to man in salvation history, and who came particularly close in Christ. Man must be all the more concerned about his relationship with God if he has been chosen by God to deliver his message of salvation. That is why, in the straits of the Christian mission, the messenger has to watch his relationship with God much more closely than his relationship with men.

After all, fear of God is uplifted into confidence in his providence. The life of Christian missionaries, like everything else, is in God's hands and at his service, at the service of his universal plan. Nothing escapes God's control; nothing is going to happen against or over his sovereign power and rule. Even the fate of the sparrows is in God's hands: none fall to the earth (Amos 3:5) without God consenting to it. And a Christian apostle is much more valuable to God than many sparrows; the implication being that God is much more concerned about them than about sparrows. This is no blank guarantee that nothing will happen. What it does mean is that whatever happens is under God's control, and the Christian messenger sustains it in the line of duty at God's service and, in this sense, in compliance with his will and wishes.

The same concept is stressed in another proverbial saying: without God's consent, no one will be able to seize you by your hair to the law-court or to death and pull it in the process. Not one hair will be lost without

God's knowledge and consent. Whenever—in his wisdom—God may consent to it, man in general, and a Christian messenger in particular, must "love" God also with "all his life" (Mark 12:30; Deuteronomy 6:5). Such a conviction, however, should spur Christians to the awareness that their sacrifice is valuable; it is valuable to God.

Christ is directly involved in all this matter. The Christian mission, with all that it entails, is a question of loyalty and faithfulness to Christ himself. Here he appears, however, not as the master who teaches his missionaries, but as the supreme judge of the world who, in the future, will evaluate the behavior of his envoys and messengers. By giving in to the fear of men in human law-courts, Christian missionaries may "disown" Christ and deny that they are Christians. These same missionaries will also be disowned by Christ in the law-court of "my Father in heaven" on the last day. Christ will say that they do not belong to him; they are not genuine "Christians," since no one can boast of being a Christian unless he is able to "hate" (value less than something else) his own life (Luke 14:26; Matthew 10:39). On the contrary, in the heavenly law-court, Christ will acknowledge those who acknowledge him in human law-courts, even when they are faced with death itself. Acknowledgment is recognition, avowal and oath of belonging to someone, to Christ in this case. It is a praise and thanksgiving for what God and Christ have done for a person. Such is the attitude that Christ expects of his "Christians" in law-courts; such is the attitude the faithful Christian can expect of Christ in God's law-court.

Thirteenth Sunday in Ordinary Time

Matthew 10:37-42

The entire chapter 10 of Matthew's gospel is devoted to missionary matters. To his missionary disciples, the Lord declares that no one should be misled. He is the

"Prince of Peace" (Isaiah 9:5); and yet it is war ("sword") —not peace—that he brought to the world (v. 34). Of course, this is not Mohammed's holy war or any other kind of "crusade," conducted and fought in the name of religion. Rather, the idea is that Jesus wants the service of his messengers. Yet he warns them that the sword, hatred and persecution will come their way: that is all he immediately has to offer to those whose service he is requesting.

He brings war to the world, because his message and the demands of his message divide and separate the tightest relationships in human society and arouse the hottest and most deep-seated passions. Son and father, daughter and mother, and in-laws will be in hot confrontation over Christ and his teaching (v. 35), first of all because of the binding and religious duties that a commitment to Christ involves; they reach and affect the deepest recesses of man's very being: the gospel is inviolable. Christ is the bearer of God's word, and "God's word is sharper than any two-edged sword; it penetrates and divides soul and spirit, joints and marrow" (Hebrews 4:12; Ephesians 6:17). No wonder it divides the members of a family! Christ's calling and teaching may confront man with a difficult choice, but there is no alternative: the sword of Christ's word will cut the bonds of blood relationships and then, the killing sword of war (persecution) will be the lot of Christians in general and of missionaries in particular: "one's enemies will be his own relatives" (see Mark 13:12f.).

It is this setting which determines the meaning of another stern statement of Jesus: when the struggle arises, "he who loves his father or mother more than me is not worthy of me, and he who loves son and daughter more than me is not worthy of me" (v. 37). The natural love among relatives is not blamed; nor is the reference to the natural tenderness and emotions of family love, as if

Christ demanded what in fact is unnatural. Rather, the term used here stresses the concept of friendly love that is grounded on frank openness, common ideals and loyal commitment to common interests. What Christ teaches is that if and when in this area it comes down to a choice between himself and even one's closest relatives, he does not tolerate any alternative choice: it has got to be him and nobody else, come what may. This is what it means to be a "Christian," to belong to Christ. If one is not able to accept this, then he is not a Christian: "he is not worthy of me," of what I am, of what I stand for, nor of being associated with me. Christ is the inflexible champion of the fourth commandment of the Decalogue against the rationalizing of the Pharisees (Mark 7:10-13), but he knows that man's loyalty must go, first of all, to God, and he is aware that loyalty to God also implies loyalty to himself. He refers to what God is doing for man in Christ, which is much more than relatives do: who can be worthy of God's and Christ's initiatives and accomplishments? Accepting a man as a "Christian" is a condescension of Jesus to man.

Being a Christian is a demanding honor. Christ's dignity demands that anyone who associates with him as a "Christian" must take up his own cross and follow him (v. 38). Christ had not yet been crucified; but his message is that being a Christian, of necessity, requires that his follower be ready to undergo the shameful, dishonorable and painful death of a common criminal. For when the other alternative is Christ, success in escaping physical death, with all the shame, pain, dishonor and "civil death" that it entails, is no advantage: it carries with it the loss of the true life in eternal damnation. The true "winners" are those who accept the "loss" of all worldly things: fame, dignity and life included.

At the end of his missionary discourse, Matthew (v. 40) turns his thought once more to the ideas leading into it (9:37—10:5). His missionaries are his delegates, ultimately they are delegates of God himself, since they convey the message or calling of God to mankind. This is why receiving the missionaries amounts to receiving Christ and God (see Galatians 4:14; John 13:20). Judaism knew the institution of the "envoy," who was an envoy or ambassador who possesses full authority in a juridical capacity to represent the one who sent him. A rule in rabbinic sources states that "a man's envoy is like to himself." The statements following these above in Matthew's account (v. 41f.), however, show that receiving the apostles is not restricted to just accepting their message, but includes accepting them as bearers of God's message in their human condition and, therefore, with their human needs. They should not be ashamed of needing support because "the workman is worth his keep" (v. 10). Not only that, they must know that God and Christ are committed to those who help in supporting them; their missionary needs, after all, do not cause any harm or loss to anyone. A service done to a Christian missionary is in no way less deserving than services done to prophets or righteous men in general. God rewards a man who "receives" a prophet because of his dignity as a prophet (see 1 Kings 17:9-24; 2 Kings 4:8-37), with a gift commensurate to the prophetic dignity; he who "receives" a righteous man will be rewarded in proportion to a righteous man's dignity. And whoever does the least of services (cup of water) to any Christian ("one of these lowly ones") —precisely because he is a Christian ("disciple"), namely a man of the Messiah—will certainly receive a greater reward—eternal life (Matthew 25:40). How much more so those who "receive" the very messengers of the Messiah?

Among other things, the boldness and assurance with which Christ claims total and absolute allegiance to himself is striking: service, loyalty, suffering, and life. And he demands this allegiance with complete disregard of any other possible claims by others, such as father, mother, etc. Christ claims to be the first absolutely, and he does not tolerate—not only relegation to the second position—but even competition for the top place.

The only obvious inference is that Jesus points to something beyond the external appearance of his person. This is the only reason why he can link eternal life or death with allegiance to himself: his word is a divine word.

Fourteenth Sunday in Ordinary Time
Matthew 11:25-30

The background of the section of the gospel in Matthew 11:25-30 is the failure of Christ in his ministry. His preaching, his word and his very person were rejected by the "learned" of the world. The learned are, first of all, the Pharisees who "are seated on the chair of Moses" (23:2) and, in Luke's understanding (11:52), have claimed for themselves "the key of knowledge," with the result that they neither enter the kingdom themselves nor let others in. Later on Paul elaborates on the same subject (1 Corinthians 1:19f.). It is the "innocent" or childlike that have come to believe in Christ, in his mission and in his word. The childlike are those who are unspoiled by learning: God is pleased with them. But they came to believe because "your eyes look intently and your ears listen" (Matthew 13:16); in other words, they pay attention and want to learn—and not to question, because they humbly and candidly trust Christ.

Their attitude teaches us how God "reveals" or "conceals." The perspective is highly theological and views things from God's side. The fact that some came to accept Christ and all that he means is evidence that God's assistance and help could and did lead them to the goal he pointed out to them from the very start. The fact that others failed to believe in Christ is evidence that God's assistance and help could not (and factually did not) lead them to the same goal. In the former case, God's assistance was not stopped or thwarted because "your eyes looked intently and your ears listened"; they opened to God's initiative and cooperated with it. Thus from man's viewpoint, they came to "know the mysteries" (Matthew 13:11); from God's viewpoint he "revealed" the mysteries to them. In the latter case (those who failed to believe), God's assistance was stopped by man's rejection; they do not cooperate with God's initiative to lead them to the goal; they refuse to look intently and to listen carefully. Thus from man's viewpoint, they refuse to reach the goal; from God's viewpoint, he "conceals" the goal, in the sense that he, in fact, fails to reveal the mysteries to them. By his initiative, God offered Christ's gift to all, both to those who happened to accept him and to those who happened to reject him: his grace and assistance were offered to all, but some accepted it and some rejected it—freely and willingly. Of course, "these things" that are revealed or concealed are Christ's significance and activity as God's envoy: the future world of God is manifested on earth in Jesus. In Jesus' words and deeds, the mystery of God's kingdom is disclosed and unveiled, but only the "innocent" grasp it.

It happened this way because such was God's "pleasure": this is how God wanted his plan of salvation to succeed. The emphasis falls—not on the fact that the learned rejected God's initiative—but on the factual reality that God's plan succeeded through the collaboration of the innocent. This was good enough for God. The theological perspective pointed out above is at work here also: it is not his pleasure that some reject his plan (and perish), but it is his pleasure that some accept it (and be saved). The latter are those who are held in contempt by men. Christ, in his turn, praises God for his wisdom. And it is more than praise: it is a "confession," it is a committing of oneself to God's plan and action. After all, Christ himself is the first of the "innocent" or unlearned; he is misunderstood, rejected and persecuted by the "learned" of the world.

In reality, in spite of the fact that "the Son" is the supreme Lord of the world because the Father already gave everything into his hands (see 28:18) here on earth, and of the fact that the Son displays his power in revealing mysteries and performing miracles—men fail to recognize him; no one knows the Son except the Father. In biblical language, "knowing" is not just having intellectual knowledge about something or someone; it connotes the concept of vital experience in interrelationship, interaction, care, love and concern. The Father has an experience of the Son in their mutual interaction, which then results in care, love and concern. This is also true of the fact that, in his turn, the Son knows the Father; and it is for this that he reveals the Father to others (open to his revelation) who in this way have an experience of the Father themselves. The learned Pharisees do not "know" what God is like; they have no experience of what God really is, because they refuse to accept his revelation of himself in Christ.

That is why Jesus now turns to the victims of this false religiosity which includes no "knowledge" of God. They are the ones who are overwhelmed by the heavy "loads" (Matthew 23:4) of legalistic imposition laid on them by the Pharisees. They are the same people as the "innocent," the people hated by the Pharisees as men who "are ignorant of the Law and accursed" (John 7:49). Whereas the Pharisees refuse God's knowledge by rejecting Jesus, Jesus' call of the innocent declares that he is the deliverer of those who are oppressed under the "yoke" of the legalistic system of the Pharisaic religiosity. To them he offers relief and rest, which are the equivalent of "peace." These notions denote a new relationship with God: in the joy of God's presence and forgiveness, insecurity and anguish are overcome. The relief and rest of Christ consist in another "yoke"; but this yoke is not just light, it is "sweet": at Jesus' school, man can learn without effort, without unbearable loads; his teaching is joy for "my commands are not heavy" (1 John 5:3). They are light and sweet, not because they are not demanding, but because they are the expression of God's and of Christ's love for man (John 14:21), and they convey the "knowledge" of God's helping interaction.

At this point, Jesus clearly discloses that he himself is one of the "meek" and the "humble" of the world, which is a reference to the spirit of the beatitudes (Matthew 5:3, 5). The inference is that he himself is completely in God's hands; he is unsuccessful, rejected by all, persecuted, on his way to the cross—and yet, enjoying the "knowledge" of the Father. He knows, by experience, what the sweetness of his yoke means. In contrast with Sirach 51:23, 26f. (31, 34f.), Jesus brings all those who labor under the Law from their toil to his rest. And when he calls them to follow and to imitate him, he proposes to them the model of Someone in whom the "lawyers" stumble, but to whom the innocent listen and whom they follow. The meekness of Christ here is the same attitude that he displayed in his passion (Matthew 21:5; Zechariah 9:9): the king who enters Jerusalem is anything but a royal ruler, he is "poor" and despised; and he enters the royal city to undergo suffering and death.

Fifteenth Sunday in Ordinary Time

Matthew 13:1-23

At a certain point in his ministry, Jesus resorted to parables as a new method to teach the Jewish crowds.

Such an initiative startled even the closest disciples: "Why do you teach them in parables?" Obviously there has been a change in Jesus' approach to his ministry. The change has to be explained in terms of the Jewish attitude towards Christ. In the foregoing chapter 12, Matthew describes in several ways, the bitter clash between Jesus and Judaism; they have already come to the point of making plans to kill him (v. 14). Jesus' reaction is a certain withdrawal or restraint. He continues to help people with his miracles but he orders them not to expose him (v. 17). At this point, the evangelist, quoting a text from Isaiah (42:1-4), teaches that in spite of the opposition "the Servant" has to carry on his teaching ministry, but without quarrels or strife: "he will proclaim justice to the gentiles, he will not contend or cry out, nor will his voice be heard in the streets." Even more, the Servant will exploit every possible change in order to fulfill his ministry and try to inflame even the slightest spark of hope left: "the bruised reed he will not crush, the smoldering wick he will not quench until judgment (God's law/instruction) is made victorious." At the beginning of his ministry, Jesus acted freely and spoke more clearly about himself and his teaching; his light dazzled the Jewish religious' "eyes" and was opposed. Yet he wants to keep in touch with the Jewish audience in the hope that an "indirect" light can bring some clarity to them. This is why Christ resorts to teaching in parables or comparisons, suggesting rather than disclosing ideas—the parables are a more obscure tool than plain and direct language (this does not mean that *all* parables in the gospel serve this purpose: see Matthew 13:35).

As a matter of fact, Christ begins his teaching by parables with the parable of the sower, which is an assessment of his ministry up to that point: most of the "seed"/preaching was wasted. With the new method, things can hardly improve, but it is not his fault. He wants his message to be received; in fact his closest disciples receive it and "in private he explains/interprets everything to them" (Mark 4:34), and in this sense "the knowledge of the mysteries of the kingdom is granted to them" (Matthew 13:11). But the reason for this is that "your eyes look intently and your ears listen"; they believe Jesus and pay attention to what he teaches and they take an interest in it. Thus it happens that in addition to what they have, both from the Old Testament and from previous instructions of Jesus, they are given more and more; they will have plenty, "He who has will be given and become rich."

It is not said, however, that Jesus preaches just for his disciples, or that he does not want others to be given the mysteries. The opposite is clear by the mere fact that he does preach. The point is that the Jewish people, particularly the Pharisees, see what is going on (miracles), but they do not look at it intently (to grasp its significance, see 12:22-32). They hear what Jesus teaches, but they do not listen, nor do they try to understand its value and meaning (see 12:3-14, 41-42; 8:3-8). Rather, they distort everything: they are dazzled by the light. Thus it happens that "he who does not have will be deprived even of what he has": he who does not get—open up to—the increasing revelation of Christ will lose even what he had from the Old Testament and from previous teachings of Jesus. When confronted with God's gifts, man cannot be selective: he either receives everything or loses everything. This is exactly the same experience that St. John reports using different terms. The Pharisees had "sight," but when they reject Christ's light they become "blind" (John 9:39-41); they lose that sight they had, "he who denies the Son does not have the Father either" (1 John 2:23). This is how "they are not given the mysteries of the kingdom"; they are not receptive.

Once more, the same reality is looked at from the viewpoints of both man and God. From man's viewpoint, the Jewish crowds are guilty and responsible for their opposition to Christ and for the ensuing result that Jesus resorts to a less clear teaching in parables—which in its turn will lead to even less understanding and to increasing obstinacy on the part of the Jews. From the viewpoint of God, his revelation through Christ did not bring about faith in the Jewish audience, and in this sense, he denied to them a gift which they were not open to receive —God denies them "the knowledge of the mysteries." On the other hand, Jesus' disciples are receptive (their eyes looked intently, etc.) and thus God's revelation brings about faith and the gift of knowledge of the mysteries. God is ready and willing to give, but man can reject or accept his gift.

This is what the long quotation from Isaiah (6:9f.) means. In sending his prophet, the Lord really wants his people to heed his message; but he knows that in their obstinacy, they won't. They will certainly hear the message, but they will not open their understanding to it; they will see clearly, but they will refuse to have any "insights" into the matter, "because the heart of this people has become insensitive/thick; as to their ears, they are hard of hearing, they have shut their eyes tightly—so as not to see with their eyes, hear with their ears and understand with their hearts, and convert." If they don't have any insights and do not listen or understand, it is their fault; they more or less actively refuse to do so. That is why the reaction of the Lord is: "and shall I heal them?" If they refuse to be healed, God gives them up to their own wishes. This was true at the time of the prophet, and God's words are fulfilled "again" and "to a greater degree" in the case of Christ's fuller revelation. If he resorts to the veiled language of the parables, it is their fault; and thus their prospects of healing are dimmer and dimmer ("shall I heal them?"). For the measure of man's guilt is the amount of God's gift.

Note that those who refuse to accept the seed/word sown by Christ do so because they yield to the suggestions of the Evil One, or because of setbacks or persecutions which occur in connection with the word, or because of worldly anxiety or love of money. Man is always open to such dangers.

Sixteenth Sunday in Ordinary Time
Matthew 13:24-43

The hardening attitude of the Jewish masses leads Christ to resort to teaching through parables and comparisons in order to keep in touch with an increasingly hostile audience. Many of the parables in Matthew's chapter 13, however, serve to illustrate the nature of God's kingdom. One of them is the parable of the weeds sown in with the wheat. The point of the parable is that confronting God/Christ, who sows the wheat (the good seed), there is "his enemy." It is not disclosed who the enemy is, but it is not hard to figure out when one realizes that in Hebrew "satan" means enemy or opponent, and it is from this term that the word Satan comes. Another point of the parable is that there is good seed but there also is bad seed (weeds) in the kingdom of God. Not everything in the kingdom of God is absolutely good and safe. Within the context of Jesus' ministry, this means that the unbelieving "weeds" in the people of God are the crop which springs from a seed other than Christ's word, or in general, from God's word, namely the seed of Satan. In the people/kingdom where God's word is supposed to be the rule, Satan, the opponent, has his following. The fourth evangelist does not hesitate to label the unbelieving Jews as children of Satan (John 8:38, 44; see v. 42). Within the context of the early Church, the same concept indicated that in the Christian community also there were both good Christians and poor Christians. But there will be a day of reckoning. And this is a third point in the parable, namely the so-called "harvest," which is a traditional metaphor for the day of judgment. Yet the idea of a judgment that takes place at the time of man's decision is clearly suggested.

The owner of the field rejects the suggestion of pulling up the weeds. The reason he gives is that the wheat might be pulled up together with them. Thus he puts off the whole work of separation until harvest time. One wonders why God permits so much evil in the world and particularly in his "kingdom." Other sayings point out that sufficient time of repentance and conversion is allowed by God: the present text discloses another point of view. Pulling up the weeds means, of course, their death. Thus God refuses to destroy evil and evildoers because an anticipated end of the world would also entail the destruction of all the good that God purposes to get from this world. Good and evil, therefore, will live together until the day of definitive separation at the end.

This parable finds a complement in vvs. 36-43: it is a complement rather than an explanation. As a matter of fact, as it has been pointed out, the explanation is incorporated into the parable itself. The complement, however, brings in new concepts, such as the Son of Man and the end of the world, that bring its apocalyptic and eschatological perspective into the open. This complement emphasizes the point of the parable: the definitive separation of good and evil men will take place at the last judgment. It is the Son of Man, namely Jesus, already constituted supreme judge and ruler in his glorification, who will conduct this judgment (Matthew 25:31-36) through his angels. The complement also discloses that the wheat and the weeds are two kinds of religious men (not two different "words"), namely those who effectively belong to the kingdom ("sons") and those who belong to Satan. In addition, it discloses that the evildoers (weeds) are active in this world: they are stumbling blocks for the others. This is why they are "children" of Satan; they are his breed and promote his interests. Therefore, they are sent to the fiery furnace (see Daniel 3:6), where the punishment is certainly severe and drives one to despair—to wail and grind one's teeth. The happiness of the righteous is described here as splendor and light, because just as darkness expresses estrangement from God so splendor and brightness express closeness to him. God is light (1 John 1:5), and his splendor is reflected on all those he has brought into his realm (see Matthew 17:2; Colossians 1:12; 1 Timothy 6:16; 1 Peter 1:9; Revelation 1:16; 21:23)—"the kingdom of their father."

Two other parables are added in order to illustrate "how it happens with the kingdom of heaven": it happens as with the mustard seed and with the yeast kneaded into flour. The idea common to these two parables or comparisons is this: what great results can be accomplished by an apparently small cause; which, in turn, discloses how powerful the small cause really is. The tall tree (springing from a small seed) is a traditional symbol for vast and powerful kingdoms (Daniel 4:9, 18; Ezekiel 17:23, 31f.). The kingdom of heaven also grows and encompasses heaven and earth. Still, his beginning is so humble: the preaching of Christ, or rather Christ himself who, alone, at a given moment was the synthesis of the true kingdom of God. The point of comparison in the parable of the yeast is the pervading and transforming power of a small amount of yeast, which can ferment great amounts of flour. The humble word of Christ gradually but surely pervades the entire world and transforms it in the process. Christ's word may appear insignificant and weak, and yet it unleashes such a power that it can no longer be contained: it grows into the all-embracing kingdom of God.

At this point another reason is given why Christ speaks in parables. He is the teacher foretold in Psalm 78:2: by means of comparisons and illustrations taken from everyday life, Christ discloses hidden mysteries involved and concealed in his person and in his preaching —namely the active presence of God at work in man's world, who commits all his power to the definitive establishment of his kingdom/rule of love and forgiveness over mankind, in spite of the opposition he encounters.

Seventeenth Sunday in Ordinary Time

Matthew 13:44-52

By several comparisons, Matthew illustrates, in chapter 13, the nature of God's kingdom and rule. The nature of God's kingdom should determine, of course, man's attitude towards it. It is within this setting and for the same purpose that three more parables are added. The kingdom/rule of heaven is like a treasure in the field; or like a fine pearl; or, again, like a dragnet that is cast into the sea.

The comparison of God's kingdom or rule with a treasure or fine pearl is inspired by the Old Testament sapiential literature, where the divine Wisdom is said to be the most precious treasure or pearl (Proverbs 8:11, 18f.; 2:4; 3:15; Job 28:18, etc.). The basic message of the two parables or comparisons is that God's kingdom and rule is so valuable that everything else must be sacrificed for it. The emphasis of the message does not fall upon the value of the kingdom—which is taken for granted—but on sacrificing everything else for it. The notion of value is just a parabolic trait, that is, it belongs to the pictorial representation. As a matter of fact, the kingdom is not a value; it is not a valuable or good "thing": it is rather a matter of the direct or close relationship of one person with another, of man with God. In order to achieve the correct relationship with God, man is required to sacrifice his entire life and being—"to sell everything he has"—which is the characteristic of a true discipleship. God's kingdom and rule are "worth" such a sacrifice.

In addition, the kingdom must be "found"; it is for those to whom the mysteries of the kingdom have been given (Matthew 11:25, 27; 13:11). Here, however, there is a difference between these two parables. In the parable of the pearl, the merchant "looks for" pearls; he tries to find them: whereas, in the other case, it is by chance that the man in question comes upon a hidden treasure, apparently unknown to everyone. One could think of how, in Jesus' words, the kingdom came to sinners and tax collectors, who couldn't care less about it, and to some pious Jews, such as John the Baptizer's disciples, who concerned themselves with a "preparation" for the kingdom.

Did the man who found the treasure act shrewdly—but unjustly? The laws of antiquity regulating such matters are not altogether clear to us. But the teaching of the parable lies elsewhere, namely in the "grotesque" picture. In regard to the kingdom, man should be as greedy/eager, shrewd and astute as those who are out to amass only the goods of this world (see Luke 16:8). In both cases also, "joy" is the natural result of the "finding" and possessing. Joy and occultation (hidden mystery) are features of Jesus and of his message.

The third parable, the dragnet thrown in the sea, conveys the same basic teaching as the parable of the weeds (13:24-30). In this world, the kingdom of God embraces both good and bad "subjects," but on the day of reckoning a complete separation will be conducted. Whereas the emphasis of the parable of the weeds falls on the growth (until the end), in the case of the dragnet, the emphasis falls on the end itself, when the separating operation is conducted. The parabolic image, of course, speaks of fish and fishermen, but it is obvious that the reference is to the "fishers of men" (Matthew 4:19), who catch men in the net of the Christian mission. The missionaries bring in men of all sorts. Even among Jesus' converts there was a Judas. Only the last judgment will disclose those who are "righteous," because those who are wicked will be picked up and hurled into "the fiery furnace," where severe torment and despair will make them grind their teeth.

At the end of his lengthy teaching, by means of these several parables, the Lord wants to make sure that the meaning of his words is clear to his disciples. This only underscores the reason why "to those" outsiders he speaks in parables (13:10ff.). Jesus' disciples ask him the meaning of the parables (v. 36); they want to learn. And Jesus adds illustrating parables upon parables in order to bring his thought into sharper and sharper focus, in order for them to see clearly. Their eyes look intently and their ears listen (13:16); thus they come to understand. Christ wants the others to understand also, but they fail to do so because of their ill-disposition toward Jesus and their lack of interest: they don't ask, their eyes do not look intently and their ears do not listen.

It is only natural that Jesus takes particular interest in the understanding of his own disciples. They have to become "scribes" instructed for the kingdom, i.e., instructed to be at the service of the kingdom, which implies an instruction in the matters of the kingdom. Judaism had many scribes, but no "scribe for the kingdom." This is a new dimension of evangelic ministers, which derives from the nature of Christ's ministry and person: the kingdom was and is grounded on Jesus himself. He remains the "rabbi," the only rabbi/teacher in the Christian community (Matthew 23:8-10), whereas his apostolic ministers must be scribes or brothers who teach what the leader taught. The head of a household has in store old and new things. Life is not disruptive, but is rather continuation and renewal; and so he administers and uses old things with the touch of new ones. This is exactly what Jesus did in his teaching through parables: he resorted to old images of common life; such as sowing, harvest, mustard seed, dough, fishing, etc., as well as to images and texts from the "Old" Testament (13:14f., 32, 35, 37, 41, 43, etc.). He wants his disciples to do the same thing: they see the old things in the new light of Christ's revelation.

Eighteenth Sunday in Ordinary Time

Matthew 14:13-21

The miracle was real and splendid. There were just five loaves and two fish, but "all" ate to their full satisfaction. Each loaf had been enough to feed one thousand men, besides a good number of women and children; and yet, at the end, no less than twelve full baskets of left-over portions (not fragments) were collected. As Jesus was "breaking" the bread, it was multiplying between his hands, before the eyes of the disciples and of the people. The disciples were taking the portions from his hands and serving them to the people; but when they were all satisfied, there were before Jesus still a good number of portions to be served, if needed. Jesus provided food easier and faster than his disciples could serve it, or the crowds eat it. This is an amazing abundance; it is the bounty of God himself. Jesus' stores are overflowing and inexhaustible. His is a creative power; and at his command/will matter is brought into being, just as it was at the beginning when God spoke his "word."

The multiplication of the loaves, as well as all other miracles on this occasion (v. 14), are a manifestation of superhuman power. It is also a manifestation of Jesus' human tenderness and living heart: "at the sight of so many people he was deeply moved with tender feelings and he cured their sick." And when the disciples tell him to dismiss the crowds that they may find food for themselves, Jesus' answer is that "they need not go"; meaning "why should I dismiss them?" And he directs his own to feed the crowds with the food supplies of the apostolic group (Jesus and his disciples) which happened to be neither uncommon nor overflowing. Still Jesus does not hesitate to skip his own meal to help others. The episode allows us a glimpse into Jesus' heart; it discloses to us how deeply human poverty, necessity and powerlessness touched him. It is this feeling of compassionate tenderness that prompts him to put his power at the service of man; and thereby, it becomes obvious to everyone that he overcomes the hunger of human masses as easily as he does individual sickness and even death. It is Jesus who supports man's life. John 6 develops this insight in considerable depth and breadth.

With its stinginess of detail, economy of words and calmness in expression, the narrative of Matthew has a ring of solemnity to it. It appears very much like an unfolding liturgical piece. Noticeably, the disciples call Jesus' attention to the fact that "the time ('hour') is 'already' past," an expression which does not necessarily mean that it is late, nor is this its usual meaning. The time within which a given action was supposed to be done is over, or the hour to start doing something is already past. Obviously, the people had been with Jesus for some time ("already"). Thus, the time for the instruction is finished, and the time for supper ("evening") has "already" come. But Jesus does not "dismiss" the people in the congregation with just the nourishment of instruction: why should I dismiss them? Now he invites them to a banquet that only his power can provide.

The disciples had mentioned, not only bread but also fish. Still, when the food is served, it is only the bread that remains in the narrative: Jesus "broke and gave the loaves to his disciples and the disciples (gave them) to the people." Obviously, it is the bread that is the evangelist's focus of attention. The notion of "breaking" obviously applies, first of all, to the bread, and the same thing is true of the portions ("klasmata," pieces) collected in the baskets. At this point, the narrative points out minute details, irrelevant to the miracle as such. The Lord "takes" the food; looks up to heaven; pronounces the (Jewish) blessing over the food; breaks the bread; gives it to his disciples—and the disciples to the people. The language is eucharistic throughout, and the description spontaneously reminds one of the Last Supper.

Matthew certainly is reporting an event in Jesus' life. But he does so in the words of the liturgical celebration of his community, thereby suggesting again, that in the eucharistic celebration of the community, Christ, after having nourished them through his word, nourishes his followers with the bread that gives life—Christ's life—also to their bodies. This bread also multiplies in Christ's hands; it never comes to an end; Christ's supply is inexhaustible; it nourishes all without ever decreasing. He feeds "all," and all obtain complete satisfaction for their hunger, for their needs. It is Christ who—in the eucharistic meal—gives man the real nourishment he needs; and he does so abundantly. Christ can feed all, even beyond his community; and this is why "twelve" baskets full of portions are left over, as in reserve, for the "twelve tribes," i.e., for the totality of the people, the totality of mankind. Christ does not want the people to leave, or to be "dismissed," he wants to nourish them himself; this is why he keeps them. But now he nourishes his people through his "disciples," whose ministerial services he uses. It is he who performs the miracle by "breaking" the bread; but then he "gives" the broken bread to his ministers, who pass it on to the people—his people—who "follow him on foot" and gather around him from every town. It is the need of man that moves Christ to pity; and out of tender compassion, he prepares this nourishing miracle for his own.

Interestingly, the miracle is introduced with the remark that, as he received news that John had been beheaded, Jesus "withdrew by boat to a desert place." No doubt he left the territory under Herod's rule and went to the other shore of the lake outside Herod's dominions. Jesus felt that he was threatened. It is the theme of persecution that overshadows his life and foreshadows his tragic end. Calvary and the eucharist are inseparable, particularly in the liturgical eucharistic celebration.

Nineteenth Sunday in Ordinary Time

Matthew 14:22-33

Jesus had just fed the crowds by miraculously multiplying a few loaves (Matthew 14:14-21). Then he wanted to be alone; so he urged his disciples to get into the same boat that had brought them to this "out-of-the-way place" (v. 13). Of course, a miracle is going to happen, and the evangelist is preparing the stage for it. The multiplication of the loaves had taken place somewhere on the northern shore of the lake of Gennesareth. Christian tradition locates the spot in the northwestern corner of the northern shore line. The disciples, therefore, were to sail east in the direction of Capernaum. In any case, in John's narrative, the Lord is found in Capernaum after the episode of his walking on the waters of the Lake (John 6:21, 24, 59).

While his disciples got under way, Jesus dismissed the crowds, and then he climbed the mountain that rises from the shore of the lake; now he was alone by himself and prayed. The evangelist notes, that as night fell, Jesus was all alone. He will reappear in the "fourth watch of the night," that is between 3 and 6 a.m. (v. 25). Jesus used to spend the nights in the open; and no doubt this time also, his withdrawal was for him an opportunity both to pray and to rest. When Jesus was left alone, the disciples' boat was already several hundred yards out on the Lake; Jesus could see how rough the water was and how hard the disciples had to row. But he did nothing to change the route or to cancel the trip; the present difficulty offers him an opportunity to disclose his power and sovereign dominion to his disciples.

As a matter of fact, there are two focal points in this narrative: Peter's cry for help ("Lord, save me," v. 30), and the profession of faith by all the disciples ("you truly are the Son of God," v. 33). In this narrative, Peter is the symbol of all the disciples in danger. Of course, all of them were at the mercy of the storm; and all of them were "upset" by the sailing conditions and at the sight of what they took for a terrifying ghost; all of them "cried out of fear." At the end, the storm is also hushed for all of them. But it is Peter who finds himself closer to drowning than any of the others: he is out of the boat, at the mercy of the waves and of the wind. He exemplifies the disciples in threatening difficulties and dangers, as well as the powerless disciples in need of Jesus' help and salvation; Peter is often the spokesman of the other disciples, and here too, he is a spokesman of sorts.

Peter's crisis is presented as a crisis of faith. The threats of the waves and strong winds must have been clear to Peter even before he got out of the boat and, therefore, even before he asked Jesus to let him go and meet him. It is not a question of walking with Christ on the water of death; nor is it an echo of the Buddhist monk who can walk on the water as long as he can concentrate on his thought. The story of Peter is reported from the viewpoint of the outcome: Peter's cry for help. Peter has "little faith," he "doubts" (v. 31). The point is that true faith in Jesus (or God) disregards even the most adverse circumstances, which to man's understanding seem insurmountable or impossible. In his temptations, Jesus states that a man can live according to God's dispositions (Matthew 4:4), even if such dispositions are paradoxical and beyond the natural means man is familiar with. Peter's faith may have been very strong at the start, but as the danger grows more and more threatening, his faith weakens and doubt sets in: one ends up with "little faith." When faith in God's word fails, man is in trouble; he sinks and eventually he drowns.

It is at this point that Peter's story reaches its most dramatic point. It is from the depths of his absolute helplessness that Peter's faith springs more vigorous than ever; it is then that he realizes that salvation cannot be found in anyone else than Jesus: "where to go? It is you who have words of eternal life" (John 6:68). And so, in his complete powerlessness, Peter speaks for all the disciples and proclaims that Jesus is the savior: "Lord, save me!" (see Acts 4:12) This is the faith that Jesus wanted and expected in order to act. And Jesus "saves": he saves Peter—and all the others—by displaying his rule over creation.

The representation of Christ walking on rough water is reminiscent of some representations of God in the Old Testament: "You strode across the sea, you marched across the ocean" (Psalm 77:18); "at your reproof the waters took to flight...you imposed the limits they must never cross again" (Psalm 104:7, 9); "he trampled the Sea's tall waves" (Job 9:8). Jesus' walking on the water and his power in abating the storm are the same features that God shows throughout the Old Testament. Thus Jesus clearly brings into the open the presence of God at work in him and through him. This is the point that he wants to make. As a matter of fact, the climax of the narrative solemnly stresses that, after what Jesus has done—walking on the water, saving Peter, and hushing the storm—all the disciples "worshiped him." They formulated a profession of faith that prepares Peter's more solemn profession formula some time later (16:16): "you really are the Son of God" (v. 33). It is the faith of the Christian community that professes the divinity of its Lord in its worship. The entire setting of the episode, however, shows that this narrative understands the divinity of Christ in terms of a helping God, who stretches his hand to those who are in danger and "saves" those who are hopelessly lost.

Twentieth Sunday in Ordinary Time

Matthew 15:21-28

Once more, the first evangelist wants his readers to understand the power of faith in Jesus and how Jesus gives in to the wishes of those who believe in him. This time, both ideas are all the more strongly emphasized since it is a pagan (non-Jewish) individual who believes in Jesus and is granted a miracle.

Jesus goes beyond the boundaries of the Jewish land and enters "the areas of Tyre and Sidon," an expression of Old Testament flavor, that denotes the pagan world: if the miracles performed in Chorazin and Bethsaida "had been performed in Tyre and Sidon" they would have converted long ago (Matthew 11:21). The narrative of the "Canaanite" woman from that area shows, in fact, that there was more faith in the pagan lands of Tyre and Sidon than on Jewish soil. In Luke 4:25f., Jesus points out that it was a widow in the area of Sidon who believed the prophet Elijah, and was granted a wonderful miracle—even though there were "many widows in Israel." In her relationship to Jesus, the Canaanite woman "from the areas of Tyre and Sidon" is the counterpart of that other woman who experienced Elijah's favor. The woman of the gospel is characterized by Matthew as a "Canaanite";

with its Old Testament overtones, the term stresses the concept of contempt and hatred which the Jews felt for the old inhabitants of their land.

From the very start, the unbelieving "pagan" woman manifests an amazing, almost "Christian" faith: "Lord, Son of David—she says—have pity on me." If she does not confess that he is supreme Lord/Ruler of the universe, she does confess that Jesus is the Messiah of Jewish expectations. But her faith is not just theoretical; she knows that he can help in a hopeless situation; that is, after all, the reason why she comes to him. At the end of the episode, Jesus will praise her "great faith." But this faith is already manifest at the outset; the narrative only discloses, as it unfolds, how firm and strong that faith was.

Christ's attitude suggests that he wanted to give the woman an opportunity to unveil all the strength of her powerful faith. This is what the readers of the gospel should learn. The first time, Jesus does not even bother to acknowledge the woman's request or her confession: "he answered her not a word." As she insisted, it is the disciples who intervene: "Dismiss her (granting her request) because she is shouting after us." It is not a suggestion of compassion but of impatience and selfishness. Matthew teaches us that the woman's faith was great enough to overcome this also. Jesus reacts to the request of his disciples, but it is a negative answer. He refuses to grant the request: "my mission regards the lost sheep of Israel," not the pagans. Thereby, the evangelist stresses once more that the woman was a pagan; she was not an heir of God's favors and gifts. The remark, however, will only heighten the condescension of a compassionate Messiah. As a matter of fact, the mere reference to the "sheep" of Israel connotes that the Messiah is a shepherd, and this is a notion that suggests concepts of love, affection, care and compassion. Christ's heart begins to soften.

The natural steadiness of a feminine heart when in distress and in search of help is the best ally of the woman's faith—a faith which now comes into the open all the more forcefully. She comes up and is now kneeling at Jesus' feet; her request is no longer for compassion in general (v. 22), but she sharpens and personalizes her distress: "Help me, Lord!" The "Canaanite" pagan woman now speaks in the language of the Psalms, where help is asked of Yahweh (Psalm 22:19f.; 79:9; etc.). Jesus must have been very pleased with the woman's strong display of faith, but he decides to strain it to the extreme with a refusal that contains a crude insult: "it is not fair to take the children's food and throw it to the dogs." Christ's sharp words offer the woman the best of opportunities to disclose all the strength of her faith. She accepts that she is not one of the "children"; she accepts that she may be a "dog." But even so, she insists that she has the rights of any dog; she accepts the fact that the "children" of the family have to get the best of the meal: "but even the dogs eat the scraps that fall from their master's table." This sounds very much like the "pearls thrown to the swine" (Matthew 7:6). The woman makes the readers of the gospel realize how much had been given to Israel, and how tenderly they had been treated by God (so many miracles in Chorazin and Bethsaida, Matthew 11:21). At the same time, she makes a confession of humility: as a hated and "impure" dog, she accepts the role of the "prodigal son" (Luke 15:12ff.) or the disobedient "younger" son (Matthew 21:30). But she wants to be treated as a dog and to get some of the scraps of the "wedding banquet" (Matthew 22:2ff.) that "the Son of David" so generously gives to the "children." The point is no longer the power of Christ to help (which was never in question), but the copious abundance of God's grace and the right that a pagan has to his gifts and, first of all, to his "compassion." Man's powerlessness and helplessness are the best titles that he can wield in order to touch God's heart.

Here is the climax of the narrative. What other proof of her unshakable faith could be required of the "pagan" woman? In the case of the Roman soldier, Jesus says that he "did not find such (strong) faith in Israel" (Matthew 8:10). In our narrative, the evangelist's meaning certainly is the same. After the test that Jesus administered to that great faith, he himself paid the highest tribute to the woman's unmovable faith in him: "O woman, great is your faith!" Christ's words are a splendid and praiseworthy recognition of something that the entire episode had demonstrated beyond any doubt. The faith of the woman "overpowers" Jesus, who now willingly grants the request. In spite of his mission, he is ready and willing to allow for exceptions whenever man's trust in him is such that it can convince Christ that the exception is God's will; when it is clear that God is at work there. For Jesus, God's will is the supreme rule.

Christ was "sent to the sheep of Israel." In his ministry, there was an order and a hierarchy of priorities that he had to comply with. His mission was universal, and as such, also encompassed the pagan world. But everything had to develop according to a plan which stressed what is "first" and what is second in chronological terms. But it is precisely this exclusion of the pagan mission from Christ's perspective, as well as the fact that pagans could be discriminated against as "dogs" which are evidence that the episode goes back to times before the Christian mission among pagans started, and even to a comparatively early stage in Christ's ministry.

Twenty-first Sunday in Ordinary Time

Matthew 16:13-20

At a certain point of his ministry, Jesus wanted to know to what extent his own disciples had pierced the mystery of his person. In pagan territory, in a place far from Jewish influence and prejudice (Caesaraea of Philippi), Jesus asked his closest disciples about what "the people" thought of him. There were many views: for some he was John the Baptizer ("redivivus"); for others Elijah who was supposed to reappear before the Messiah; for others Jeremiah or one of the old prophets who had come back to life. The variety of interpretations only underscores that Christ was an outstanding religious person who was difficult to characterize: his mystery was difficult to penetrate.

At this point, Jesus was not particularly interested in "the people." After all, he knew and taught that "the mysteries of the kingdom" are not given to the people but "to you" (Matthew 13:11), to his disciples, and that "no one knows the Son except the Father" (Matthew 11:27). That is why, in reference to the various opinions of the people, he asks his disciples: "but you yourselves—who do you say I am?" He wants to know how far his own ministry has disclosed the knowledge of the Father to his disciples. Interestingly, Jesus is described here as "the Son of Man," which characterizes the Messiah as the heavenly, universal judge of supreme authority, whom "the people" take for a simple man (this is what "son of man" means philologically). He is presented as universal and supreme judge because he is going to make use of his supreme authority (v. 18f.).

It is Peter who has the deepest insights into Jesus' mystery: "You are the Messiah, the Son of the living God." Peter's confession marks one of the peaks of the narrative. He has perceived that Jesus is above all other prophets and God's envoys: he is the Messiah, the object of Israel's expectation, the fulfillment of the prophetic dreams, the goal and end of salvation history and the subject of the entire Old Testament. Peter's confession, however, is phrased in supremely solemn words: "the Son of the living God." God is characterized as the "living God" on particularly serious occasions, when he plays an actual role as the active one, the judge, or the present one. In the understanding of the evangelist, Peter's insight into Christ has grasped the deepest reality of Jesus: his divine being and his vital relation with the living God. That is why Jesus understands that Peter has been given a "revelation," i.e., a share in God's very knowledge about the Son—"only the Father knows the Son." Such a knowledge could not come from Peter's merely human capabilities ("flesh and blood"). Peter "was given the knowledge of the mystery," no doubt because his eyes looked intently and his ears listened (Matthew 13:16) to what Jesus did and taught; he trusted Jesus absolutely. Peter may have been weak in his attitudes, but he had very clear ideas and very deep-seated convictions about Christ. It was these qualities which made him strong later on. It is this future strength that renders Peter worthy of Jesus' congratulations (blest) because his hopes are very good.

The other related climax of the narrative is Christ's reward to Peter for his brilliant profession of faith. It is a true reward: "in my turn." The Lord answers Peter's confession by bestowing upon him a new name, a new function and a new authority. The apostle's civil and official identity was Simon bar-Jona, but from now on, the apostle will be known by a new name, which is a functional name: Cephas. This is an Aramaic word which means "the rock," of which the Greek translation is "Petros," namely Peter. Thus Peter means "the rock": "you are Peter ("the rock") and it is on this rock (which is Peter) that I will build my church." Such is the new function bestowed upon Peter: as "the rock" that he is, he must carry a building and provide the solid foundation for it. The building is, of course, the Christian community. In the biblical language, a social unit is usually described as a building; think, v. gr., of "the house" of Israel, of Jacob, of Judah. In other passages, the Christian community is the "temple" of God (1 Corinthians 3:16; Ephesians 2:22; 1 Peter 2:5, "house"). Peter is a very strong and firm base: when a house was grounded on rock "rain came down, floods rose, gales blew and hurled themselves against that house, and it did not fall: it was founded on rock" (Matthew 7:25). By Jesus' choice and strengthening power, this is what "Peter" provides to "my Church": the Church may be assailed by all the powers of the "city of evil" ("gates of Hades"), the forces of Satan or Dragon (Revelation 20:7-10), but they will not prevail because it is founded on "the Rock." In Matthew 7:24f., the firmness of the "house" derives from the rock of man's faith in Jesus' words. The firmness of the Church derives from the rock of Peter's faith in Jesus' divinity.

Peter is also given a new authority. He is given the "keys" of the kingdom. The Pharisees had claimed for themselves "the key of knowledge" (Luke 11:52), and with this key of religious knowledge, far from opening the gates of the kingdom for themselves and for the others, they "locked them" (Matthew 23:13). They excluded themselves from the kingdom and prevented others from entering. Peter will be given these keys in order to open the kingdom to all who want to come in; he will do so by teaching the true knowledge of Christ's teaching and mystery. This is the same key that Christ himself uses for the same purpose. What follows, however, indicates that giving the key to someone connotes the idea of full authority in government (Revelation 3:7; Isaiah 22:22): "whatever you bind on earth shall be bound in heaven; whatever you loose on earth shall be loosed in heaven." Binding and loosing are legal expressions of the time that convey two ideas: first, to allow and to forbid; second, to condemn and to acquit. One wonders if the expression is not one of those comprehensive sayings, where by mentioning the two "ends" of a given subject, fullness and totality is indicated (day/night, heaven/earth, light/darkness, etc.). Peter is given the supreme authority in the kingdom; it is the functional aspect of his role of being the Rock of the Christian community.

Jesus is very pleased with Peter's insights into his mystery. Evidence for this is that he rewards the apostle so generously. But the new knowledge must remain a secret, and no outsider should come to know about it. In the Jewish mind, many concepts and hopes were associated with the notion of Messiah which did not fit into Jesus' "messianic" understanding and mission; it would certainly be misunderstood, as it was by the disciples themselves (see John 6:14; Acts 1:6). A nationalistic propaganda of his messianism would certainly raise problems for Christ in his relations with the ruling Roman power, and his authentic messianic work (preaching, etc.) would run into serious trouble. After all, this was the ultimate reason why he was condemned to death (John 19:12). Immediately afterwards (v. 21), Jesus begins to teach his disciples that he is a "suffering" Messiah.

Twenty-second Sunday in Ordinary Time

Matthew 16:21-27

Peter has solemnly declared that Jesus is the Messiah, the Son of the living God (Matthew 16:16). Christ has stated that Peter's insight was perfectly correct; that, in fact, it was a revelation of "my Father in heaven" (v. 17); and he rewards the apostle for his admirable faith. Still, Jesus does not want this aspect of his person to be divulged, because it is bound to be understood in terms of the popular Jewish concept of a political, powerful and nationalistic Messiah.

This is why, "from that time Jesus 'the Messiah' (Christ) began to disclose to his disciples that he had to go to Jerusalem and suffer grievously at the hands of the elders, chief priests and scribes—and die." That Jesus is the Messiah is the basic faith of the Twelve. But they shared the messianic ideal of their countrymen (Matthew 20:20ff.; Acts 1:6). Still, on the basis of their firm faith in the messianic dignity of Jesus, he moves on to correct their views on the Messiah; he now "begins" to disclose to them a dimension of the Messiah that they did not even suspect. The name of Jesus which Matthew uses here is deliberately solemn: "Jesus Christ," i.e., Jesus the Messiah. Thus Jesus is the Messiah; but he is—as he teaches his disciples—a Messiah who by divine disposition "had to go to Jerusalem," not to usher in the splendid messianic kingdom in the royal "city of David," but to suffer grievously and to die. He was to suffer and die precisely at the hands of those who were the religious and political leaders of the messianic people, and the guardians of their messianic hopes and expectations: it is they who will put the object of their faith to death. The disclosure is shocking.

Shocking as it is, the disclosure does not get the message across. Peter—who has just proclaimed Jesus as Messiah—now starts to remonstrate with Jesus, doing his best to prevent him from accepting such a lot: "God is gracious to you"; that is, God has nothing against Jesus, so he will not tolerate any evil coming upon Jesus. But Peter does not try to prevent him from going to Jerusalem.

Peter's suggestion touches off a sharp reaction from Jesus. Peter has become a satan, a tempter or opponent (this is what the Hebrew word "satan" means), and as such is rejected and turned down ("go away from me"). Jesus' sharp reaction allows us a glimpse into the turmoil of his soul. The anguish of his life comes to a head in the garden of Gethsemane; but it is there throughout his ministry from the start, as the three temptations of the synoptic tradition serve to evidence. Mount Calvary, looming large at a distance, overshadows Jesus' career and weighs down his soul with anxiety and anguish. That is why he is so sensitive to any suggestion that adds to his problem, to the turmoil of his spirit (see John 12:27). Peter's suggestion is an invitation to Christ to follow his own inclination, "my will" not "yours," to get around the arduous duties ("have to go" to Jerusalem, etc.) requested of him. This is why Peter becomes a tempter; he reasons in terms of a popular ("men's," see v.13) messianism; he has no feelings for God's terms; he helps the human side of Jesus that was all too active already; and in this sense, he becomes a "stumbling block" that could lead Jesus to disobey God and fall. Christ's over-reaction is an exercise of will power in order that "not my will but yours be done."

What Jesus wants his disciples to understand is that he is a "suffering" Messiah; he is "the Servant" of the Lord portrayed in Isaiah 53. It was a hard message, extremely foreign to the Jewish mind and exegesis and, therefore, also foreign to the disciples themselves. It will take all the convincing power of the Spirit—and of events—to render the disciples receptive to such an idea. And yet, from this very moment, Jesus wants them to become acquainted with still another disappointing idea. Being a "Christian," a subject, follower or minister (the reference is to the ministers, "disciples") of the Messiah means to share his own fate, namely, to renounce one's own understanding, pleasure, inclinations, possessions, life ("oneself"), and to accept all the shame, dishonor, etc., of a criminal's death on a cross in imitation of the Messiah. Jesus applies—to himself and to his disciples—the principle that using one's own arts and capabilities to keep one's physical life is a loss if the true life of eternity is forfeited. Christ himself could use his supernatural powers to bring the entire world under the control of the

Messiah; in their ministry, his disciples could achieve something similar by resorting to their human arts. But "what is the gain if one wins the whole world but forfeits his (true, eternal) life?" There is no way of repairing the damage, or of reversing the situation (v. 26). The only alternative is to prevent the damage from occurring, by one's obedience to God, by accepting his will even if it includes self-denial, the cross, and loss of physical life. This is true of all Christians, but even more so of Christian ministers.

While disclosing his sufferings in Jerusalem, Jesus added at the end a reference to his resurrection: Jesus the Messiah "will be raised on the third day" (v. 21). This reference is ignored throughout the entire episode, but it is picked up at the end: "the Son of Man will come in the splendor of his Father with his own angels, and then he will reward each one according to his behavior." Jesus the Messiah will suffer and die, but this is not the end of his career nor of his dealings with mankind. His resurrection opens up a new perspective and an even more decisive task of the Messiah. Through his resurrection, he is constituted supreme and universal judge in heaven ("the Son of Man"), and as such, he will come with all the magnificence of his heavenly glory ("the glory of his Father"), no longer as "the Servant," but with angels at his service; and the supreme Judge will evaluate the deeds of each individual and reward them accordingly. Obviously, "sparing one's (physical) life" will not be a plus, and "gaining the entire world" will not be of merit if it means doing "my will, not yours" (God's). The yardstick to know God's will and to pass judgment is Christ's word, particularly his word on suffering, the cross and death (see Revelation 3:8-11).

Twenty-third Sunday in Ordinary Time
Matthew 18:15-20

The first evangelist devotes chapter 18 of his work entirely to the duties of the leaders in the Christian community. He warns them about careerism and its ruinous effects ("scandal") for the "little ones": ambition for "being greater" makes no sense in the kingdom of heaven (vvs. 1-10). Then he reminds them that "it is not the will of the Father in heaven that any of the little one's perish"; they are expected to go and search for "the straying sheep" (vvs. 11-14).

It is in this context that in vvs. 15-20 the evangelist writes a few practical rules to help the leaders deal with the "sinners" in the community. These rules can be properly evaluated and understood only when one realizes that sin is not just an offense against God; it is also a breach of the law of holiness that governs the Christian community and, in this sense, it is an offense against the community itself, against the "society" of the holy ones. The case contemplated in the text is that of a Christian ("brother") who "sins," i.e., trespasses the law of the kingdom, and not the case of a Christian who sins or offends "against me," against an individual. This is why the rule concerns the leaders, those in charge of the holy life of the community. Three steps are considered in dealing with such sinners.

The first step is a personal approach and somewhat informal procedure: "Go and have it out with him alone, between your two selves." The leader is supposed to argue the case and convince/convict the sinning brother that he is wrong because he is offending against the law of the community. The informal approach is first, because if the brother "listens to you, you have won back your brother," and the problem is settled. The brother is "won back" in view of, and in comparison with, the worst alternative possible, which is envisaged in the third step

(v. 17). Excommunication is a practice known also to the Pauline churches (1 Corinthians 5:3ff., 12f.).

It may happen, however, that the offender pays no heed to the informal correction of the leader, and then the second step applies: "take one or two others along with you" (v. 16). At this point, the evangelist quotes a rule of Jewish procedural law, which is stated in Deuteronomy 19:15, and which is widely followed in the early Christian community, even by St. Paul in his Greek communities (2 Corinthians 13:1; 1 Timothy 5:19; see 1 Corinthians 5:3f.; Hebrews 10:28). The leader is ordered to take along one or two others, "that the whole action be established on the testimony of two or three witnesses." This is a legal and judicial process instituted to convict the offender of his wrong-doing and pass the suitable sentence. The implication is that there are such judicial powers in the community, as St. Paul himself abundantly shows (1 Corinthians 6:1ff.; 5:12). The implementation of this second step represents an official and authoritative exercise of the judicial powers of the community.

The offender, however, may ignore even this second step. Noticeably, the evangelist understands that if the first step is ignored, the offender "does not listen" to the leader; but if he disregards the second step, he "disobeys" the judges of the community: it is a sort of rebellion against the law of the community and against the community itself. This leads to the more serious and decisive step. The leader is instructed to "report (the case) to the community; but if he (the offender) disobeys even the community, treat him like a pagan or a tax collector." Obviously, the reference is to an assembly of the local community, open to all its members, where the community as such pronounces the verdict. In the case that even this verdict is disobeyed, excommunication or dismissal from the community follows; the offender is to be treated as those who do not belong to the Christian society—a pagan, or a tax collector who by his business was the exemplification of collaboration with the enemies (Romans) of God's people.

The source of such judicial authority in the community is then stated: whatever the community, through its leaders, binds or looses on earth, will be bound or loosed in heaven; God will ratify the judgment passed by the authority in the community. Binding and loosing (recall a "binding" injunction or being "released" from an obligation) were legal terms meaning "to forbid/permit" and "to condemn/acquit." It is on this legal principle that Peter's supreme authority is grounded. What this process means is that, as in every society, in the Christian community also there are various levels of jurisdiction.

In support of the same general practice of justice in the community, the evangelist reports another saying of Jesus. Clearly referring to the two or three witnesses of v. 16 and to the binding or loosing "on earth" or "in heaven" (v. 18), Jesus is reported as teaching that when "on earth" (where else?), two or three judges/witnesses (the terms often cover the same areas of meaning) reach an agreement on any matter (it is a legal term in Greek) they "ask for," it will be granted to them by the Father "in heaven." The reason for this is that where "two or three" assemble "in my (Jesus') name I am in their midst." The judicial aspect of this passage derives from the immediate context, where the same expressions are used. But it becomes even more apparent when it is illustrated with the actual practice followed in the Pauline communities. From Ephesus, Paul gives instructions to the Corinthian community regarding a man of that community involved in a case of public incest: "absent in body but present in spirit, I have already reached a verdict: together with my spirit 'convene in the name of the Lord Jesus' and with the power/authority of our Lord Jesus" excommunicate the man (1 Corinthians 5:3f.). A few verses down, the apostle emphasizes that both he and the community have jurisdiction over the community, and therefore "drive out this evil-doer from among you" (v. 12f.). The community (even in a minimal expression of two or three of its members) convenes in the name of the Lord Jesus, and by invoking his power/authority they "ask" that this "matter" of real excommunication be granted to them. Since they act in the name and by the power of Jesus, they are certain that it will be granted to them by the Father in heaven.

Twenty-fourth Sunday in Ordinary Time

Matthew 18:21-35

In his "ecclesial" treatise (ch. 18), Matthew warns the leaders of the Christian community against ambition for a career (vvs. 1-10), against disregard or neglect of their pastoral duties toward "straying sheep" (vvs. 12-14), and against softening in the use of their authority with stubborn offenders (vvs. 15-20). In the form of a parable, the treatise closes with a strong lesson of forgiveness. The closing episode is part of the subject discussed in the entire chapter. It is not irrelevant in this context, that it is precisely Peter, "upon whom I shall build my Church" (Matthew 16:18), who brings up the subject: "how often will my brother wrong me and I shall forgive him?" No doubt, the question is related to the leaders' pastoral duties towards "straying sheep," and to their judicial interventions in cases involving stubborn offenders. Since a Christian sinner trespasses, not only against God, but also against the law of holiness of the community, he somehow wrongs the representative or "foundation" of the community who must defend it and its law; he wrongs "me." The prospective offender is a "brother." It is Matthew himself (23:8) who stresses that no one in Christ's community should be called "rabbi" (teacher/leader) because Jesus remains the only rabbi, "but all of you are brothers." The instruction that follows is in answer to Peter's question and is addressed to him: in matters of forgiveness, "seven times" are not enough, the leader is supposed to go as far as "seventy times seven." Lamech (Genesis 4:24) wanted to be avenged, not seven, but "seventy times seven times." In sharp contrast to such vindictiveness, Jesus teaches that it is to forgiveness that no limitation or number should apply—no number, because the expression means innumerable, countless times. The following example illustrates the point.

Originally, the parable in vvs. 23ff. visualized the mutual forgiveness among Christians. By reporting it in the present context, Matthew turns it into a rule of pastoral practice concerning offending Christians.

Because of the rule of unlimited forgiveness, it happens with the reign of God as it does with a "king" who wants to settle accounts with his "servants" or ministers. In the following parable, several elements are not in agreement with historical realities. The prevailing practice in Palestine did not suggest that any person who was unable to pay his debts sell his property or his wife or children; the detail is meant to bring out the idea of extreme distress and helplessness of the servant in question, as well as the mercifulness of the forgiving king. The amount of money that could be obtained by selling everything and everyone connected with the servant is completely insignificant when compared with the huge debt, and, therefore, there is no real point in resorting to such cruelty; the detail emphasizes the seriousness of the situation and the determination of the king to punish mismanagement. Also, unlikely is the sudden change of the king from the maximum penalty to maximum forgiveness: the king lets himself be influenced and overcome by humility and prayer. All these are parabolic elements that render the picture all the more vivid and the teaching all the more poignant.

The most unlikely feature is the huge amount of the debt: ten thousand talents, which represent a laborer's wages for sixty million work days. The revenue of Herod's dominions (Galilee and Transjordan) amounted to approximately two hundred talents. This element stresses that such an amount simply could not be paid back by any individual; the servant was absolutely not able to pay his debts. This element, together with the fact that this servant is accountable to the "king" himself, further suggests that it is a high ranking servant who is contemplated—some sort of "minister," and not a simple subject. In view of the huge debt, the promise "I shall pay you back in full" can only express a desire to placate the king right now, and put off his final decision.

It is at this point that the decisive element is brought into the picture: "the king was deeply moved" as he saw his servant at his feet pleading for understanding and patience. And out of his deep "emotion," he let the servant go and cancelled his debt.

It is time to "develop" the parabolic negative and unveil the positive. Verse 35 teaches us that the king is "my Father in heaven." In reference to God, man is always unable to pay his debts; his "debt" always runs into the prohibitive millions. Every man fails at one time or another, and once he fails he cannot blot out his "debt"; as far as he is concerned, his failing remains forever. It will be blotted out only when God forgives. Man can ask for forgiveness, and pray and weep and do penance, but none of these represent a real right to be forgiven; no one has any right to God's forgiving "grace" or gift. God forgives "out of compassion," or loving tenderness (such is the meaning of the Greek term), or out of sheer goodness. Admittedly, the "king" says in v. 32 that he forgives all of the amount "because you pleaded with me," but this only means that God's heart is compassionate and sensitive to man's needs and poverty.

God's loving tenderness for sinners is boundless; it forgives huge amounts, and makes his justice so flexible that it is altogether bent toward mercy and forgiveness. Noticeably, God's forgiveness is not just a financial operation or adjustment; it is the result of true, compassionate love which leaves no resentment behind, but represents a complete and total gift.

The second and predominant point of the parable is now clear. It is directed to the relations among the members of the Christian community, particularly between the leading elements and offending "fellow servants," common Christians. The "debt" of a man to another never exceeds an infinitesimal fraction of man's debt to God (in the mathematics of the parable, it is but one six-hundred-thousandth). Still, in contrast with God's generosity, with regard to his fellow human beings, man urges his rights violently and cruelly. Such a selfish and "inhuman" attitude hurts both God's and other men's feelings. God surrenders to man's pleading, but man doesn't. Therefore, the "king" punishes the inhuman servant because he is expected to treat other men as God has treated him. He hands him over to the torturers, "till he should pay all his debt"—which, in view of the huge amount and of his total inability to pay, points to a torment without end.

The message is contained in the last sentence: "that is how my heavenly Father will deal with you unless you each forgive your brother from your heart"—from your heart, with a total gift and "grace," without any residual rancor or resentment. The teaching of the parable re-echoes the Lord's prayer: forgive us our trespasses (Greek, "debts") "as we forgive those who trespass against us" (Greek, "our debtors") (Matthew 6:12), which is briefly commented upon in vvs. 14f. This does not mean that God's forgiving power and love is tied up by man's lack of mercy. Rather, it means that a merciless man refuses to imitate God by his acting without mercy, and so he deserves to be treated by God as he treats others. It means, furthermore, that from the way he deals with others in his life, a man can know how God will deal with him at the last Judgment; in fact, the reference is to the future: this is how he "will deal with you."

Twenty-fifth Sunday in Ordinary Time

Matthew 20:1-16a

At the end of chapter 19 (v. 30), in connection with other ideas, the evangelist concludes that "many who are first will be last, and many who are last will be first." The parable which follows, that of the laborers sent to the vineyard at different times of the day, is devised as an (partial) illustration of the statement. The parabolic story is simple and easily understandable. In order, however, to grasp the meaning of the lesson at the end, one has to bear in mind that the first group of laborers is hired at six in the morning, whereas the last group is hired at five in the evening; those of the first group are right in that "we have borne the brunt and heat of the day" (v. 12). Only those of the first group had a binding contract on which they "agreed": "one denarius a day" (v. 2); to the others, the employer one-sidedly promises "to give whatever is fair" (v. 4), but there was no agreement, no contract.

The point of the parable appears in its second part. At the end of the day, the wages are distributed beginning with the "last" arrivals and proceeding to the "first." It is the "last" and the "first" that really count in the parable: all the other groups in between disappear, they are just a pictorial element in the story and have no contribution to make towards the understanding of the narrative. The difficulty of the drama is that the last arrivals are paid as much as the first (one denarius); this is what, in the absence of any contract, the master thought was a "fair" remuneration. Such lavish generosity arouses great hopes in the first group: a proportionate generosity will increase their agreed-upon wages many times. They are disappointed: "they, too, received each one denarius."

Clarity of the exposition requires replacement of the image by what it represents. This parable has a great deal in common with the parable of the prodigal son in Luke 15:11-32, and the basic lesson is also the same. The "landowner" and employer is God himself; those who come "first" to the vineyard are the Jewish people, the community of the Old Testament; they are, first of all, the Pharisees. Those of the "last" shift are the pagans who, only later, turn to God, after a life of complete disregard of God's demands—like the prodigal son of the parable.

Having been disappointed, those who formed the "first" group complain: the "last" ones have worked just one hour, "but you have treated them the same as us," or rather, "you have equated them with us." Of course, the denarius stands for God's full gift of salvation and inheritance. The Pharisees and the other Jews could not expect to receive more than that, the denarius. But the burning problem is the "equation"—God considers the last ones as good as the first, and treats them equally. It is too much for a Jew or a Pharisee, in view of their convictions of superiority or "priority" in God's heart and dealings with mankind. It is this leveling-off that rankled. Whatever God's "fair" payment could have implied, they expect it to be *less* than their own share. It is with this understanding that the first of the employer's three answers is unobjectionable and paves the way for the two following answers, "I am not being unjust to you; did we not agree on one denarius? Take your earnings and go." This answer clearly indicates that in his dealings with mankind, God's justice is his own, even if it does not agree with man's justice. As for man's justice, God always complies with it (here is your denarius); but he also always goes beyond it.

God's justice is always a matter of forgiveness, affectionate generosity, and love. That is why he is always just, because he always goes beyond man's justice, giving more than is required—even to the Pharisees, whose religiosity he does not deny.

Once the matter of justice is settled, the second answer discloses the central idea being taught in the parable: "I choose to pay the 'last'-comers as much as I pay you. Have I no right to do what I like with my own?" It is not a matter of human justice and retribution. What is at work is God's munificence and liberal generosity; God freely and with no obligation "chooses" not to pay the "first"-comers *less* than the others (or less than stipulated), but to pay the last-comers *as much* as the first-comers. They may not deserve it, but the first-comers do not deserve it either, since God's gift and "covenant" are God's initiative and pure grace, sheer condescension. Even in his first covenant, God demonstrates that "he had the right to do what he liked with his own," he is the "giver"; and he still has the same right to do the same thing again and again. Conversely, no one has any right to God's gifts.

The third answer allows us a glimpse into the psychological side of the story. Dissatisfaction shows in one's face and looks, particularly when a self-righteous person is disappointed; he "grumbles" and complains because he thinks he is deprived of some privilege and brought down to a lower level, where he is "equated" with sinners, tax collectors and prostitutes (see Matthew 21:31, etc.). That is why the "land-owner" retorts: "or is your eye/look evil because I am good?" The target of the evil and furious looks is not so much God as the "last"-comers, who were upgraded to the level of the first. The goodness and generosity of the master leads them to hatred and to evil-doing.

The parable proves what the evangelist has set out to demonstrate: "the last-comers become the first, and the first become last." The story certainly intends to show God's generous forgiveness, mercy, and love for all men. But the last sentence also shows—perhaps because of the "grumbling" and "evil eye"—that in his mysterious plan, God gathers for himself a people of "last"-comers; and the first-comers, by their own fault, do not enjoy God's most splendid gifts. The first-comers are not denied God's gifts, but they refuse them because they reject any idea of an "equation," which certainly did not imply their degradation but rather the upgrading of others to their level. Within the context of the Christian community, it means that no advantage or rank represents any guarantee: God is not unjust with any one, but he is free to use his gifts as he pleases.

Twenty-sixth Sunday in Ordinary Time

Matthew 21:28-32

Interestingly enough, the parable proposed by Jesus in Matthew 21:28-32 ends with a strong statement in support of John the Baptizer: "John came to you with a pattern of justice." But while sinners "believed" in him, the leaders of the Jewish community did not, and they did not change their minds even after seeing the conversion of sinners (v. 32). In point of fact, the direct purpose of Jesus' words is to defend John's religious significance and the people's conviction that John is a real prophet. All this, however, is done for the sake of Jesus himself and for the sake of his ministry.

The parable is prompted by a question addressed to Jesus in reference to the events of his triumphal entry into the temple on Palm Sunday: "What authority have you for acting like this?" Jesus responds with a question of his own: "John's baptism, where did it come from: heaven or man?" This short dialogue took place between Jesus and "the chief priests and the elders of the people," i.e., the leaders. They refused to give an answer because, among other reasons, everybody held John for a real prophet, and therefore, whatever they said could condemn them. It is the prophetic character and religious significance that is involved in Jesus' question: if John was a prophet ("baptism from heaven"), as he really was, then the leaders had paid no attention to his "heavenly" authority and disobeyed God's message by not receiving his baptism. Why do they want to know Jesus' authority, when their minds are set on disobeying any message or authority that does not agree with their own views? Furthermore, the preaching of John has already disclosed the authority of Jesus: he is the Messiah. Under these circumstances, Jesus' denial of an answer has the same motivation as his silence before Pilate later on: his answer wouldn't change a thing, it would just provide the questioners with an opportunity to distort reality.

In the parable that follows this episode, Jesus does not answer the question of the Jewish leaders, but addresses to them a disquieting and unambiguous message: "on the way to the kingdom of God tax collectors and prostitutes are ahead of you" (v. 31). In other words, in God's evaluation, tax collectors and prostitutes are closer to God than the elders and "the chief priests." The sentence is a scathing indictment of a religious establishment that, in its pride and shallowness, is deaf to God's true message, blind to his glaring splendor, and insensitive to his overwhelming presence.

This answer enlightens the terms of the parabolic image. The sinners are that "second" son who, to the "father's" invitation to go and work in the vineyard, answers with a flat no, "but after all he thought better of it and went." It is the "first" son who personifies the chief priests and elders: with a flattering "certainly, sir" he says yes, but he never goes to the vineyard, as the "Father" has requested that he go. "Which of the two did the 'Father's' will?"

The real question is the Father's will. In John 9:31 the clear suggestion is that a genuinely religious person is "he who does God's will." All the pride, arrogance and triumphalism of an organized religion that does not do God's will is not true religion; such a religion does not worship God but itself. This is the point of this parable. Neither John the Baptizer nor Christ himself mean anything to the "chief priests" and other leaders; they couldn't care less about God's message/will as it is proclaimed by the prophets or envoys of God. In the message preached by John and by Jesus "everybody" (v. 27) could perceive the voice of God—everybody, that is, except the chief priests and the elders. John—Jesus tells them—appears, showing God's way of "justice," namely, the way in which God "justifies" man. John proclaims a "baptism of repentance" and a change of heart; it is through repentance, penance and "metanoia" that God justifies tax collectors and prostitutes, because they heed his appeal. God's justice and justification is his forgiveness, his forgiveness to those who accept it. In their aloofness, the leaders of the religious establishment are careful to counter any threat to their "authority," but they completely disregard God's authority as it appears in his "authorized" envoys. The popular masses and even "the children" (vvs. 9, 15) were able to perceive the messianic authority of Jesus, but the dull narrow-mindedness of the chief priests and elders was not; they do not ask about his authority—they challenge/deny it. Their spiritual attitude prevents them from understanding and "seeing" God's way of justification, to which tax collectors and prostitutes resort in their humility and sincerity of heart.

It is also because of such a spiritual attitude that, "on the way to the kingdom tax collectors and prostitutes" are ahead of self-righteous chief priests and other leaders. They accept their weakness, and in their weakness they "confess their sins" and accept God's forgiveness. This is how they "believed" in John. It is a matter of faith, a faith that is a complete commitment to God and that, therefore, is the guiding light of its own darkness: it is an enlightened "instinct" to discover God and his saving plan. The sinners believe immediately. The leaders, however, not only pay no attention to John at first, but even after "having seen" God's grace and power at work in the conversion of tax collectors and prostitutes (the prototypes of irreligion and immorality)—even then—they refused to "give some thought to it after all—and to believe." It is not just a matter of failing to believe; the real question is a deep-seated attitude of man's spirit; they refuse even to give some thought to the religious "revolution" and renewal that was taking place. On some other occasion, some other religious leaders explain Christ's miracles as a clear manifestation of Satan's powers (Matthew 12:24ff.). Any other spiritual attitude is more conducive to God's kingdom than religious arrogance and self-sufficiency.

Twenty-seventh Sunday in Ordinary Time

Matthew 21:33-46

In a series of sharp messages to the Jewish religious leaders, Jesus also addresses the parable of the faithless vinedressers to the "chief priests and leaders of the people" (v. 23). As the introduction to the parable itself says: "listen to another parable" (v. 33). At the end of the present narrative, it is "the chief priests and Pharisees" who understand that this and other parables are "meant for them" (v. 45). It is they, furthermore, who exchange words with Jesus as his teaching unfolds (v. 41).

In terms that certainly refer the reader to Isaiah 5:1ff. and other passages of the Old Testament (Psalm 80:8ff.), Jesus takes up the traditional metaphor of the vine and uses it to characterize the Jewish community or the People of God in general. By implication, the "landowner" is God. The vine, however, is "planted" somewhere. As a matter of fact, Psalm 80:8f. states that the vine was uprooted from Egypt and planted somewhere else, where "it covered the mountains...the cedars of God with its branches, its tendrils extended to the sea, its offshoots all the way to the river." The vine was "planted" in the Promised Land, but the vine is not the land. The land remains God's property, and the people ("vine") are just tenants; an idea that denotes, in the first place, the religious leaders ("chief priests and Pharisees"). In rabbinic literature, the teachers of God's Law are often described as vinedressers and also as "builders." The "vine" includes the notion of the Covenant with all its stipulations and gifts ("fence, winepress, and tower") which can make the Covenant work and the vine bring forth the fruits God expects. The "landowner" entrusted the vine to its leaders ("tenants") and "went abroad"; in a sense, he let things take care of themselves.

From time to time, God sent prophets and righteous men ("servants") to his vine to "collect the produce," to obtain the fruit of genuine religiosity that God expected, and not the ritualistic performance of an organized religion, that "rendered God's word ineffective" (Mark 7:13), with all its doctrinal and moral results. God "expected it to yield grapes, but sour grapes were all that it gave" (Isaiah 5:2).

The tenants, however, beat and killed God's envoys. This parabolic element uncovers all the tragedy and all the inconceivable faithlessness of the "tenants," that permeates the history of Israel and that Matthew portrays, however briefly, in some other place: "alas for you, scribes and Pharisees, you hypocrites! You who build the sepulchres of the prophets and decorate the tombs of holy men.... You are the sons of those who murdered the prophets.... I am sending you prophets and wise men and scribes: some you will slaughter, crucify, scourge...you will draw down on yourselves the blood of every holy man that has been shed in the land...Jerusalem, Jerusalem, you that kill the prophets and stone those who are sent to you!" (23:29, 31, 34f., 37; see Acts 7:51; 1 Thessalonians 2:15)

It is within this setting that after several "servants" had been killed, as a last and best favor and chance, "at the end" (Hebrews 1:1f.) the landowner sends "his own son." Admittedly, he thinks that "they will respect my son," but even so, rather than by human wisdom and likelihood, this detail is dictated by divine wisdom, or better, love for the vine: "God so loved the world...!" (John 3:16) It was the last resort God could think of. But the outcome shows that God was wrong in his expectations, because he expected too much. Far from being respected, his "son" was "thrown out" of the vine, he was declared an outcast in his own property/house, and as an outcast he was killed outside the vine ("outside the gates, outside the encampment," Hebrews 13:12f.; Acts 2:23). The "tenants" want to be left alone; they regard themselves not as tenants, but as owners of God's vineyard. Religion is not for God, it is for themselves; it is their own estate and for their own advantage. No one should intrude into their castle.

The point Jesus is making is explicitly stated by those in the audience themselves: " 'What will he (the owner) do to those tenants?' They answered, 'He will bring those wretches to a wretched end and lease the vineyard to other tenants...' " (v. 40f.). This is what God will do. The wretched end is certainly a reference to the destruction of the Jewish state and religious establishment by the

Romans in 70 A.D. But the main thrust of the parable is aimed at the religious aspect: the owner "will lease the vineyard to other tenants." Since the fig tree had no fruit, it was ordered/accursed "never to bear fruit again; and at that instant the fig tree withered" (Matthew 21:19). Since for so long, the tenants obtained no genuine fruit from the vineyard, they are denied even the chance ever to obtain it. Both metaphors portray the failure of the Old Testament community to live up to God's rightful and reasonable expectations. That is why God tries something new and turns to the pagan world, where he expects to find a community of "tenants" who will put the gifts of his "new covenant" to a better use.

At this point, Jesus is reported as bringing a quotation from Psalm 118:22-23 into his teaching. The passage of the Psalm is supposed to illustrate the preceding parable. In this quote, the primary emphasis falls on the "rejection" of the stone by the "builders," by the leaders. Of course, the tenants rejected the "son" of the landowner. Jesus calls the attention of the chief priests and Pharisees to the Scriptures they were supposed to know. The Scriptures should teach them that their "rejection" of Christ has been foreseen by God; it is in keeping with their "stubbornness" throughout history: "in the past they killed those who foretold the coming of the Just One, and now you have become his betrayers, his murderers" (Acts 7:51f.). This is all God could expect of them: he is not betrayed by his lack of knowledge, but by his heart.

The other concept in the quotation marks a transition to the conclusion: the rejected stone became the pivotal element in God's saving plan; it "became the key stone" of God's "building/temple" in his community—something that only God's power can do; man can only stare in amazement at God's marvelous work. The reference is to Jesus' resurrection and glorification as supreme Lord and ruler of men's History. Those who fight against it and fall upon such a "stone," will be dashed to pieces (see Isaiah 8:14; Daniel 2:34, 44; Romans 9:32). It is hard to kick against the goad (Acts 26:14), and those upon whom such a "stone" falls, with all the weight of his authority and power, will be crushed. The reference is to the Jewish downfall in 70 A.D. That the chief priests and Pharisees of Jesus' day were "the children of those who killed the prophets" is evidenced by the fact that they "sought to arrest him," Jesus, for the purpose that, at last, they were able to pursue to the end.

Twenty-eighth Sunday in Ordinary Time
Matthew 22:1-4

The narrative of Matthew 22:1-14 is part of a longer context in which the unfaithfulness and faithlessness of the Jewish community towards God's saving plan in Christ is brought into the open and warmly reproached. Chapter 23 marks the peak of this violent attack. Our passage is the last in a series (21:23-46) of three parables devoted to the same subject and, in this sense, it carries the same concept further, particularly the concept of the parable of the faithless vinedressers. As it is today, the parable in Matthew 22:1-14 is considerably complicated, and additional elements lead to a conclusion that, in fact, can only apply to the last part of the narrative: "many ('polloi') are called but few are chosen."

Obviously, our parable has two focal points. One is the "invitation to the wedding feast" and the other the expulsion of one guest from the wedding celebration who is "thrown into the dark" because he has no wedding garment. It is in these two focal points that the entire narrative is clearly expressed.

The background of the entire narrative is the feast that a king gave on the occasion of his son's "wedding." The king is God, the son is Jesus Christ. The wedding is the consummation of Christ's relationship with his (and

God's) community in the eternal happiness, which is the final and most important phase of the "kingdom of heaven." The passage of Revelation 19:7-9 offers a suitable background or parallel: "This is the time for the marriage of the Lamb. His bride is ready, and she has been able to dress herself in dazzling white linen, because her linen is made of the good deeds of the saints.... Happy are those who are invited to the wedding feast of the Lamb." This is why, in the New Testament, Christ is sometimes characterized as a bridegroom and his community as a bride (Mark 2:19f.; John 3:29; Revelation 21:2, 9; 22:17), and the eternal happiness is sometimes described with the image of a banquet (Matthew 8:11; Luke 22:30). The beginning or "preparation" for the final banquet takes place in this world through the "invitations" that the king sends out. He, not the "son," is the real host.

There is reference to a first mission of "servants" who go to invite the guests. Of this mission, it is only said that it was "fruitless" (Matthew 21:24f.) because the invitation went unheeded. This is the invitation that God extended to the Old Testament community through the prophets and other religious leaders; of course, the invitation was for the final feast, the entire messianic event/kingdom is included. This, as well as other parables, show that the community refused the invitation (see Matthew 21:34-36). There is a second mission conveyed with a sense of urgency: "I have my banquet all prepared... everything is ready. Come to the wedding." The "servants" on this mission are the Christian missionaries among the Jews, starting from the days of Christ (see Matthew 10:5ff.). The sense of urgency derives from the fact that the "son" is already there, and the messianic event is already unfolding and headed for its consummation.

They "were not interested" for various worldly reasons (see Matthew 13:22); the Jewish masses disregarded the Christian message. Others among them, however, were not satisfied with mere disregard: "the rest seized his servants, maltreated them and killed them" (v. 6). These are the "tenants" of the vine (21:33ff., "chief priests and Pharisees" v. 45). This is what Matthew 23:33 discloses: "serpents, brood of vipers.... I am sending you prophets and wise men and scribes: some you will slaughter and crucify...." They now meet the fate they themselves described on another occasion: the king "will bring those wretches to a wretched end" (Matthew 21:41). The king "dispatched his troops, destroyed those murderers and burnt their town" (see Revelation 11:13ff.). The reference is to the downfall of Jerusalem and of the Jewish state in 70 A.D. "The king was furious."

Now the king sends his "servants," or missionaries, to wherever people could be found ("crossroads," or better, the points where streets become roads at the "city limits") and invites everyone who can be found, without any preference for Jews. The king is determined to go ahead with the wedding feast; and "God can raise children for Abraham from these stones" (Matthew 3:9). The new order is a universal mission, already beyond the "city limits," beyond Israel; it is the pagan world that is now invited by the Christian missionaries to come to the wedding feast, to eternal happiness, and to the Father's inheritance. God is determined to honor his "Son," and he will certainly raise a community for him. The "vineyard" is given to other tenants (21:41, 43).

It is at this point that a new perspective emerges. In their mission, the servants "congregated" everyone they could find: in the congregation, however, there were both "good and bad" elements. At any rate, the wedding hall was full of guests. The high celebration is about to start, but has not yet begun. According to the Oriental custom, the king comes to the hall to welcome his guests and to make sure that they don't lack anything, and that everything is all right. He catches sight of a guest who was not wearing the wedding garment. Admittedly, the detail does not settle very well with the story: the guests had been gathered in a hurry and almost forced into a situation that they did not expect. The teaching intended justifies the inconsistency of the story. The author has already pointed out that not all the guests are good, there are also "bad" guests.

The passage of Revelation quoted above states that the "white linen dress" of the bride/community is "the good deeds of the saints." In a wide context, the New Testament teaches that a Christian "puts on Christ" at his baptism (Galatians 3:27; see Ephesians 4:26; Revelation 6:11; 7:13f.; 22:14) and refers to the "white robe" of Christians; it is the expression of a life according to God and according to the "purification/washing" of man at baptism. This is the wedding robe for anyone to be admitted to the eschatological "wedding feast." What the parable teaches at this point is that in God's Church there are many guests invited to the final feast. But not everything depends on the initial invitation or on the initial steps. A Christian must keep his baptismal "robe" clean and shining. What the king does is to carry out a separation between the "good and bad" guests, just as it happens in other passages of the gospel (Matthew 13:41, 49). It is in this sense that "many are called, and few are chosen." The notion of "many" is not restrictive, it stands for "all," the multitude; no one is excluded from the invitation. The "choice," on the other hand, is not an arbitrary decision. Those who wear the wedding robe—all of them are chosen. The robe is given by God; wearing it until the end depends on each one of those who have been called or invited.

Twenty-ninth Sunday in Ordinary Time
Matthew 22:15-22

Jesus put an end to the discussion by declaring that Caesar must be given his due; and God given his own due. It is both the historical and religious background which renders the discussion alive. The Jewish commonwealth is under Roman rule ("Caesar") and the Jews bear the burden only with reluctance, resentment—and rancor. The Pharisees share and feed popular resentment; the Zealots are the militant extremists of the time, and murder is a matter of policy. Several false Messiah's spring up from time to time, creating serious problems for the Roman overlord (see Acts 5:36f.; 21:38; Matthew 24:5, 24). One of the grounds operative in Christ's death sentence is his claim of being the Messiah (Matthew 26:63; John 18:33ff.; 19:12; Luke 23:5). On the one hand are the nationalistic feelings of the Jewish masses; on the other, is all the weight of the ruling power.

In their hatred for the new religious reformer, Jesus, the Pharisees decide to "entrap him in some statement," so as to discredit him in the esteem of the Jewish people, or to entangle him in judicial troubles with the Roman authority. The move comes from the leading ("council") Pharisees, who send to Jesus a delegation made up of their own disciples or adherents and of "Herodians." The Herodians are a group who support the policies of Herod the Great (the ruler at Christ's birth). Their presence on the Jewish religious scene, at a time far removed from his death, would give some support to early statements that they considered, or flattered, Herod as Messiah and that Herod himself entertained such dreams. At any rate, they side with the Romans, whose protégé and dedicated servant Herod had been. The presence of the Herodians further sharpens the espisode: two opposite factions could testify against Jesus, no matter (they thought) what his answer may be. The agreement of two antagonistic parties would have an overwhelming juridical weight. The plot is skillfully devised.

The question is the payment of tribute to a pagan establishment, which worships idols and divinizes its emperors, when such tribute has to be paid by a community that, theoretically speaking, recognizes Yahweh as its only true ruler, and is committed to God's worship, regarding idolatry as an "abominable" evil (Romans 2:22), and any communion with pagans an impurity. The question certainly has political and nationalistic undertones, but its very wording ("is it permitted...?") clearly suggests that the predominant concern is religious. Clear evidence for this is Jesus' answer: the questioners ask only if it is permissible to pay taxes to Caesar, but Jesus' answer also includes man's duties to God. Of course, no answer of Jesus will be regarded as binding or even acceptable. All the praises of Jesus by the questioners (v. 16) are part of the "trap" and are intended to encourage Jesus to speak out his own mind without fear. They know that he is a sincerely religious man ("you teach God's way with sincerity") and that he takes no sides with either party; he is objective ("you show no partiality"). This is how Jesus understood the whole thing: an enticement for him to fall into the trap, and this is why he calls them *hypokritai*, which in this case does not mean a meticulous interpreter of the law, but a real actor who pretends one thing but intends and plans another.

The coin shown to Christ is common currency throughout the Roman Empire; it is used by the Jews themselves in their commercial transactions and in paying taxes. It shows the head of the emperor and his name (Tiberius). Jesus' answer is grounded on the common understanding that the monetary system is based on the authority and power of the empire and, ultimately, on the emperor himself. As a matter of fact, the right of stamping money is an indication of independence and sovereignty. The figure and name of the emperor on the coin is clear evidence that he is the ruler and that the coin belongs to him and to the empire; it is the expression of his (and its) power and authority. By merely pointing out the facts, Christ makes his Jewish questioners realize that they are not independent, that they themselves are using the resources of the empire, and that they are living according to the institutions of the empire. The question is, therefore, pointless: when you are paying taxes, you are "giving back," as something which is due to the emperor, something that you have previously received and accepted from him. So what is new? Jesus' answer could displease neither the Herodians who supported Roman policies, nor the Pharisees and the Jewish masses because paying taxes is a fact of life. This is the kind of answer they do not expect; Jesus goes around the "trap."

Jesus' answer, however, sets a principle of great consequences, that the Jews had to learn. Social and earthly realities do not interfere with God's rights. Jesus does not say that the Jews could not have their own monetary system and their independence. He does say that right now they are integrated within the monetary and social/political system of the Roman Empire (where the Jewish religion is respected and guaranteed by the Roman legal system as "lawful religion"). And when religious (God's) rights are respected, then being independent or being integrated into this or that social, economic, or political system, as well as using this or that monetary system is irrelevant from a religious (God's) point of view. Jesus' answer is religiously minded; he ignores the political implications of the question. He does not question nor discuss whether the Jews should gain independence or not. He would go along with that, but such is not his concern because his mission is religious, not political. His concern is that, in whatever political situation, a Jew must be a true Jew and give God what he is supposed to give God. The Romans are wrong in equating Caesar/empire with God, and the Jews are wrong in opposing God and Caesar. Christ makes a clear distinction, separating the realms of God and Caesar. Christ does not canonize or condemn any merely political or economic system (he just disregards this aspect), but he does establish and affirm the rights of God in any possible system. The Jewish tendency is (theoretically at least) to stress God's rights against the interests of the earthly power; it seems that the tendency today is to emphasize the interests of Caesar at the expense of God's rights.

Within the general context of Jewish "traps," Jesus' answer to the Pharisees and other Jewish leaders means that their zeal for God is not genuine. They disregard God's calling to repentance, to serious religiosity and to the "wedding feast" (Matthew 21:28—22:14), when they try to entrap (and ultimately kill) the bearer of God's message and forgiving love—God's "thing" would be to listen to Jesus.

Thirtieth Sunday in Ordinary Time

Matthew 22:34-40

Jesus brings into the forefront the basic principle of man's religious and moral conduct: it is the principle of love. In Matthew's gospel, Jesus' clarification on this point comes in the form of an answer to his enemies, who wanted to trip him up. The episode belongs in a context where Jesus' enemies come up to him with tricky questions aimed at ensnaring him in political problems (vvs. 15-22) or at discrediting him as a teacher (vvs. 23-40). In the latter episode, Jesus closes the mouths of the Sadducees who propose to Jesus an academic problem that in their opinion ridiculed the idea of a bodily resurrection. Note that Sadducees and Pharisees are at odds with each other on many issues, and the doctrine of the resurrection is one of them: the Pharisees believe in it, the Sadducees reject and ridicule it. This explains Matthew's introduction to our episode: "when the Pharisees heard that he had shut the mouth of the Sadducees, they came together to the same place and one of them, a lawyer/theologian put a question to him." Still, what he intends is not to learn, but "to probe" him; namely, to probe Jesus' thought, opinion, or knowledge: Jesus is addressed as "doctor." The question is this: "which is the greatest commandment of the Law?"

In the historical setting of the time, the question is rather academic, but it is very actual and very vividly debated in academic centers. The Jewish "canon lawyers" have meticulously analyzed the Law and have come up with a classification of its commandments: 365 negative commandments or prohibitions ("not to do") and 248 positive commandments or orders to do something. The next step is to establish some sort of hierarchy in so many rules, and possibly to find the basic principle from which all other prescriptions flowed. A later rabbi, Simlai (c. 250 A.D.), will find some guidance in the Bible towards an answer to such a question: on Sinai Moses received 613 commandments; David brought them down to 11 (Psalm 15:2-5), Isaiah to 6 (33:15), Micah to 3 (6:3), Amos to 2 (5:4), and Habakkuk brought all the commandments back to a simple principle: "The righteous shall live by faith" (2:4). Long before this, some Jewish teachers have come very close to Jesus' insight. About 20 B.C., Hillel had formulated a principle that in its basic meaning is confirmed by Jesus (Matthew 7:12): "Do not do to others what you don't want others to do to you; this is the entire Law, all the rest is an explanation of it." About 135 A.D., Akiba is reported as saying that, "you shall love your neighbor as yourself: this is a great principle of the Law." It is this on-going academic discussion that provides some reason to "probe" or explore Jesus' knowledge or opinion.

Jesus' answer is sharp and unambiguous. Love is the answer. Love of God and of one's neighbor. But in his answer, Jesus points out that love of God is "the great and the first commandment." As a matter of fact, without qualifying the question he is asked at all, Jesus quotes the text from Deuteronomy 6:5: "you must love the Lord your God..."; it is to this quotation that he attaches his comment, "this is the great and first commandment." Then he adds that "a second" commandment is "similar" to this: "you must love your neighbor as yourself" (Leviticus 19:18). Obviously, Jesus gives priority to love of God; it is the most significant and important ("the great") commandment in the Law, the idea being that it is the most decisive and relevant for man's religious life and spiritual development, and therefore, the most basic and pressing obligation. Beyond that, and as a result of that, the commandment of God's love comes "first." The top priority for man's heart is God himself, and everything man does and is must be related to God in the first place.

Love for one's neighbor comes "second." This does not mean that there is a chronological sequence between these two expressions of man's love. Nor does it mean that love for one's neighbor must be a "second" class love. What it means is that there is a logical and causal order in man's loving activity. One's neighbor can be loved in many ways, and among these many ways there are numberless wrong ones. Man's love for his neighbor must be grounded on man's love for God and enlightened by it; a love which is respect for God, interest in God's plans, and filial obedience to his will. Only then can man love his neighbor properly, that is, both according to God's will and in order to promote God's saving interest (love of God) in man; loving man in this way (for God's sake) represents the promotion of man's genuine interests and of man himself as a person with a supernatural destiny. This is how God's love comes first as a logical necessity and as an inspiring principle to love man as he is supposed to be loved.

Analysis is important in order for us to understand, but in real fact, true love for man is, at the same time, love for God. God wants us, commands us to love our neighbor; and, furthermore, he teaches us how his love for man should be expressed: that is why obedient and filial love for God prompts us to love our neighbor. St. John (1 John 4:20f.) understands that man cannot love God if he does not love his neighbor, and he points to a single commandment of love: "this is the commandment we have from him, that he who loves God love also his own brother." But the sense of direction, finality and motivation of love for man comes from one's love for God, and not conversely.

The notion of love in the bible is not so much psychological and emotional as it is practical and factual. The love of *agape* stresses the realities of genuine, helping and giving sacrifice; it is an unselfish love that intends to make the other, not oneself, happy. It is in this context that, according to Matthew, love for God requires a "total" gift of man's will, life and mind to God—the gift of everything man is and, therefore, of all the activities of his being, even when these activities are related to one's neighbors. Now, man's love for his neighbor is "similiar to this." The similarity consists in that man has to put at his neighbor's service what he puts at God's service—namely, himself, with his "total" will, life and mind. Even his life. In 1 John 3:16, St. John writes that "this has taught us love: that he gave up his life for us, and we, too, ought to give up our lives for our brothers."

Thirty-first Sunday in Ordinary Time
Matthew 23:1-12

The first evangelist devoted one of his main discourses or treatises to Jesus' views on the Pharisaic religiosity; it runs through the entire length of chapter 23. In Matthew 5:20, Jesus has stated that the "justice" of Christians must be more complete or comprehensive than that of the Pharisees. In this discourse of chapter 23, he discloses what is wrong with the Pharisaic "justice" or religious system. In the section vvs. 1-12, we have a partial comparison between the Pharisaic and the Christian systems: Jesus expects his followers to avoid some prominent mistakes of the Pharisees. Here his teaching is addressed to the leaders of his community, who are the counterpart of the Pharisees and scribes, the latter being the lawyers/theologians of the time, usually affiliated to the Pharisaic party.

As a matter of fact, the Pharisees are seen as those who "occupy the (teaching) chair of Moses"; they are the spiritual guides of the Jewish community. This is neither questioned nor objected to. But they are blamed because they teach one thing but do something else; they do not live up to their own teaching. According to the entire context of the gospel (see Matthew 15:1-9; Mark 7:1-23), this means that they teach the Law of God, but, exploiting their teaching position, they surround it with explanations and supplements of "human" traditions that turn the Law to their own advantage and selfishness in different ways. Their zeal for God's law is just lip-service. They render the Law as difficult as possible for the others, but not for themselves. This is how they do not move a finger to lift the burdens they load on the shoulders of others: they take advantage of what they think and teach is the meaning of the Law; it is the others who have to carry the burdens or "loads" that the Pharisaic religiosity imposes on the Jewish community. The image is that of a heavy burden (the Law plus the Pharisaic traditions, etc.) that is supposed to be carried by a group (by all the community). But some find a way to skip their responsibilities; what is more, they take advantage of what they teach is common law.

"Everything they do is for the purpose of attracting attention"—not God's but men's. The Pharisees do not lack interior religiosity; but they emphasize exteriority and appearances too much, and thereby empty God's word of its power and content. In 6:1-18, the evangelist has listed some such external practices. In our text he adds some other details. In Deuteronomy 6:8, the instruction of keeping God's commandments in mind (and work) is expressed in the form of "fastening them on your hand as a sign and on your forehead as a circlet." The instruction is physically implemented, with written sentences of the Law on tapes ("phylacteries") that are then fastened to hand and forehead. The Pharisees wear broader tapes, as an expression of greater religiosity. Again, according to Numbers 15:37ff., the Israelites are ordered to "put tassels on the hems of their garments...this will remind you of all my commandments." Jesus himself complies with this commandment (Matthew 9:20; 14:36. parall.). But the Pharisees wear longer tassels, which are more conspicuous to men. Taking advantage of their teaching position, they claim the places of honor in banquets (see Luke 14:1, 7ff.) and in the synagogues, where—archaeological evidence shows —there is a chair in the front that is called the chair of Moses. They take pleasure, furthermore, in being acknowledged as distinguished persons by the greetings of the common people gathering around them in the public places. But it is the title "rabbi" (teacher, doctor) that they treasure most; in their view the common people are "this crowd ignorant of the Law" (John 7:49; see 9:28f., 34). Theirs is the kind of religiosity that Jesus could not put up with.

That is why some instructions follow, that should mark the difference between the Pharisees and the leaders in Christ's community. They must not allow themselves to be called rabbi/doctor ("doctor of the Church"), because "your (Christians') doctor is only one, but all of you are brothers." No one in the Christian community is supposed to found his own school of thinking; all they are supposed to do is to hand down the teaching of the "one" teacher who founded the "school" of Christian wisdom/revelation. There must be "scribes instructed for the kingdom" (Matthew 13:15), but "the teacher" or thinker is only one; and all other "scribes" in the Christian community are just "brothers," namely, schoolfellows. The one "doctor" may be God; more probably, it is Christ himself in view of v. 10 where, very likely, we have another translation of v. 8, using different words. The Greek term for "teacher" in v. 10 can be another translation of rabbi; and in this case, there is no question that "your (Christians') teacher is the Messiah"—he is the founding thinker of the Christian school.

In this same teaching, Jesus commands the leaders of his community that they "must call no one on earth your (Christians') father, for only one is your Father, the heavenly one." The term "father" was a real title, and a highly honorable one; it applied to outstanding Jewish religious thinkers of the past, to the point that the talmudic tradition includes a treatise entitled "Sentences of the Fathers." Not infrequently, the views of the "fathers" were given more authority than God's word itself. Jesus does not want the leaders of his community to be called "fathers"; they have just to hand down the teaching/revelation of the source/Father of all Christian thought, expressed through Christ the revealer—who is "the Logos," Word, and Thought of the Godhead.

The closing sentences in our section show that, after all, it is pride and arrogance that Christ blamed in the Pharisaic system of religious exhibitionism. Christ wants the leaders (the greater) among Christians to understand their greatness as service ("servants") to their fellow Christians (20:20-28), and not as a matter of "imposing heavy loads"—on "others," or making a display of colorful "tassels," or "phylacteries," or showy emblems, or both worldly and "holy" titles, or ambition for social distinction and attention, etc. To all this, the Lord adds an eschatological perspective of exaltation or humiliation of Christian leaders on the day of reckoning: "anyone (leader) who exalts himself will be humiliated, and anyone who humbles himself will be exalted." The example of a Christian leader remains, "the Son of Man who came not to be served but to serve, and to give his life as ransom for many" (20:28)—as the "Servant of the Lord" (Isaiah 53). This is what the Pharisees did not do.

Thirty-second Sunday in Ordinary Time
Matthew 25:1 13

In a long section of his gospel (chs. 24-25), Matthew offers a panoramic view of the Kingdom of God, from Jesus' days to its consummation. In the first place, the kingdom appears in its struggle with the antagonistic Jewish state of the time, which ends up in ruins for its opposition to God's plan in Jesus (24:1-35). In the third place, Matthew describes the end of the earthly phase of the kingdom, with the last judgment conducted by the "Son of Man," in which the final separation of "lambs and goats" is made, and each group sent to its eternal destiny (25:31-46). In between (24:36—25:30), Matthew describes the existence of the kingdom from the downfall of Jerusalem to the last judgment; but he describes it from a particular angle, with one eye on the past judgment/punishment of the Jewish state, and the other on the coming judgment at the end of time. That is why "watchfulness" and "achievement" are so strongly stressed in this central section, which is basically constituted by three parables, aiming at different, but not unrelated, targets.

It is within this general framework, and within this central section, that the parable of the "ten virgins" is reported (25:1-31). The main point emphasized in the parable is clearly indicated by the conclusion: "stay, therefore, awake, because you do not know either the day or the hour" of the Lord's coming for judgment. It is watchfulness that is called for in one's life as a Christian in view of the second and decisive coming of the Son of Man. Besides the need for watchfulness, the narrative contains many other doctrinal points.

The parable, obviously, draws its inspiration from the customary ritual of wedding celebrations of the time: in a joyous cortege of friends and admirers, the already betrothed bride, led by her bridesmaids, is accompanied to the bridegroom's home where the wedding feast is celebrated. The representation in the parable, however, does not square with the custom, which on several points is, indeed, reversed. The most significant deviation from custom is that there is no bride at all in the parable—no bride as an individual figure. Then, it is the bridegroom who "comes," who moves into some place. At the end, he becomes some kind of doorkeeper, who answers the bell, but rejects those who come late (there isn't much celebration or politeness). The bridesmaids do not accompany any bride, but wait for the bridegroom to come; and at a certain point, they—all ten of them—fall asleep; the bridegroom is very late (it looks like a very dull and disorganized wedding). Finally, the bridegroom makes an ill-timed appearance, right at midnight, when apparently no one expected him any more; and even more oddly, precisely at midnight, the shop attendants were at their counters to attend the foolish bridesmaids. These, and other inconsistencies, are only parabolic elements, chosen for the sake of the teaching they are meant to convey.

The parable receives much light when it is related to the scene of the last judgment described in 25:31ff. The bridegroom is Christ, who "comes" to his "bride," in order to celebrate the wedding of eternal happiness, after the long period of betrothal throughout the history of the Christian community. The ten "virgins" are, of course, thought of as bridesmaids in the parabolic negative of the wedding feast; in the positive, however, they are not just girls, they are virgins, because they themselves are the "bride," a collective bride—who is the entire Christian community. It is well known that in the New Testament, the community sometimes appears in the figure of a bride (see Revelation 19:7ff.; 21:2, 9; 22:17; John 3:29; Mark 2:19) and Christ as the bridegroom. Therefore, they represent this "virgin" bride (2 Corinthians 11:2), before the real marriage of total communion is celebrated. This already explains why some are "wise" and some are "foolish," and why the former are admitted to the wedding and the latter are excluded. The Christian community is a mixture of "wheat and weeds" (Matthew 13:37ff.), of "good and useless fish" (13:48), of wise Christians and of foolish ones. Only the wise virgins go into the wedding hall, because they are the part of the community who enjoys the total communion and gift of Christ to his community after the betrothal of its earthly existence; bad Christians, during this earthly existence, are excluded from the joys of intimacy in the heavenly phase of the kingdom. This is why the bridegroom becomes the doorkeeper; the closed door is not so much the door to the banquet hall, as the door to the bridal chamber, from which those "virgins" are excluded who do not enjoy the favor of the Lord.

What we have here is a wedding that becomes a judgment. It is for judgment that the bridegroom comes, and he makes the separation in this particular way. Because of their carelessness, the foolish virgins miss the train, and that is how they are excluded from it. The characterization of the virgins as wise or foolish is relevant; it is, after all, the criterion for the choice. Both "wise" and "foolish" are sapiential terms: wisdom is that quality or combination of qualities that make someone successful in life; foolishness is the lack of those qualities or the presence of some shortcomings that lead to a lack of success, to failure. In a religious context, wisdom is the ability to please God, and thus, to reach one's eternal goal; foolishness is the opposite. Wisdom and foolishness are not related to falling asleep (all the virgins do); this is just a descriptive element and brings out that the bridegroom comes "at midnight," when he is not expected. Wisdom and foolishness are related to the oil, to having or not having oil—it is oil that the parable is all about.

The lamp is the symbol of one's own person and life, as these may be considered from different angles; here they are considered from the viewpoint of one's relationship to Christ and to God. In Revelation, the "seven lamps (1:12) are seven churches" (1:20), i.e., the totality of the Church; if a local church does not live according to Christ's principles, "I will come and remove your lamp from its place" (2:5). This living according to the gospel is the oil that feeds one's Christian life, one's Christian personality; no doubt, it includes a reference to the "anointing" of the Spirit in baptism, whose presence in the Christian person is the guarantee of a good Christian life. It is of decisive importance to be in possession of such oil when the bridegroom/judge comes; and his coming may happen at any time of one's life, even at "midnight," when one least expects that anything may happen.

On the other hand, the oil is a strictly personal possession; it cannot be given to others; no one can expect to obtain it from somebody else. This is why the wise virgins refuse to share what they have, they just cannot. So one must be in possession of good Christian living at all times. If something happens at "midnight," and one has run out of oil, it may be too late to get some more. Note that the foolish virgins are said to have gone for oil, but it is not said that they were able to buy any. It is a matter of "readiness." It is in view of this readiness—with an abundant supply of oil—that the Lord earnestly warns everyone: "stay awake, because you do not know either the day or the hour." He comes "like a thief in the night" (1 Thessalonians 5:2; Revelation 3:3; 16:15).

Thirty-third Sunday in Ordinary Time
Matthew 25:14-30

Like the parable of the "ten virgins" (Matthew 25:1-13), the parable of the talents belongs to the central part of Matthew's eschatological discourse, where the evangelist contemplates the earthly phase of God's kingdom between the downfall of the Jewish state in A.D. 70 (24:1-35) and the day of the last judgment (25:31ff.). The parable of the talents teaches us that the kingdom can be likened to a man who, on his departure for foreign lands, entrusts his property, in different proportions, to "his servants," with the aim that they increase it by means of wise and active investments. Upon his return, "after a long time," he settles accounts with his servants. The parable provides its own interpretation, at the same time that the parabolic figure unfolds.

Again, as in the parable of the virgins, this one has one eye on the history of the past and another on the coming of the "Son of Man" for judgment, at the end (25:31ff.). Obviously, the "man who travels abroad" and comes back "after a long time" is the Lord, who, through his passion and following developments, leaves this earthly existence, coming back only at the end of time. He will come back on the day of "reckoning"; on that day, he will evaluate the deeds of his servants, and assign rewards and punishments accordingly. His "own servants" do not seem to be all Christians at large—even if the teaching of the parable is also applicable to them —but those to whom the Lord assigns some special activity in his community. This is what the parallel parable in 24:45-51 suggests, where the "servant" is someone "whom the Lord placed over his own household to give them their food at the proper time," and who is in the position of "beating his fellow servants." Furthermore, this servant is described as "faithful" when he does exactly as the Lord expects him to do; and when he does, the reward he receives is a promotion: the Lord "will place him over everything he owns." This also seems to be the case in our parable.

Those who are entrusted with some activity in the community are particularly equipped, "in proportion to their power," for the authority or job they are given. This equipment are the "talents" they receive. Of course, the talents are all kinds of graces and supernatural powers that Christ entrusts to his "ministers" in order to further his own interests by making those powers fruitful. A talent weighed about 80 pounds in silver or gold. So the traveling man was not only rich, but also generous and trusting—his servants were granted an abundant and valuable equipment.

The teaching of the parable is that Christ's gifts to his ministers must be kept in active trade; they must be regarded as an investment made by Christ, who wants his "capital" to bear fruit. Conversely, his minister must realize that his equipment is not given to him as a spiritual luxury that confers status in the community. He is expected to "trade" with it and to increase its value. After all, these are not his interests but Christ's interests. This is why, when he arrives home, the traveling man settles accounts with his servants; and they have to render their accounts. The man wants his money back—"with interest" (v. 27). The point is not only that wrong deeds are sin; doing nothing also is sin.

Importantly in this parable, the "interest" is not the external work and accomplishments of ministers, but the spiritual enrichment of the minister himself. His reward, in fact, is an increase of this same enrichment in eternal happiness; he "goes and joins in his master's happiness," he enjoys the full and direct communion of Jesus' gifts in complete rest and joy; there is now no question about ministerial "work" and fruit. The external work of the minister is matched by an internal enrichment by Christ.

This is how the gifts given for ministerial work, no matter how valuable, can be said to be "little things," whereas now, "greater things" are given. It is not a matter of absolutes, but of relative evaluation. No matter how great and invaluable Christ's gifts are on this earth, St. Paul could say that "no eye has seen, no ear heard...what God has prepared for those who love him" (1 Corinthians 2:9), and that "in Paradise he heard words which cannot be uttered" (2 Corinthians 12:3f.; cf. Romans 8:17ff.; Colossians 3:4). In comparison with present supernatural realities, St. John writes that "we are already children of God, but what we are to be in the future has not yet been revealed" (1 John 3:2). In comparison with the gifts of Christ on earth, those to be enjoyed in the future life are far better: Christ's minister will receive a much greater spiritual enrichment/reward for his active trade with his master's talents.

The notion that the "interest" is one's spiritual enrichment, also explains why the lazy servant has lost this interest, as well as any further enrichment that he might have been given as a heavenly reward. It is in this context that the sentence in v. 29 makes sense: he who is already spiritually rich will be rendered richer in heaven; he who has achieved no spiritual enrichment in his ministry will have even the basic "capital" taken away from him. If the basic capital of the lazy minister is said to have been given to the one who already has the highest amount of capital, it is merely a parabolic element, exemplifying the fact that the rich become even richer.

Another merely parabolic trait is the excuse of the lazy minister—who is lazy because he is the opposite of the "faithful" one, who does what he is expected to do. The proverb, by which he expresses his views about his master's severity and sternness (v. 24), is just an excuse—a poor one at that. It is intended only to point out that the Lord really wants his gifts to bear fruit ("interest")—he is greedy, and to provide him with an adequate opening to state his criterion for judgment: "he who does not have will be deprived even of what he has."

Thirty-fourth Sunday in Ordinary Time (Christ the King)
Matthew 25:31-46

The message of Matthew's gospel closes with the scene of the last judgment. After that, the passion narrative follows. With the last judgment, the entire message of Matthew comes to rest. The earthly phase of the kingdom evolves into its heavenly and definitive form; the separation of "wheat and weeds," so often spoken of throughout the gospel, now becomes effective and final: those on the left "will go away (from Christ) to eternal punishment, and the virtuous to eternal life" (v. 46). And thus the curtain falls over man's History.

The final judgment is conducted by the "Son of Man" (v. 31) who, just two verses later in the chapter (v. 33), is described as "the king." The "Son of Man" is a messianic title deriving from Daniel 7:13; it portrays Christ as sovereign judge and ruler over the entire universe and, therefore, over man and man's History, which also explains why he is called "the king" absolutely. He now comes "in glory," with all the splendor of his power and dominion; an expression of which is the fact that the angels themselves are his servants, and that he takes his seat on the "throne" of glory. The absolute power of the Son of Man appears, not just in his splendid display but, first of all, in the fact that he seals the eternal fate of the whole of mankind. There is no appeal against his sentence. And his sentence means eternal happiness or eternal punishment; it means the final, encompassing, scrutinizing and evaluating look at centuries and millennia of human History; a look at all the accomplishments and failures of the human race, but also at every single deed of every single individual. This is the last and final evaluation of man's actions, projects, etc.—and the only one that counts.

The supreme king and judge suddenly becomes the "shepherd" (v. 32) who conducts a separation in his flock. The metaphor indicates the shepherd's loving and caring tenderness for the "sheep" at his right hand; it is for these, after all, that he labored on earth, and it for these that he now comes in order to bring them to their final destination, their final and definitive salvation. The sheep are the fruit that he expects from the field of man's history; once the fruit expected is collected, history may be brought to an end. Those on the left are not the real concern of the "coming" shepherd; they belong to the nonprofitable produce from the field of man's History; it is just discarded.

Significantly, however, "all nations" are to appear before the universal judge, and among all nations the shepherd finds "sheep" and "he-goats." The sheep represent meekness and powerlessness, namely, those spiritual attitudes that Matthew himself points out in his beatitudes (5:3ff.); whereas the he-goats, according to a broad biblical background (see Daniel 8; Isaiah 34:6, etc.), are the symbol of power, overbearance and haughtiness, namely the opposite of the spirit breathing in the beatitudes. In point of fact, the sheep are those who are, first of all, "merciful" or compassionate (Matthew 5:6): they are sensitive to the needs of others (hunger, thirst, hospitality, clothing, sickness and dejection in jail). This is why, according to the promise of the beatitudes, they obtain mercy on the day of reckoning (see James 2:13). It is the he-goats who are insensitive to human needs, and refuse to be instruments of God's love for man. The spirit of the beatitudes is the criterion or law on which Christ's verdict will be based; it is on such criterion that man's entire history will be evaluated, and, wherever the spirit of the beatitudes will be found, the reward of the "inheritance" of the kingdom will be granted.

Another great message of Matthew's narrative is the new dimension that he discovers in the outcast of this world, in those who suffer: it is those who are hungry, thirsty, homeless, naked and sick whom Christ calls "my little brothers" (v. 39). Even deserved suffering establishes brotherhood with Christ: "I was in jail." All who suffer, all who are outcast, are Christ's brothers, because he, better than anyone else, knew what suffering was, what contempt and what being an outcast meant. Those who suffer share his own fate, his own life, his own sorrow, his own helplessness and his own powerlessness before human arrogance, carelessness and overbearance. Communion in suffering generates unbreakable bonds; it is this communion that binds Christ with those who suffer, with his "brothers." This is why he is so grateful to those who show mercy to those in distress. Jesus himself was grateful to the thief who felt compassion for him on the cross, and he rewarded him with "his company in Paradise" (Luke 23:40ff.).

Christ is the brother of every human being through his communion in human "blood and flesh" (Hebrews 2:14, 17, 12); suffering seems to be one of the essential ingredients of that human condition "in blood and flesh," which is also why all who suffer are human—and Christ is one of them. Suffering is human and is communion with Christ, even when it is the result of deserved punishment. This is the reason why human love and compassion must go to those "in jail" and to those who suffer other forms of just punishment: God's love goes to "evil and good" men, "to righteous and unrighteous" (Matthew 5:45).

The righteous seem to be unaware of their good deeds, and the news that they did good works seems to come to them as a surprise (v. 37f.). Their surprise, of course, is a literary device that paves the way to Christ's disclosure that all who suffer are "his little brothers." But the detail emphasizes also that "your left hand must not know what your right hand is doing" (Matthew 6:3). True compassion and mercy do not take note of what they do: they spring naturally and spontaneously from the heart, and flow into practical life and action, as the oil that smooths one's neighbor's existence and burns up, shedding light on the world (Matthew 5:16).

Solemnities

January 1
Feast of Mary, Mother of God

Luke 2:16-21

See the commentary on the gospel passage on the Feast of Christmas (At Dawn). Here follow some reflections.

God called Mary to do him the "service" of being the mother of the Savior. Mary's motherhood is related, not to one more instrument of God's salvation, but to the "son of David," to "the Messiah," he is "the" Savior of the old promises and of the old expectations of God's people. Mary's maternity happens to be related to the most important person of the entire biblical history and of tradition. What is more, it is related to the person who marked the direction, goal, purpose and end of Old Testament history and religion and, for that matter, of the entire salvation history. Such a perspective is clearly indicated in the text of the message to Mary in Luke 1:30-33 (see 2 Samuel 7:12-16). Mary is requested to be the mother of a unique person in God's design who is "Jesus," namely the Savior. Clearly this is a unique dimension. Thus the collaboration Mary is requested to offer is related directly and immediately to the most important person in the entire history of salvation, it is related to the most precious instrument of salvation God had in store, to the key element of God's design on which his whole plan hinges. Here lies the importance of Mary's "service."

The terms of the message and the operation of the Spirit in the conception of Mary's Son open up a wider perspective: this man will be called "son of the Most High, of God." If the exegete goes a step beyond the present text, he will discover that he has to deal, as Paul (Galatians 4:4) puts it, with "the Son of God born of a woman," "with his Son born of David's seed according to the flesh" (Romans 1:3). In other words the man whose mother Mary is requested to become is no less than the real Son of God. This was certainly clear to God when he conveyed his message and request. The inference is that Mary's service is directed to a most unique person with unique, special and exclusive relations with God. It is in these terms that the uniqueness of Mary's motherhood appears. She provides God with "the" Savior and, first of all, she provides a human nature to God's very Son and has to deal with him in a "familiar" relationship. Besides, Mary's motherhood is unique because of its virginal character.

Motherhood, however, spells sacrifice, suffering and self-denial. Mary was no exception. After a childbearing in a strange home and in poor circumstances, the "presentation" narrative in liturgical language, and without any legal obligation, shows Mary, with Joseph, bringing the child to Jerusalem "and *offering* him to the Lord" (Luke 2:22). Simeon's statement "but a sword will also pierce your very soul," which is addressed to Mary even though Joseph also is present (Luke 2:34ff.), is not easy to evaluate in detail, but it certainly discloses that suffering and sacrifice are part and parcel of Mary's motherly role. One early manifestation of the "piercing sword" was no doubt the "anguished" (*odynomenoi*) search for the twelve-year-old boy and, particularly his startling reaction "why do you search for me? Don't you know that I have to care for my Father's interests?" It is immediately after such an episode that the evangelist notes that "Mary was keeping all the words in her heart" (Luke 2:48-51; see v. 19). The gospel of Matthew informs us of Joseph's uncertainties and plans because of Mary's conception "by the Spirit" (1:18f.). The life of her child is menaced and "the child and *his mother*" become exiles on the earth and wander until they finally settle in Nazareth (2:14, 20ff.). At a certain moment Jesus engages completely "in the interests of his Father," the inevitable implication being that Mary has to let him go, that she sees him only occasionally, and then Jesus, once more, declares his independence (Mark 3:31-35; see Luke 11:26).

Just as Moses' and Samuel's mothers did (Exodus 2:10; 1 Samuel 2:26), Mary gives up her Son totally to God's work, a renunciation which climaxes in the scene on Mount Calvary (John 19:25-27), where Jesus, who through the cross is going to "where he was before" (John 6:63; 13:1; 16:28), signifies that the support a mother could give him is over and some others could benefit from his mother's support.

The relationship between Mary and her child is different from the normal relationship between mother and son. It is not to be understood as a mere affective communion or interplay of a mother towards her son. From the very outset the relationship here is determined not by the mother but by the child. In the infancy narratives of Matthew five times the following expression occurs: "the child and his mother." Mary is respected, venerated, holy, because her child, the Messiah, is respected, etc. The gospels indicate that in this relationship there was intimacy as in any living relationship between mother and child. But they also indicate that there was a necessary distance between Mary and Jesus.

The mysterious relationship between Mary and Jesus can be grasped and understood from the viewpoint of the Incarnation. The child is the Creator and Lord of his mother. It is the Son that creates or brings about this relationship, it is not determined by the mother. The authority is with the Son, not with the mother. What tradition handed down and was written down in the gospels is not the customary and human communion deriving from the relations between a mother and a son, but rather what was extraordinary between "this" son and "this" mother. The gospels bear witness to the veneration and respect of Mary as the "Mother of my Lord" (Luke 1:43). But at the same time they record also those sayings of Jesus that proclaim his absolute sovereignty, and his consciousness of being directly related to God.

Such is the Church's vision of Mary. "The Blessed Virgin...the Lord's humble handmaid...in an utterly singular way cooperated by her obedience, faith, hope, and burning charity in the Savior's work of restoring supernatural life to souls. For this reason she is a mother to us in the order of grace.... By her maternal charity, Mary cares for the brethren of her Son who still journey on earth. The Church does not hesitate to profess this subordinate role of Mary. The Church experiences it continuously and commends it to the hearts of the faithful, so that encouraged by her maternal help they may more closely adhere to the Mediator and Redeemer, our Lord Jesus Christ" (Vatican II, Const. on the Church, 61f.).

Mary's maternity was a "service" to God by which she provided and brought up a Savior for God. This is what the divine maternity of the Blessed Mother should teach all human mothers and particularly all Christian mothers. They are supposed to bring up instruments of salvation in God's hands, to raise their children in such a way that God can avail himself of them to carry out his plan of salvation. In theological terms, being a mother means to raise a man preparing him to be able and willing to be at God's service, to be useful to God in his saving undertaking.

Feast of St. Joseph

Luke 2:41-51

The episode of Jesus lost and found in the Jerusalem temple is a genuine illustration of the statement in v. 40, which in all truth is an introduction to the temple story and, in this sense, it looks forward, not backward. In v. 40 the evangelist writes that "the child was developing and gaining strength as he was being filled with 'wisdom,' and God's 'grace' was with him." The following account will show how "wise" and "favored" (grace) the child was.

As Mary and Joseph were introduced to the reader the emphasis fell upon the virginal nature of Jesus' birth, the marital status and Joseph's family bonds with David and with Bethlehem. Now the author emphasizes that they were pious Jews who complied with God's law; Jesus' "parents 'used' to go to Jerusalem for the feast of the Passover—every year." The author insists again (v. 42) that this was the "usual" practice with the couple. The law of going to Jerusalem (three times a year: Exodus 23:14-17) was binding on the Israelite man only (Exodus 34:23; Deuteronomy 16:1). Women had no obligation to comply with this law, but they often complied with it out of devotion and sincere religiosity (see Mark 15:41). Rabbinic regulations determined that a boy became "a son of the Law," i.e., subject to the demands of the Law, when he turned 12 years old. This must have been the reason why this time (perhaps the first time) Jesus went to Jerusalem for the pilgrimage. The celebration of the feast lasted one entire week, but pilgrims were not required to stay the seven days. They could leave on the third day. It was when the parents left with a group of Galileans (according to custom) that Jesus remained in Jerusalem. The following will show that he did not stay behind unintentionally or just by accident. He was a "wise" child.

Another tribute to the wisdom of the child comes precisely from his parents' lack of concern. The evangelist wants to show that Jesus was a wise child, he could handle situations like those involved here and was smart enough to find his way around. In the writer's mind the apparent carelessness of the parents is not evidence of their lack of concern but of their full trust in the child: they must have known that he was a "wise," smart child. Thus they covered the distance of one day's journey in the conviction that the child was in the group on his way to Galilee, but as they went, they tried to trace him among relatives and acquaintances. When the search turned out unfruitful, they returned to Jerusalem where they found him "after three days," i.e., on the third day from the initial departure or the day after their second arrival in Jerusalem; the suggestion being that locating the child was not an arduous task. Of course, nothing is said about where the child was all that time, where he stayed overnight, why Joseph and Mary expected to find him in the temple.

The only important element in all this is the basic teaching of the entire narrative. In the first place the child was in the company of the "teachers" of Israel attentive (listening) to what they said and interested (asking questions) in what they taught. For a child of twelve going to school when nothing or nobody puts pressure on him is rather unusual. It is precisely here that the "wisdom" of the child excelled; he acted judiciously and showed an interest for what really matters. But the talent of the boy is brought into a sharper relief by the "surprise" of all who heard him talk, because of his intelligence and of his answers. The surprise is, of course, a pleasant one: it is here that the "grace" of God enters the picture. The question is not one of theological grace in God's eyes, but of favor and pleasant acceptance that God gives to the child in men's eyes. For the biblical world also, the child is the father of the man, and this was true also of Jesus. The present episode foreshadows the wise and surprising answers that Christ gave to his friends and opponents, e.g., in regard to the resurrection (Mark 12:18ff., parall.), taxes to the Roman emperor (Mark 12:18ff.), much of his parabolic teaching, etc. See also the words of "grace" coming forth from his lips in Luke 4:22.

The climax of the infancy narratives in Luke is the answer that the boy gave to his parents: "What does it mean that you were looking for me? Did you not know that I have to devote myself to my Father's interests?" This time the "wisdom" of the child is such that he surprised even his parents and gave them an answer far above their heads—"they did not understand." The remark is intended to let us know how smart and clever the boy was. Still, his answer is as enigmatic to us today as it was to his parents. The translation itself of the original Greek is uncertain: the clause "to devote myself to my Father's interests" can be legitimately replaced by "to be in my Father's house" or home. In either case, moreover, the meaning of the answer can be that the parents had no need to go around in search of him, they should have gone to the temple right away, it was there that he was supposed to be; or the meaning can be that they should not worry about him but let him alone, he knew what his duty was and how to discharge it. Again, the ambivalent answer of the child foreshadows some of the ambivalent expressions of the grown-up man: how can the Messiah be "Son of David"? (Mark 12:37); "you say so" was Jesus' answer when Pilate asked if he was king (Mark 15:2); even the rulers or judges are said to be "gods" (John 10:34f.). It is the wisdom of the child that shines through. One thing, however, is clear in the answer: that Jesus is more directly related to God himself than to any human relationship. The answer throws the narrative of the "virgin" birth (Luke 1:26-38) and of the "presentation" of the child to God (2:22) into a sharp relief.

This episode of Jesus' childhood was handed down not just to inform the readers of the gospel about a curious incident in the life of the child where he does not come out precisely as a model of obedience; nor was it handed down to inform us of the parental plight of Mary and Joseph. The whole episode was designed and reported in order to let us understand something about the child himself. It is within this perspective and against this background that the entire episode must be read. The story prepares the reader for the Jesus of the public ministry.

As a matter of fact, the author closes the episode (v. 52) with the same concepts that opened it (v. 40). Even after the temple story "Jesus increased in wisdom, in stature, and in grace/favor with God and men"— throughout the years that elapsed between his childhood and the day of his ministry during his manhood: the Jesus of the public ministry continues to develop just as every man does. After all God's interrelations with man expand at the pace that the human capacity also expands.

Obviously the evangelist did not see any conflict between his narrative of the virgin birth (1:34; 2:5) and the fact of speaking of Jesus' "parents," and even of Jesus' father in reference to Joseph. He does so only after the child came to find himself, and to be found by others, within a family structure; casual language naturally leads to such phrasing. Furthermore, Jesus is never called son of Joseph in these narratives (see Luke 3:23). As for the knowledge of Mary and Joseph concerning the child nothing can be concluded from the narrative. As significant as the remark "they did not understand" is the child's expression "did you not know?", with the implication that they did know.

Feast of the Annunciation
Luke 1:26-38

A commentary on the gospel is found in B, the Fourth Sunday of Advent. Here some other reflections follow.

As far as the Blessed Mother is concerned, the message of today's gospel is not that Mary was just served notice that she was to conceive and give birth to the Son of God. She was not served notice, she was "called" by God to cooperate with him in his saving plan. Mary was requested by God to do him a service that he needed. The difference between both concepts is considerable. In the first place, the request made by God shows that Mary is called to accept willingly and freely the request of service to God; in the second place, an acceptance of God's request implies a personal resolve and involvement of Mary in the discharge of the service requested; it requires a personal and conscious commitment to God's work, to God's service; in the third place, a request of God freely and willingly accepted by Mary discloses the real meaning of the self-definition of Mary as "the servant of the Lord."

This "title" of the Blessed Mother is not so much an expression of humility and lowliness as a "soteriological" technical term, deeply rooted in the biblical tradition that proclaims that Mary in her maternity was an instrument of salvation in God's hands; she did God a saving service, a service that he needed in order to implement his redeeming design. The title, therefore, underscores, not so much Mary's humility as her conscious and courageous resolve to discharge the service that the Lord wanted. Her answer is to be compared with that of the prophet Isaiah at the time of his calling: "Here I am, send me" (Isaiah 6:8). As a servant of the Lord in a saving project, Mary becomes a redeeming instrument in God's hands, that makes its own contribution to the total and final purpose of God.

This perspective discloses the true meaning of key expressions in the narrative. The divine messenger announces to the Blessed Mother that "the Lord is with you." In the contexts of the Old Testament that provide the literary model of today's reading from the gospel the expression "the Lord is with you" is not a wish, it is a statement. It is not a mere greeting formula, it is a promise or rather a declaration of divine assistance for some commission which is regarded as difficult and arduous. When another angel appeared to Gideon (Judges 6:11ff.) and greeted him with the words "mighty man of valor, the Lord is with you," Gideon retorts: "If the Lord is with us why is it that we are helpless and oppressed by the enemy?" Later on when Gideon tries to find an excuse to shun the divine commission, the Lord tells him: "I will be with you, and you shall be able to defeat the Midianites." This also is true of Moses (Exodus 3 and 4), of Jeremiah (1:5; 11), and of the "Servant of the Lord" in Second Isaiah. This is even true of non-religious narratives. One example is Potiphar of Egypt in regard to Joseph (Genesis 39:2ff.): Potiphar saw that "the Lord was with Joseph" because he succeeded in everything he undertook, and this was the reason why "Joseph found *grace* in the eyes of his master" and was appointed steward of his master's household. Later on, Pharaoh himself did the same thing for the same reason.

This leads us over to the other expression of Luke's narrative: "you have found grace with the Lord." Joseph "found grace" because he was chosen, he was picked up, to be appointed to some office. Moses, Gideon, the Servant of the Lord also "found grace in the eyes of the Lord" because they were picked up to be instruments of salvation in God's hands. This is a notion which usually is bound up with the fact that the Lord is with his elect giving them assistance and help. The assistance of the Lord is needed whenever a human being is chosen to serve the Lord, because the service of the Lord is always demanding. That is why the Blessed Mother is deeply upset, not because of the vision, as in the case of Zechariah (Luke 2:12), but because of the greeting itself as she tried to find out the concrete meaning of God's calling.

God's calling is that Mary serve God as a mother; this is the specific service that he needs and requests. Mary accepts to do this service, and it is this that the definition of "the Servant of the Lord" expresses. From another point of view, however, Mary is requested to be the mother of the Messiah, the person towards whom all the aspirations and expectations of the Old Testament were directed, the purpose and goal of the entire salvation history, the key element in God's salvation projects, and, in fact, the greatest redeemer and savior of all times, at the service of God.

It was this saving instrument that Mary had to provide. Far beyond that, God was choosing and requesting Mary to be the human mother of his divine Son: "in the fullness of time God sent his Son born of a woman" (Galatians 4:4), and this woman was Mary of whom the Son of God was born "according to the flesh" (Romans 1:3).

Theologians will continue to debate whether such a privilege could be merited. The liturgy teaches us, at any event, that when God rewards the merits of his beloved he glorifies the work of his own grace, power and mercy. From our point of view, however, it is all too obvious that a mere human creature of our large human family was distinguished with such a privilege; it was Mary of Nazareth, and no one else, who was picked by the Lord to serve in such a close, familiar and intimate collaboration with God in his grandiose saving project. It is a distinction and a privilege beyond all imagination. As a daughter of our human family, however, Mary is one of us, she is one of our sisters in this large human family, and this is why we feel that her distinction is an honor for all of us, and her privilege is a glory for all of us.

This is the foundation of our reverence, of our veneration, of our pride and of our love for this admired sister chosen among thousands and millions to be elevated to that intimacy with God and to be entrusted, not with the household of God, but with what God himself treasured most: his only beloved Son. Mary, the Blessed Mother, is in all truth "the exaltation and the pride of our people, the highest boast of our human race."

(See also solemnity of the Immaculate Conception, December 8.)

Saints Peter and Paul
John 21:15-19

Peter was a temperamental and impetuous man. He would not let Jesus wash his feet—"ever" (John 13:7f.); thereby Peter was determined not to let the Lord accomplish his work of "Servant" of the Lord (the Johannine version of Matthew 16:22). A few minutes later Peter solemnly declared his readiness to die for Jesus: "why cannot I follow you 'now'? I will give my life for you" (John 13:37), which is a mild rendering of the synoptic statement: "even though 'all' will be disloyal to you, 'I' will never be disloyal" (Matthew 26:33). But some time later, when Jesus was in trouble Peter three times disclaimed to have any connections with Jesus at all. He did exactly what all the others did (they abandoned Jesus)—and worse.

Against this background, Jesus asks Simon Peter: "Simon, son of John, do you love me 'more than these'?", the reference being to the other disciples present there. Peter gets the message, and he answers just "yes, Lord, you know I love you." The comparison with anybody else ("all") drops from Simon's lips; he just states that he loves the Lord. And even this is done without any reference to his own achievements. Peter makes an appeal to him who knows the warmth of man's heart—as well as its weakness: "You know, Lord, that I love you." Jesus' knowledge of man's heart should find an explanation of man's incomprehensible apparent inconsistency between his will and his factual deeds, between his love and his weakness. Thus Jesus should be able to understand that Peter really loves him in spite of his cowardice. He may not be better than anybody else, but Jesus can certainly understand what Peter cannot: his own sincere and genuine love and his inconsistent attitudes. Jesus got his message across, and in the following questions addressed to Peter he drops any comparison with the "others."

But two more questions on top of the first add up to three, and "three" was a number that rankled in Simon's heart and mind: he had disowned his Master three times. Obviously, Jesus wants a redress of the three denials by a triple declaration of love. Jesus does not remind Peter of his senseless bravadoes in his comparison with "all" others; he gently but consciously touches a wound still bleeding in Simon's heart. The message could hardly be grasped at the second question, and this explains why Peter's answer this time was exactly the same as the first. But when the "third" question came, the message could not be missed and it cut Peter to the quick: now it is only too obvious to him that the Lord really "knows everything"—not only his love, but also his cowardice and his denials. After everything the Lord knows, can he believe Peter's reassurances of love? At this, "Peter saddened because he (Jesus) for the 'third' time asked" him the same question—just as before somebody else had asked Peter the same question three times, and three times he had disowned the man he now faces. More than ever Peter is at a loss and has no explanation for his behavior, but he is sure of one thing and this he emphasizes with all the strength of his heart: "you know that I love you." What about my failings? Well, I have no explanation for them, but "you know everything" and you know all the abyss of man's poverty and powerlessness, which does certainly not mean that I do not love you. You know both things as you also know how they can exist together at the same time in the same heart. Peter is the impersonation of every sincere Christian who dearly loves his Lord and yet is weak and fails. Peter teaches us the only correct and possible attitude open to a sinning Christian.

The Lord gently reminds Peter of his weakness, but at the same time that he does so he also lets Peter know that love is more powerful than weakness and sin, that Peter's failings have not diminished Jesus' trust and faith in the committed apostle. As Peter gradually tries to assure the Lord of his love, the Lord lets Peter feel that he enjoys the full trust and confidence of the Lord: "Tend my little lambs, tend my little sheep." If Peter was reminded of his failure three times, he also was reassured of the Lord's trust in him by a triple reaffirmation of the Lord that Peter had to tend "my" own little sheep. What is dearest to Jesus' heart is entrusted to Peter. This is the clearest evidence of Jesus' trust in Peter; the apostle cannot only see, but experience that confidence has been fully restored. In Jesus' eyes, loving faith or faithful love are not offset by weakness and failings.

Peter, however, has to learn what being a shepherd/pastor means. When Jesus was about to set out on his painful way to Calvary and, by washing their feet, he taught his disciples that he—"the Master and Lord"—was the "Servant of the Lord," Jesus told Peter that he could not understand that lesson "now," at that moment; but he had a prediction for the apostle: what I am doing you do not understand now, "but you will understand it later" (John 13:7). After a few minutes the Lord insisted with Simon: "you cannot follow me 'now,' but you will follow me 'later' " (13:36). When Jesus appoints Peter supreme shepherd of his flock he is explicit: at an old age, after a life spent at the service of "the Master and Lord," Peter will follow him all the way to the cross. This is what being a shepherd in Christ's community means: absolute and total commitment to the Lord and to his flock—in sacrifice, self-denial and complete surrender of one's total being and life. This time Peter was absolutely loyal and faithful, he showed himself to be worthy of Jesus' trust. He set an example for all the shepherds/pastors who supposedly tend the Lord's flock—and not themselves.

In his first letter Peter characterizes the Lord as the "chief shepherd" (5:4). He may have been thinking of that memorable moment when Jesus told him: tend "my" flock. At that time, in fact, he acts as the real shepherd who cares for his sheep—one of Jesus' prominent features in the fourth gospel (John 10)—he is a loving shepherd who with infinite tenderness and affection speaks of his "little lambs," of his "little sheep." Jesus has to leave his flock, but he cannot see his flock unattended; his care prompts him to look for a shepherd, but he needs a "good shepherd," and much better than anyone else Jesus knows that a good shepherd is only "he who gives his life for the sheep." And he knew that, in spite of all his weaknesses,

Peter was such a shepherd because "Simon, son of John" really "loved" him and cared for his Lord's interests and wishes, and not for himself.

August 6
The Transfiguration of the Lord
Mark 9:2-10

See a commentary to the gospel, Mark 9:2-10, in B, Second Sunday of Lent. Here some other reflections are added.

The Transfiguration of the Lord is, in some way, an anticipation, a foretaste and a sort of sign of his Resurrection. If we were to translate the synoptic description of this event into the language of John, we would say that in the Transfiguration Jesus regained for a while the "glory" or splendor that he had as his own and personal possession with the Father before the world began (John 15:5-24). The Lord's Transfiguration allowed his disciples a glimpse of who Jesus really was. The splendor and life of the divine permeated the humanity of Christ.

For a while in his state of slave the Lord releases the glory that he had when he was living in the condition and state of God and when he was equal to God in splendor and glory. For a while he shows to his closest friends what he had before, what he is going to have later on, thereby suggesting what he *is* even *now* in his state of slave. John says that in Christ—in Christ's deeds, teaching, etc.—he "saw" the "glory" or splendor of the Logos, a glory which is that of the only Son of a Father who is God himself. The author of the second epistle of Peter (1:16ff.) mentions the fact of Christ's Transfiguration to demonstrate that the Christian preaching concerning Christ's power and second coming, i.e., his divinity and pre-existence, is not based on sophisticated myths; it is well established upon the testimony of eyewitnesses, namely the testimony of those who at that time were with him on the holy mountain and saw his majesty, when he received honor and glory from God the Father, and the voice was borne to him by the Majestic Glory (i.e., God): "This is my beloved Son, with whom I am well pleased."

This also is the theological thought in the synoptic tradition: Christ's Transfiguration is a disclosure or a "revelation" of what Jesus really was—"my beloved Son"—it is a revelation of his divine power and glory. For an instant the divinity of Christ shone through his body. The splendor proper to divinity, which was not granted to his humanity during his earthly life as a permanent possession, for a short while was given to him, i.e., to his humanity, the body being included.

At the Resurrection of Christ, however, this splendor of the divine being was given to Christ's humanity, including his body, as a permanent donation and, therefore, as a personal and permanent possession. It is particularly in this sense that the Transfiguration appears as an anticipation and sign of Christ's resurrection. The body of Christ permeated by the divine splendor at the Transfiguration is the same human body that existed both before and after the brief moments of that Transfiguration. To the biblical mind it is inconceivable that Christ's body, i.e., his physical dimension, would vanish for a moment. What this biblical mind understands is that the same body can exist in different modes of existence: it existed as an "earthly" natural body before and after the Transfiguration itself, and it existed in another way, which may be called "spiritual" or heavenly (see 1 Corinthians 15:44-47), during the time of the Transfiguration itself. It is the same body which can receive various forms of existence. This is, in fact, the language of Mark and Matthew; their Jesus *metemorphothe* in the presence of his disciples, i.e., Christ underwent a "metamorphosis" in their presence. Luke says that the appearance of his face (or presence in general) became different, though he was the same person, with the same body too. It is along this thought pattern and on the basis of this fact that we have to conceive of the Resurrection of the Lord: among other things, the Resurrection of the Lord means that his body underwent a "transfiguration" (or a metamorphosis, see Philippians 3:21; 1 Corinthians 15:50-54), it did not vanish.

Another feature common to both the Transfiguration and Resurrection of the Lord is the authenticating value of both events. The relationship—both literary and theological—between the narrative of Christ's Transfiguration and the narrative of his baptism is obvious, and has always been pointed out by the scholars. The baptismal theophany takes place at the beginning of Christ's ministry, and it is meant to disclose that Christ has God's approval and assistance as a divine envoy who proclaims God's will and doctrine to man. Christ's missionary work is guaranteed by God: man can and must trust Christ. At the Transfiguration, God's statement explains: "this is my beloved Son, *listen to him.*" Again, the display of Christ's glory and splendor is not just a show, there is a didactic dimension to it. Once again God authenticates and guarantees Christ's teaching, and wants us to listen to what he says. At the Transfiguration God wants the witnesses to the event and us all to know that Christ is backed and supported by God's full authority, and that whatever he says and teaches has to be accepted and complied with: "listen to him."

In this regard also the Transfiguration of Christ is an anticipation of Christ's Resurrection. It is, in fact, through the Resurrection that God authenticates and ratifies the entire career of Jesus; by the resurrection God declares that justice and righteousness are on the side of Jesus and not on the side of those who opposed and put him to death (John 16:10; Acts 3:13-15; 4:10; 5:30f.). One can say that the Transfiguration of Christ is a sort of sketch or rehearsal of the Resurrection of Christ.

In both cases, however, the practical inference is this: "listen to him." This is perhaps the most important message of today's reading for us. Our faith professes that Christ is God's divine Son; our faith professes, furthermore, that Christ's teaching is God's doctrine. Now, our intellectual faith must be made truth and life in actual living. And concerning this particular point our faith has to be actualized by ourselves listening to Christ; by ourselves trying to hear what he says to us in his gospel, in his community, in his envoys; by ourselves trying to hear what he has to tell us as individuals with a personal mission in this world and in his community.

Assumption of Mary
Luke 1:39-56

When Mary received her heavenly call to be the Messiah's virgin mother, the angel gave her a sign that her calling was really coming from God: her unfruitful relative, Elizabeth, was in her sixth month. But the angel added that the power of God can go beyond that and give Mary a virginal maternity: "nothing will be impossible to God." That Elizabeth was with child truly was a family event, an occasion of joy and congratulatory visits. In the existing circumstances, furthermore, particularly in Elizabeth's circumstances, the help of a young lady of the family was most welcome by the expectant mother, and mandatory in reference to her relatives. So Mary went to see Elizabeth and stayed with her "some three months" (Luke 1:56), namely until the child's birth. She was unaware of the surprise waiting for her.

The episode is usually called the Visitation. In the purpose and intent of the evangelist it was much more than a courtesy visitation. After all, it is not the family event that the evangelist wants his readers to know about; he rather uses the event to make his point, which is this: the revelation of Mary's maternity to herself. She had given her consent to become a virgin mother. Now the happenings that took place when she met Elizabeth reveal to her that she already is a mother. She became mother by "the Power of the Most High," and now the same Power acts again to show her that she carries the "son of the Most High" in her womb. It is the Spirit of God who through Elizabeth's child—who becomes a prophet from his mother's womb (see Luke 1:15, 76)—and through Elizabeth's words declares to Mary that her maternity is under way: she has conceived a child, she is an expectant mother. The author wants his readers to know that it was the Holy Spirit that had to make such a disclosure since Mary's had been a virginal conception, and after her call she had left for Judea "in haste."

It is at the realization of her motherhood that the young lady bursts forth into joyous songs and praises that are only too inadequate to bring forth all the happiness, elation and bliss that fill her heart and flow over: "my soul sings the greatness of the Lord, my spirit is overjoyed in God my Savior." The young girl who becomes a mother for the first time finds delight and pleasure as she dwells on the thought that "the Mighty One has done great things to me." In view of her realized motherhood, she resorts to the highest attributes of God in order to praise him for such a wonderful gift: he is transcendent/divine ("holy"), he is for ever a loving God ("mercy") to those who show him filial respect; he is powerful, and has resorted to his power to exalt the girl of the village and bless her with a child in her womb.

It is the natural joy of knowing herself to be a mother that springs in Mary a rapturous exultation. But the rapture is boundless when she realizes all the goodness of the Lord, all his love, all his commitment, all his selective process involved in the case of Mary's motherhood. The Mighty One really did "great things" to her—great beyond man's imagination. He really looked upon the "lowly condition of his servant," he was really gracious and loving. The virginal maternity is to Mary a source of joy and bliss beyond all telling; her maternity is unique, fully and exclusively hers, glorious, miraculous, absolutely wonderful and fulfilling.

Through Elizabeth the Spirit not only discloses Mary's maternity but he also tells the young mother the meaning and significance of her motherhood. She is "the mother of my Lord," she is the mother of the messianic king whom David himself addressed as "my Lord" (Psalm 110:1; Mark 12:36f.); thus Mary realizes that she is "the mother of the king," the queen-mother of the Davidic dynasty. "The mother of the king" was a relevant dynastic figure in the royal family of Judah. She is consistently mentioned in the presentation of every king who ascended David's throne, whereas in the northern kingdom the mother of the king is never thus mentioned. The *almah* of Isaiah 7:14 and "she who has to give birth" in Micah 5:2 point to that dynastic figure. The "mother of my Lord," therefore, appears as the last of the queen-mothers in the Davidic dynasty from whom the glorious Davidic king of the promise was descended: she is the mother of the messianic king. This is why Elizabeth deems it a privileged honor that such a mother, "the mother of my Lord," the queen-mother of the Messiah, pays a visit to her. Mary is declared blessed because "the fruit of her womb is blessed"; it enjoys God's particular blessing and protection and, therefore, it will be glorious and "great."

It is precisely on account of the greatness and blessedness of her child, and on account of the fact that she is "the mother of my Lord," that Mary comes to the realization that "from now on," from the very moment she came to realize the joys of her motherhood, "all generations will call me blessed"; just as the psalmist addresses the king and sings to him, "I shall make your name to be remembered in all generations, the peoples, as a result, shall praise you for ever and ever" (Psalm 45:8). Mary catches a glimpse of the praise and honor that all generations everywhere will give her, but she is aware that all that is grounded on the distinguished privilege of her maternity, it is grounded "on the blessed fruit of her womb." The definition of Mary as "the mother of my Lord" is reminiscent of the entire episode reported in 1 Kings 2:19: Solomon's mother, "Bathsheba, went to king Solomon to speak to him...the king rose to meet her and bowed down before her; he then sat down on his throne; a throne was brought for 'the mother of the king,' and she sat down at his 'right hand' " (see Psalm 110:1).

It was on the occasion of her dutiful visit to expectant Elizabeth that the Spirit disclosed to Mary that she was a mother, the mother of a highly significant child. At such a discovery joyful emotions overwhelm Mary's soul and in immortal words that "all generations" will endlessly re-echo she herself sings the bliss of her motherhood. Really, "the Mighty One has done great things to me. My spirit is overjoyed in God my savior."

Feast of All Saints

Matthew 5:1-12

The Sermon of the Mountain in Matthew (5-7) opens with a series of solemn statements in which the Lord pronounces "blest" those who in various ways suffer and endure the hardships of this life. These are the Beatitudes. The Greek word translated by "blest," and its Hebrew background, rather convey the concept of congratulation: those who suffer are to be congratulated. The meaning is not that they are to rejoice in their suffering, but this: their hopes are good, their future (afterlife) is bright, on account of the promise attached to each one of the statements. In each of them, in fact, the second half (even in vv. 11-12) contains a "reward" that stands for eternal happiness in its various aspects—it is a "reward in heaven." It is for this reason that the Beatitudes in Matthew appear as the eschatological reason for the ethics of the gospel: please sustain sufferings and hardships in view of the eternal reward.

The Beatitudes, however, are not a comprehensive list of virtues describing the Christian ideal of morality. Nor do they portray social or religious groups committed to a given ideal (e.g., poverty) or affected by a given condition. They describe various aspects of one and the same spiritual attitude that is supposed to be found and to prevail in each individual Christian: religious openness to God's will amidst, and in spite of, the hard conditions of the present life. The Beatitudes represent a complete reversal of worldly values; this paradox is one of the essential enigmas of the gospel but it also is its essential message (see 1 Timothy 2:15ff.). They carry further an Old Testament line of thought to be seen, e.g., in Isaiah 61:1, 13; 49: 6-13; 29:18; see Matthew 11:4-6.

The poor of the first Beatitude are a religious, not just social, category as can be seen in James 2:5-7. They are the Old Testament *anawim* who not only were destitute but also oppressed by the rich who trusted in their wealth and disregarded God (see Psalms 82; 52:9ff.). The poor are really poor and religious people who put their trust in God and expect help and deliverance from him alone. They are promised the possession of the Kingdom which is the sum total of the messianic blessings in their eternal fullness. The sorrowful of the second Beatitude (see Isaiah 61:1ff.) are those for whom life is not pleasant at all, is not joy and happiness, and yet accept their lot in submission to God's design and expect their consolation from God alone—consolation in eternal happiness (see Revelation 21:4).

The meek or mild in the third Beatitude are those who are not arrogant, proud, haughty, insolent (see Zechariah 9:9 in Matthew 21:4), and respect God's right to rule history as he pleases: they do not try to oppress others in order to make room for themselves. The land promised to them in perpetual possession is the land of Israel considered as the symbol of the messianic Kingdom in its projection of heavenly joy and victory. The hunger and thirst in the fourth Beatitude is an ardent desire for justice, i.e., for being just or righteous—justice is one's perfect compliance with God's will expressed in his Law. The reward is that those hungry and thirsty for justice will find themselves doing God's will blamelessly without any effort or strain in eternal life. This is the same thought of the petition "thy will be done on earth as it is in heaven" (Matthew 6:10).

The parable in Matthew 18:21-35 (especially vv. 33 and 27) discloses the meaning of the merciful in the fifth Beatitude. Merciful are those who are compassionate and forgiving in every regard but particularly in regard to offenses received. It is the same idea of the petition "forgive us our trespassses as we forgive those who trespass against us" (Matthew 6:12, 14). The mercy promised to them is God's mercy at the last Judgment (see 2 Timothy 1:18; James 2:13). The purity of heart in the sixth Beatitude indicates (just as in the case of pure gold, etc.) man's sincerity and uprightness by which he totally, unreservedly, undividedly, without any admixture devotes himself to God. The "vision of God" promised to such a man is the happiness of enjoying God's benevolent and beatifying countenance in heaven.

The peacemakers of the seventh Beatitude are those who in themselves enjoy God's peace and spread it around themselves by actively trying to make peace between antagonistic individuals. They will be treated as God's children in heaven by the God of peace (Romans 15:33; 16:20) and the Prince of peace (Isaiah 9:15; Zechariah 9:9); they will be heirs of God and co-heirs of Christ (Romans 8:17). The persecution in the eighth Beatitude is for the sake of justice, i.e. (as in the fourth Beatitude), for complying with God's will that, this time, is God's will manifested through Christ—it is the gospel and its herald, Christ. The promise here is the same of the first Beatitude. The Beatitude in vvs. 11f. is an expansion of the eighth (v. 10): Jesus' disciples endure persecution just "because of me." There is reason for rejoicing, however, in persecution: Christians emulate the glory of the Old Testament prophets whose successors they are. They deserve to be congratulated because their reward will be great, not here on earth but in heaven.

December 8
Feast of the Immaculate Conception
Luke 1:26-38

The commentary on the gospel passage is found on the 4th Sunday of Advent, cycle B; see reflections on the Feast of the Annunciation, March 25. Here follow some other reflections on the same gospel passage.

The narrative in Luke 1:26-38 is a calling narrative to be compared with the callings of outstanding "servants of the Lord" through whom God had determined to carry out his saving plan. The calling of Mary by God in Luke's gospel is projected against the background of the callings of Moses (Exodus 3 and 4), Gideon (Judges 6:11-18), Jeremiah (1:5-11), and the Servant of the Lord in Second Isaiah.

It is against this background that the biblical thought and the expressions of the gospel passage provide a suitable setting for the unique privilege of the Immaculate Conception of the Blessed Mother. In fact, when God intimates his calling to the prophet Jeremiah, he does so in these suggestive terms: "Before I formed you in the womb I knew you; before you came forth out of the womb I sanctified you: I have appointed you a prophet unto the nations." The text teaches us that the prophet had been chosen by God long before he had been born, and even long before he had been formed, or shaped—conceived, we should say. Long before the prophet came to exist, he was known, he was sanctified by the Lord. This is, more or less, the concept of predestination of later theology—though not exactly so. The concepts "to know" and "to sanctify" are important in this context. In the biblical language, to know is not to have an idea about someone or something; to know includes the aspect of affection rather, the motion and inclination of one's will. Thus "to know" means to grasp the significance and the claims of the known person and, as a result, to know expresses a provident concern for such a person. It is all the more so when God is said to know someone, for God's knowledge of this person is the true foundation and source of the (saving) significance of that person who, thereby, becomes the object of God's care, love and election. This is how Jeremiah was known by God even before his conception: God cherished him and chose him as his messenger.

In keeping with this is the concept of "sanctification" of Jeremiah before his birth. Admittedly, this concept here is not related to moral or religious saintliness; it rather expresses the concept of dedication to the service of the Lord, it is a *consecration* to the Lord. What is consecrated here, however, is not an object but a person who is set apart for a human and intelligent mission, namely to be a prophet. On the other hand, it is God himself who consecrates, the implication being that it is not a question of any sort of ritual consecration; it is rather a question of a causal and effective consecration that equips a human person for some specific mission, for a prophetic mission in this case. This sort of consecration was somehow effected by God even before the prophet was born.

The same theological conceptions are expressed in the calling of the Servant of the Lord in Second Isaiah: he was formed and chosen as "the Servant" from his mother's womb. That is why he says: "the Lord has called me from the womb, from the womb of my mother has he made mention of my name...he formed me from the womb to be his servant...for I am honorable in the eyes of the Lord and my God has become my strength" (Isaiah 43:4; 44:2; 49:2, 5). In view of his "predestination," the Servant is honorable or, rather, according to the original language, he is something precious in the eyes of the Lord. The prominent feature, however, in the relationship between the Servant and the Lord is that of love: he "is my elect (= beloved)—says the Lord—in whom my soul delights; I have put my spirit upon him" (Isaiah 42:9); to the point that the Lord addresses his Servant in these terms: "since you are precious and honorable in my sight, I have loved you" (Isaiah 43:44). Samson, another saving instrument in God's hand, had to be a *nazir* in his mother's womb, namely he was consecrated to God even before his birth (Judges 13:5).

Projected against the background of these calling narratives in the Old Testament, the terms in which the calling of the Blessed Mother is reported obtain a new perspective and a new depth. That the bestowal of divine gifts before birth is present to the mind of the evangelist is beyond any question, since, in the same narrative, he refers to John the Baptist as being filled with the divine Spirit in his mother's womb. In the context of her calling, furthermore, the Blessed Mother is said to enjoy God's grace, or even the fullness of grace according to the received translation; the Lord is with her, she is invited to rejoice. The narratives of the Old Testament teach us that those chosen and called for some saving mission were somehow equipped by the Lord for that mission even before their birth. The same thing is true of John the Baptist in the New Testament.

Such is the theological setting and the literary framework in which the "fullness of grace" of the Blessed Mother is placed by the evangelist. In the context of a calling, such a grace is, not just a benevolent feeling, but the expression of a choice to which tangible and concrete expressions of grace, i.e., love, are attached; this grace consists of special gifts for the appropriate discharge of a divine commission. In point of fact, the Blessed Mother is said to enjoy God's grace even before she becomes the Savior's mother. In one way or another, this points to the spiritual equipment of the Blessed Mother to become that instrument of salvation God wishes her to become.

In this narrative of a divine calling addressed to Mary, the concepts of grace in God's sight and of God's assistance can hardly mean anything less than the spiritual equipment of John the Baptist who was an object of God's care and gifts from his mother's womb. The concepts of grace and favor in God's sight as well as of divine assistance are the expression of God's care, gifts, love for the Blessed Mother in a theological context where many "servants" of the Lord before her had been "known" and "sanctified" by God before they had been shaped each one in his mother's womb, i.e., before they had been born.

Admittedly, the tools that an exegete handles do not allow him to determine further the contents and depth of Mary's grace. But the exegete can certainly show that the privilege of the Immaculate Conception rests on solid biblical grounds, and that such a privilege becomes more understandable when it is placed in the appropriate biblical setting, namely the callings of those instruments of salvation who became "servants" of the Lord. This is how the Blessed Mother understands herself in her relationship to God: as "the servant of the Lord." The biblical thought provides a doctrinal background for the Christian faith and for the theological effort of Christian generations which came to grasp and to propound with clarity and lucidity that the Blessed Mother from the very first moment of her existence as a human life had enjoyed God's friendly assistance, God's favor, God's grace and God's provident love: because, even before she was formed in the womb, God had chosen her to be "the servant of the Lord" and, as such, to serve as an instrument of God's salvation in her role of Mother of the Savior.

Index of Sundays and Sequential Feasts

Advent Season
1st Sunday (Mt. 24:37-44)	15
2nd Sunday (Mt. 3:1-12)	18
3rd Sunday (Mt. 11:2-11)	21
4th Sunday (Mt. 1:18-24)	25

Christmas Season
Christmas Day	
—at night (Lk. 2:1-14)	29
—at dawn (Lk. 2:15-20)	32
—during the day (Jn. 1:1-18)	35
Sunday after Christmas, Holy Family (Mt. 2:13-15, 19-23)	39
2nd Sunday after Christmas (Jn. 1:1-18)	42
Epiphany (Mt. 2:1-12)	45

Lenten Season
1st Sunday (Mt. 4:1-11)	49
2nd Sunday (Mt. 17:1-9)	52
3rd Sunday (Jn. 4:5-42)	53
4th Sunday (Jn. 9:1-41)	58
5th Sunday (Jn. 11:1-45)	61
Passion (Palm) Sunday (Mt. 21:1-17)	64
Holy Thursday (Jn. 13:1-15)	67

Easter Season
Easter Sunday (Jn. 20:1-9)	71
2nd Sunday (Jn. 20:19-31)	75
3rd Sunday (Lk. 24:13-35)	80
4th Sunday (Jn. 10:1-10)	83
5th Sunday (Jn. 14:1-12)	87
6th Sunday (Jn. 14:15-21)	90
Ascension (Mt. 28:18-20)	94
7th Sunday (Jn. 17:1-11)	98
Pentecost (Jn. 20:19-23)	102
Holy Trinity (Jn. 3:16-18)	105
Corpus Christi (Jn. 6:51-58)	108
Sacred Heart (Mt. 11:25-30)	111

Ordinary Time
1st Sunday, Baptism of the Lord (Mt. 3:13-17)	116
2nd Sunday (Jn. 1:29-34)	120
3rd Sunday (Mt. 4:12-23)	122
4th Sunday (Mt. 5:3-13)	125
5th Sunday (Mt. 5:13-16)	128
6th Sunday (Mt. 5:17-37)	131
7th Sunday (Mt. 5:38-47)	134
8th Sunday (Mt. 6:24-34)	138
9th Sunday (Mt. 7:21-27)	142

10th Sunday (Mt. 9:9-13) 144
11th Sunday (Mt. 9:35—10:8) 148
12th Sunday (Mt. 10:26-33) 151
13th Sunday (Mt. 10:37-42) 154
14th Sunday (Mt. 11:25-30) 158
15th Sunday (Mt. 13:1-23) 161
16th Sunday (Mt. 13:24-43 165
17th Sunday (Mt. 13:44-52) 168
18th Sunday (Mt. 14:13-21) 171
19th Sunday (Mt. 14:23-33) 174
20th Sunday (Mt. 15:21-28) 177
21st Sunday (Mt. 16:13-20) 180
22nd Sunday (Mt. 16:21-27) 184
23rd Sunday (Mt. 18:15-20) 188
24th Sunday (Mt. 18:21-35) 191
25th Sunday (Mt. 20:1-16a) 195
26th Sunday (Mt. 21:28-32) 198
27th Sunday (Mt. 21:33-46) 201
28th Sunday (Mt. 22:1-14) 205
29th Sunday (Mt. 22:15-22) 208
30th Sunday (Mt. 22:34-40) 212
31st Sunday (Mt. 23:1-12) 215
32nd Sunday (Mt. 25:1-13) 219
33rd Sunday (Mt. 25:14-30) 223
34th Sunday (Mt. 25:31-46) 226

Index of Solemnities

January 1, Mary, Mother of God (Lk. 2:16-21) 230
March 19, St. Joseph (Lk. 2:41-51) 234
March 25, Annunciation (Lk. 1:26-38) 237
June 29, Saints Peter and Paul (Jn. 21:15-19) 240
August 6, Transfiguration of the Lord (Mk. 9:2-10) 244
August 15, Assumption of Mary (Lk. 1:39-56) 247
November 1, All Saints (Mt. 5:1-12) 250
December 8, Immaculate Conception (Lk. 1:26-38) 253

Alphabetical Index of Solemnities

All Saints	250	Holy Thursday	67
Annunciation	237	Holy Trinity	105
Ascension	94	Immaculate Conception	253
Assumption	248	Joseph, St.	234
Baptism of the Lord	116	Mary, Mother of God	230
Christ the King	226	Palm (Passion) Sunday	64
Christmas	29	Pentecost	102
Corpus Christi	108	Peter and Paul, Saints	240
Easter Sunday	71	Sacred Heart of Jesus	111
Epiphany	45	Transfiguration	244
Holy Family	39	Trinity Sunday	105

Index of Gospel Passages

Matthew

1:18-24, 4th Sun. Advent	25
2:1-12, Epiphany	45
2:13-15, 19-23, Sun. after Christmas	39
3:1-12, 2nd Sun. Advent	18
3:13-17, 1st Sun. OT (Baptism of the Lord)	116
4:1-11, 1st Sun. Lent	49
4:12-23, 3rd Sun. OT	122
5:3-13, 4th Sun. OT	125
5:13-16, 5th Sun. OT	128
5:17-37, 6th Sun. OT	131
5:38-47, 7th Sun. OT	134
6:24-34, 8th Sun. OT	138
7:21-27, 9th Sun. OT	142
9:9-13, 10th Sun. OT	144
9:35—10:8, 11th Sun. OT	148
10:26-33, 12th Sun. OT	151
10:37-42, 13th Sun. OT	154
11:2-11, 3rd Sun. Advent	21
11:25-30, 14th Sun. OT and Sacred Heart	111
13:1-23, 15th Sun. OT	161
13:24-43, 16th Sun. OT	165
13:44-52, 17th Sun. OT	168
14:13-21, 18th Sun. OT	171
14:23-33, 19th Sun. OT	174
15:21-28, 20th Sun. OT	177
16:13-20, 21st. Sun. OT	180
16:21-27, 22nd Sun. OT	184
17:1-9, 2nd Sun. Lent	52
18:15-20, 23rd Sun. OT	188
18:21-35, 24th Sun. OT	191
20:1-16a, 25th Sun. OT	195
21:1-11, Passion (Palm) Sunday	64
21:28-32, 26th Sun. OT	198
21:33-46, 27th Sun. OT	201
22:1-14, 28th Sun. OT	205
22:15-22, 29th Sun. OT	208
22:34-40, 30th Sun. OT	212
23:1-12, 31st Sun. OT	215
24:37-44, 1st Sun. Advent	15
25:1-13, 32nd Sun. OT	219
25:14-30, 33rd Sun. OT	223
25:31-46, 34th Sun. OT, (Christ the King)	226
28:18-20, Ascension	94

Luke

2:1-14, Christmas, night	29
2:15-20, Christmas, dawn	32
24:13-35, 3rd Sun. Easter	80

John

1:1-18, Christmas, day	35
1:29-39, 2nd Sun. OT	120
3:16-18, Holy Trinity	105
4:5-42, 3rd Sun. Lent	53
6:51-58, Corpus Christi	108
9:1-41, 4th Sun. Lent	58
10:1-10, 4th Sun. Easter	83
11:1-45, 5th Sun. Lent	61
13:1-15, Holy Thursday	67
14:1-12, 5th Sun. Easter	87
14:15-21, 6th Sun. Easter	90
17:1-11, 7th Sun. Easter	98
20:1-9, Easter Sunday	71
20:19-23, Pentecost	102
20:19-31, 2nd Sun. Easter	75

Also available from St. Paul Editions

Good News for the Liturgical Community
A, B and C Cycles

Valentino Del Mazza, SDB

"Father Del Mazza presents his biblical and doctrinal reflections in a clear, straight-forward manner. His meditations contain many noteworthy citations of the words of the late Pope Paul VI, the documents of the Second Vatican Council, and the writings of St. Augustine and other significant authors as well. Each of his reflections is followed by some brief suggestions of the pastoral dimension of the message" (from the Preface).

cloth $5.95; paper $4.95 — SP0203

In the Light of the Bible
(Vols. I & II)

Sr. Concetta Belleggia, DSP

"These little books present basic teachings for Catholic living in Christ and (as their title indicates) present them in the clear light of the written Word. Anyone interested in studying or teaching the Christ-life will find these books helpful and authoritative, because their authority rests on God's inspired Scripture."—Most Rev. John F. Whealon, Archbishop of Hartford

Vol. I—141 pages; $1.25 — SC0060
Vol. II—117 pages; $1.00 — SC0061

Introductions to the Books of the New Testament

Daughters of St. Paul

Based on the most recent studies in Scriptural exegesis, these introductions offer information on the author, the socio-historical and cultural background of his times, his purpose and the theme of his work. Thus the reader of the New Testament will gain a deeper spiritual insight into each of the sacred books and be induced to make frequent, even daily use of God's holy word as a means of growth in supernatural wisdom and divine grace. 76 pages
paper $1.00 — SC0080

Living and Growing Through the Eucharist

Compiled by the Daughters of St. Paul

This volume contains everything you need on the liturgical reforms, and on the deep spiritual meaning of the Holy Eucharist—sacrifice, sacrament and Real Presence—as taken from theological, Scriptural and Patristic sources.

Includes a collection of 32 liturgical documents from 1902-1976. 575 pages
cloth $7.00; paper $6.00 — EP0710

Meditating the Sunday Gospels

Rev. P.J. McHugh

"...For the most part they are my own musings as I tried to make my daily meditation before the Lord." The author.

Priests, religious and laity alike will find these reflections of great comfort, inspiration and help.
331 pages
cloth $5.95; paper $4.95 — SP0410

Meditation Notes on Paul the Apostle, Model of the Spiritual Life

Rev. James Alberione, SSP, STD

These writings of Father James Alberione, Founder of the Pauline Family, were discovered after his death in November, 1971. They are meditation notes and resolutions made during a course of spiritual exercises. The theme is St. Paul and the priest. Every priest and spiritual guide can find in these pages a great wealth of material. 100 pages
cloth $2.00 — SP0420

The Paschal Mystery and Christian Living

Rev. James Alberione, SSP, STD

Meditations on the passion, resurrection and ascension of our Lord Jesus designed to deepen the Christian's understanding of that pivotal event in time—the Paschal Mystery—and the event's transcendence of time and space to permeate the lives of each of us at every moment. An excellent volume of meditations for everyone—religious and laity alike—for to the living of this Mystery all of us are called.
pages
cloth $3.95; paper $2.95 — SP0570

Reading the Acts, Epistles and Revelation

J. Kingsley Dalpadado, OMI

Anyone interested in Scripture will find, along with hours of enjoyable reading, the results of the latest exegetical studies.

"The Gospels present to us what Paul calls 'the mystery of Christ.' The *Acts* and *Epistles* proclaim it, explain it and apply it to our daily lives. The book of *Revelation* written in a time of crisis and persecution, is a magnificent declaration of faith in this mystery which dominates history and transcends time." 432 pages
cloth $6.95; paper $5.95 — SC0431

Reading the Bible—a Guide to the Word of God for Everyone

J. Kingsley Dalpadado, OMI

Each chapter offers an introduction to a book of the Bible, giving background, setting and explanation, select passages for reading and thoughtful applications. Charts, quizzes, answer keys, suggested hymns and prayers make this an ideal text for school, adult study, or individuals desirous of understanding Scripture better. 325 pages
cloth $5.95; paper $4.95 — SC0430

Reading the Gospels

J. Kingsley Dalpadado, OMI

Providing a good background for understanding or explaining the Sacred text, the author takes one Gospel at a time, presenting each scriptural passage with scholarly comments and points

for reflection and discussion. He intends to stimulate a life-giving encounter with Jesus, Way, Truth and Life. 311 pages
paper $4.00 — SC0432

Seek His Face
Brother Anthony J. Pfarr, SJ

The broader view of Scripture afforded by the three-year cycle of Sunday liturgical readings is newly applied to contemporary thought and life in this meditation/homily material arranged for each Sunday, and for major feasts. The author's tone is simple and clear, almost conversational, as he presents varied reflections on the message of God's Word. 260 pages
cloth $4.95; paper $3.95 — SP0690

Sunday Liturgy Themes
Prepared by the Daughters
   of St. Paul

An ideal aid for the assimilation of the Scriptural readings for the Sunday and holyday Masses throughout the full three-year liturgical cycle. The words of Vatican II and post-conciliar documents alternate with the Spirit-filled counsels of His Holiness, Pope Paul VI. Together they provide an authentic font of strength for a perennial springtime in living the liturgy and, through it, our dedication to God and His People. 300 pages
cloth $5.00; paper $4.00 — SP0730

Please order from any of the addresses on the following page, specifying title and item number.

Daughters of St. Paul

IN MASSACHUSETTS
  50 St. Paul's Ave. Jamaica Plain, Boston, MA 02130;
    617-522-8911; 617-522-0875;
  172 Tremont Street, Boston, MA 02111; **617-426-5464;**
    617-426-4230
IN NEW YORK
  78 Fort Place, Staten Island, NY 10301; **212-447-5071**
  59 East 43rd Street, New York, NY 10017; **212-986-7580**
  7 State Street, New York, NY 10004; **212-447-5071**
  625 East 187th Street, Bronx, NY 10458; **212-584-0440**
  525 Main Street, Buffalo, NY 14203; **716-847-6044**
IN NEW JERSEY
  Hudson Mall — Route 440 and Communipaw Ave.,
    Jersey City, NJ 07304; **201-433-7740**
IN CONNECTICUT
  202 Fairfield Ave., Bridgeport, CT 06604; **203-335-9913**
IN OHIO
  2105 Ontario St. (at Prospect Ave.), Cleveland, OH 44115; **216-621-9427**
  25 E. Eighth Street, Cincinnati, OH 45202; **513-721-4838**
IN PENNSYLVANIA
  1719 Chestnut Street, Philadelphia, PA 19103; **215-568-2638**
IN FLORIDA
  2700 Biscayne Blvd., Miami, FL 33137; **305-573-1618**
IN LOUISIANA
  4403 Veterans Memorial Blvd., Metairie, LA 70002; **504-887-7631;**
    504-887-0113
  1800 South Acadian Thruway, P.O. Box 2028, Baton Rouge, LA 70821
    504-343-4057; 504-343-3814
IN MISSOURI
  1001 Pine Street (at North 10th), St. Louis, MO 63101; **314-621-0346;**
    314-231-1034
IN ILLINOIS
  172 North Michigan Ave., Chicago, IL 60601; **312-346-4228;**
    312-346-3240
IN TEXAS
  114 Main Plaza, San Antonio, TX 78205; **512-224-8101**
IN CALIFORNIA
  1570 Fifth Avenue, San Diego, CA 92101; **714-232-1442**
  46 Geary Street, San Francisco, CA 94108; **415-781-5180**
IN HAWAII
  1143 Bishop Street, Honolulu, HI 96813; **808-521-2731**
IN ALASKA
  750 West 5th Avenue, Anchorage AK 99501; **907-272-8183**
IN CANADA
  3022 Dufferin Street, Toronto 395, Ontario, Canada
IN ENGLAND
  128, Notting Hill Gate, London W11 3QG, England
  133, Corporation Street, Birmingham B4 6PH, England
  5A-7 Royal Exchange Square, Glasgow G1 3AH, England
  82 Bold Street, Liverpool L1 4HR, England
IN AUSTRALIA
  58 Abbotsford Rd., Homebush, N.S.W., Sydney 2140, Australia